"BONDS of SILK"

"BONDS of SILK"

THE HUMAN FACTOR IN THE BRITISH ADMINISTRATION OF THE SUDAN

Francis M. Deng and M. W. Daly

Copyright © 1989 Francis M. Deng and Martin W. Daly

All Michigan State University Press books are produced on paper which meets the requirements of American National Standard of Information Sciences—Permanence of paper for printed materials ANSI 239.48-1984.

Michigan State University Press
East Lansing, Michigan 48823-5202

Printed in the United States of America

Library of Congress Cataloging-in-Publication Data

Deng, F. M.
  Bonds of silk : the human factor in the British administration of the Sudan / Francis M. Deng and Martin W. Daly
    p. cm.—(African series : no. 1)
  Includes bibliographical references.
  ISBN 0-87013-279-2
  1. Sudan—Politics and government. 2. British—Sudan. 3. Sudan—History—1899-1956. 4. Oral history. I. Deng, Francis Mading, 1938-   . II. Title. III. Series: African series (East Lansing, Mich.) ; no. 1.
DT156.7.D33   1990
962.4'03—dc20   89-43113
                                                                     CIP

CONTENTS

Contributors vii
Foreword ix
Introduction 1

PART I
THE RULERS
The British and the Sudan

1. Pre-Conceptions and Early Contacts 13
2. Official and Personal Relations 33
3. Working Conditions and Attitudes 61
4. Nationalism and Independence 71
5. Post-Colonial Contacts and Perspectives 85

PART II
THROUGH THE EYES OF THE RULED
The Northern View

1. Early Contacts 101
2. Official and Personal Relations 109
3. Working Conditions and Attitudes 119
4. Nationalism and Independence 131
5. Post-Colonial Contacts and Perspectives 147

PART III
THROUGH THE EYES OF THE RULED
The Southern View

1. Pre-Conceptions and Early Contacts 163
2. Official and Personal Relations 175
3. Working Conditions and Attitudes 185
4. Nationalism and Independence 195
5. Post-Colonial Contacts and Perspectives 205

Appendix A 213
Appendix B 219
Index...241

List of Contributors

British

Sir Gawain Westray Bell
P. P. Bowcock
G. R. F. Bredin
L. M. Buchanan
D. C. Carden
Anthony W. M. Disney
Sir A. D. Dodds-Parker
James Donaghy
W. M. Farquharson-Lang
Jean-Pierre Greenlaw
V. L. Griffiths
E. C. Haselden
K. D. D. Henderson
Robin Hodgkin
P. P. Howell
A. W. Ireland
J. W. Kenrick
Maurice Stanley Lush
J. F. Madden
J. G. Mavrogordato
W. C. McDowall
F. D. McJannet
T. H. B. Mynors
H. A. Nicholson
T. R. H. Owen
J. F. S. Phillips
A. W. Polden

G. E. R. Sandars
A. B. Theobald
R. C. Wakefield
John Winder

Northern Sudanese

Ahmed Mahgoub
Amin Hassoun
Babo Nimir
Daud Abd al-Latif
Jamal Muhammad Ahmed
Muhammad Abu Ranat
Muhammad Abu Sinn
Sorror Ramley
Yusuf Bedri
Zubayr Ahmed al-Malik

Southern Sudanese

Abd al-Rahman Souley
Andrew Wieu
Benjamin Lang Juuk
Chier Rian
Gordon Muortat Mayen
Manoah Majok Deng
Santino Deng Teeng

Foreword

The Anglo-Egyptian condominium government in the Sudan lasted for only fifty-seven years, from the Anglo-Egyptian agreement of January 1899 (following Kitchener's victory over the Khalifa 'Abdallahi near Omdurman in early September 1898) to New Year's Day 1956. During this short period of time the Sudan was technically under British and Egyptian rule, but the British were in fact the dominant influence. After the November 1924 assassination in Cairo of Sir Lee Stack, the governor-general of the Sudan, all Egyptian military forces and many Egyptian officials, clerks, technicians, and teachers were withdrawn from the Sudan, and few returned until after the Anglo-Egyptian treaty of 1936. Thus in the interwar years the British ruled the Sudan, relying significantly on local (native) authorities under the precepts of "indirect rule." With the onset of the Second World War in 1939 the situation changed again, and embryonic political parties, one of which sought to unite the Sudan with Egypt, began to call with varying degrees of stridency for the end of colonial rule and direct Sudanese participation in their country's political future.[1]

The book which follows grew from a collaboration undertaken at the Woodrow Wilson International Center for Scholars in Washington, D.C. during 1986–1987 by two of the foremost authorities on the modern Sudan. Martin Daly was then a fellow at the center and Francis Deng was a senior research associate working on African affairs with me in my, then, capacity as deputy director of the center. The interviews and questionnaires which form the basis for this book were conducted and collected by Francis Deng over the years between 1973 and 1981. He brought them together into a full first draft for a book. Thereafter, Francis was extraordinarily busy with other books and issues,[2] and it was only when Martin Daly read through the manuscript at the center in 1986, making a number of editorial suggestions, that he and Francis decided to collaborate on the final editing of the book, while retaining its character as a particularly personal record of British imperial rule in the Sudan. As a minor catalyst in this process who had assisted Francis in a major conference focused on the possibility of ameliorating the deep and tragic division within the contemporary Sudan,[3] I agreed to write this foreword.

The book is based on a small number of respondents—thirty-one British, ten northern Sudanese, and seven southern Sudanese. Brief biographical summaries are collected at the end of the volume. Despite the small number who speak or write of their personal experiences in these pages, their collected testimony is powerfully suggestive of some generic themes. My role here is to call attention to the general import of several of these themes.

This book is most assuredly not history from the bottom up. The views presented are those of elites—both British and Sudanese—who dealt in some degree directly with each other, primarily during the years from 1930 to 1956. In this quarter century, the length of one human generation, the government of the Sudan evolved from a colonial administration to independence. The thirty-one British respondents with whom the book deals served in the Sudan for an aggregate of 626 years, an impressive average of over twenty years per person. As a group they come from middle- and upper middle-class origins, they hold solid academic degrees primarily in history and classics from good British universities—seventeen from Oxford—and a few became truly distinguished administrators. In this respect they are representative of the Sudan Political Service, an elite corps within the Sudan Civil Service, emerging as a recognizably special entity after 1919. The Political Service recruited heavily from Oxford and Cambridge (nearly 90 percent of the total of approximately 310 graduates recruited to the service)[4] and drew disproportionately from varsity athletes (30 percent) as well as excellent scholars (10 percent held first-class degrees). Only the Indian Civil Service before the early 1930s could claim a better-qualified group of political officers.

The attitudes reflected by the thirty-one British respondents in these pages show the preference of many British administrators for rural districts. Given the large distances in the Sudan and the great diversity of its peoples, the single officer in a large, thinly-populated district had to depend on the cooperation and consent of those he governed—a practice which Lugard had elevated in Nigeria to a doctrine of "indirect rule." In this situation, personal relationships of trust and even admiration developed, yet, characteristically, in most cases they simultaneously remained formal and impersonal; the British reacted to the intellectual isolation of their positions by concentrating on tasks of the moment and delving into the history and laws of their localities.[5] There is a notable absence in these pages of a discussion of Sudanese cultures or poetry or social relationships. There is little serious attention to the function of religion in shaping society or to the nature of belief, little thought about the role of women, and an almost unbelievable lack of expressed sexuality, especially between British and Sudanese, although sexual relationships are discussed more by southern respondents than by others. What comes through equally clearly is the distaste many British officers felt for the newly emerging Sudanese urban intellectual elite of the 1930s with their frequent Egyptian sympathies and their desire for participatory politics. The British recruits who joined the Sudan Political Service after the Second World War were more sympathetic to nationalist activities, but even they were surprised at the speed with which political devolution occurred. Independence came in 1956, only ten years after the reorganization of administration following the war.

Arguably of greatest moment for the Sudan is the British distinction which comes through in these pages between the northern and southern parts of the country, a distinction which became elevated by January 1930 into the "Southern Policy." Although the policy was articulated officially in 1930, two of its cardinal elements had evolved over the prior decade out of necessity. These were the use of tribal rulers to assist in the courts and in sustaining security (which became in official language the use of native authorities for the purposes of indirect rule), and the use of missionary schools to provide education in the region. Flowing from these usages, made mandatory by lack of personnel or funds to do otherwise, were three other aspects of the Southern Policy: the use of eight languages of the south (Dinka, Nuer, Bari, Moru, Ndogo, Shilluk, Madi, and Zande) for instruction in primary schools, the exclusion to as great a degree as possible of Egyptian or northern Arabized personnel from administrative or commercial functions in the south, and the use of English as the official language.[6]

These policies, implemented with some enthusiasm during the 1930s, stimulated much amateur and some professional anthropology (e.g., Evans-Pritchard, *The Nuer*, 1940; S. F. Nadel, *The Nuba*, 1947), much anguish over the role of Italian Catholic Verona fathers as missionary teachers during the Italo-Ethiopian war, some good dictionaries and grammars of southern Sudanese languages, and a sense of heightened difference between the administrations of the north and the south. Unfortunately, these policies also brought to the fore certain contradictions: indirect rule designed to strengthen tribal authorities, almost all of whom were illiterate and committed to traditional values, was seldom compatible with economic development and modernization; the ejection of trained northern staff was not possible if there were no trained southerners with literate English to take their place. Lack of economic infrastructural development, lack of secular government schools (especially at the secondary level), and the attenuation of the use of Arabic meant that the southern provinces were increasingly cut off from the issues which agitated the north in the late 1930s.

The interviews in this book make clear that tribal leaders, such as Babo Nimir and Deng Majok, were highly intelligent, much involved in judicial and administrative matters, deeply concerned about the relations between the Arabized peoples of Kordofan and their southern neighbors, and skilled in mediating conflicting values. Many British officers admired these qualities and appreciated the extraordinary character of these men. But there is little discussion here with southern respondents of the liabilities resulting from the lack of skilled and educated staff, or the need to plan a transition to a new kind of leadership, or of the role of Arabic in knitting the Sudan together. There is a pride, a confidence, and a cohesiveness among the Nilotic tribes that enabled them to remain relatively self-contained. Good personal relations, even trusted friendships, could ease the tasks of governance between northern and southern Sudanese and with the British, but good relations could not overcome the structural and educational deficits of the south in its need for equal treatment at the time of independence.

What is the ultimate value of the opinions and reflections recorded here? It is not that they give a true view of the Sudan; more accurate and more comprehensive history is presented by professional historians. But they convey a direct feel for the situation, a filtered sense of which memories and experiences have lasting meaning and which in their multiple lives now seem evanescent and incidental. As Francis Deng makes clear, the oral tradition still lives, vibrantly among some peoples and residually in all of us. The Anglo-Egyptian Condominium existed for a brief moment in the sweep of history of the Nile Valley peoples—fifty-seven years of another wave of imperial rule among the many tides that have washed for millennia across the region. The accounts in this book embody the relationships of colonial rule in the personae of real people, with the result that these relationships are neither simple nor caricatured. They are complex, ambivalent, for the most part honorable, primarily formal, with consequences at odds with their intentions, spiced with irony, and often overtaken by events. The British clearly intended that the northern and southern parts of the country be treated differently, in part because they found them to be different, in part because British administrators with different proclivities gave their character to the administration. But there is no evidence that they foresaw or desired a result that would end in mutiny, revolt, and prolonged civil war. Protection was not intended to result in rejection. Fifty-seven years is a small interlude in the long military and commercial intrusion of Arabic and Islam among African peoples, and the British contribution may in the long term have been only to build a temporary dike against the encroaching tide.

A second forceful impression derived from the aggregate weight of these responses is the speed with which the assumptions underlying governance changed. Within one person's working career the self-assertions of nationalism went from a maverick intellectual critique to an accepted majority opinion. Views about the Egyptian contribution to the Sudan varied from co-responsibility through anathema to nationalist political assistance and then desired separation. Few individuals could maintain in the course of these winds of change a steady path or a consistent explanation of their destination. Sand blew in their eyes, grit got in their teeth, rains changed an apparent road to gelatinous mud. That personal relations sustained the character described in these pages is a tribute to the integrity of individuals and the psychological separation, even in times of great political change, of personal from political commitments. Perhaps the British and the Sudanese are better at maintaining these distinctions than are most of us. As the title suggests, these are lives lived in the full maturity of ambivalence, hoping to do good, realizing that we possess neither the knowledge nor the control to ensure that what we intend has the desired result. We are left with the bittersweet taste of reality.

Prosser Gifford
June 1988, Washington, D.C.

Notes

1. The most complete history of the condominium period is M. W. Daly, *Empire on the Nile. The Anglo-Egyptian Sudan 1898–1934* (Cambridge: Cambridge University Press, 1986) which is volume 1 of a two-volume work. Volume 2, taking the history through 1956, is forthcoming. A briefer history is P. M. Holt and M. W. Daly, *A History of the Sudan*, 4th ed. (London: Longman, 1988). For the growth of the educated elite and their participation in the Graduates General Congress, see Muhammad Omer Beshir, *Educational Development in the Sudan 1898 to 1956* (London: Oxford University Press, 1969); for the growth of nationalist politics, see Muddathir 'Abd Al-Rahim, *Imperialism and Nationalism in the Sudan* (London: Oxford University Press, 1969).

2. Francis Mading Deng, *Recollections of Babo Nimir* (London: Macmillan, 1982); Francis Mading Deng and Robert O. Collins, eds., *The British in the Sudan, 1898–1956* (London: Macmillan, 1984); and *The Man Called Deng Majok. A Biography of Power, Polygamy and Change* (New Haven: Yale University Press, 1986).

3. Francis Mading Deng and Prosser Gifford, eds., *The Search for Peace and Unity in the Sudan* (Wilson Center Press, 1987).

4. See Collins and Deng, eds., *The British in the Sudan, 1898–1956*, appendix, 244–50 by A. M. H. Kirk-Greene giving "an educational profile of the Sudan Political Service."

5. See, for example, among the respondents in this volume, K. D. D. Henderson, *The Making of the Modern Sudan* (London: Faber, 1952), and *Sudan Republic* (New York: Praeger, 1965); or the series of articles in the periodical *Sudan Notes and Records* by P. P. Howell, "The Shilluk Settlement," 24 (1941), "The Death of a Reth of the Shilluk, 27 (1946), "Notes of the Ngok Dinka," 32 (1951), and "Death and Burial of Reth Dak Fadier," 33 (1952). There were many more articles and books on northern than on southern Sudanese peoples and history. See, e.g., H. A. MacMichael, *A History of the Arabs in the Sudan*, 2 vols. (1922; reprinted London: Frank Cass, 1967).

6. The most complete discussion of Southern Policy is Robert O. Collins, *Shadows in the Grass* (New Haven: Yale University Press, 1983), 148–248 and *passim*; see also Daly, *Empire on the Nile* 396–419; Henderson, *Sudan Republic*, 161–202; and Dunstan M. Wai, *The African-Arab Conflict in the Sudan* (New York: Africana, 1981), 33–52. A different but useful perspective addressed to the resistance of southern peoples to the spread of Islam is J. Spencer Trimingham, *Islam in the Sudan* (London: Oxford University Press, 1949), chaps. 3, 7.

Introduction

Colonialism has been condemned as a fundamental subjugation and exploitation of people, akin to slavery, and a negation of basic human rights. But this intense human experience, notwithstanding the indignities of dominion, brought together peoples otherwise very far removed from one another. It therefore poses challenging issues about the values that inform human interaction, especially when viewed from the perspective of the interacting individuals. As we move further away from the trauma of colonialism, this point, which has in any case often been overlooked, must increasingly be remembered in order to achieve a balanced view of the period and of its substantive bequest to future generations. In this book we attempt to provide information necessary for this purpose. Its subject is the colonial experience of the Sudan, which from 1899 until 1956 was ruled by an Anglo-Egyptian condominium.

The Sudan is geographically the largest country in Africa, with an area of nearly one million square miles and a population of some twenty million fragmented into several hundred tribes. Located at the heart of the continent, the Sudan borders eight countries: Egypt to the north; Libya to the northwest; Chad, the Central African Republic, and Zaire to the west and southwest; Uganda and Kenya to the south and southeast; and Ethiopia to the east. Across the Red Sea lies Arabia. Surrounded by states with various racial and cultural characteristics, the Sudan reflects internally the immense diversities represented along its extensive borders. These diversities divide the country, somewhat inexactly, into two parts: the northern two-thirds in land and population is mainly Arab and Muslim, while the remaining third is Negroid and pagan, with an educated elite that is overwhelmingly Christian.

It is true that the majority in the north represent an Islamized

Arab mold, but there is also a considerable non-Arab element. Many of the tribes of Darfur in the west are conspicuously Negroid; the Nuba of southern Kordofan were barely touched by Arabism and Islam. Even the Nubians of the extreme north, with the longest history of contact with Arab civilization and Islam, have retained their language. The same is true of the Beja in the east.

A long history of hostility and deep-rooted animosities have so conditioned the peoples of both north and south that they cannot see anything in common. While both the Arabs and the Nilotics have been liberal in assimilating those they captured as slaves, their prejudices against intermarriage and social mixing are profound and mutual. What gives the prejudices of the Arabs a greater strength is that they are sanctioned by Islam, which permits only the Muslim man but not the woman to marry outside the faith. The threat of assimilation from the north has had the added effect of strengthening the Nilotic sense of identity, ethnic pride, and resistance to Arab Islamic influence. Of course, the peoples of the south have, over the centuries, adopted some cultural traits from the north, but they have tended to integrate and assimilate these traits into a cultural mold that has retained its indigenous flavor.

The racial and cultural division between the south and the north has been formalized and reinforced by political interventions. The Turco-Egyptian regime of the Ottoman Empire, which was established in the north in 1821 and continued until 1885, was Muslim, and although it could not extend effective control to the south, except for a flourishing trade and a succession of terrorizing expeditions, its policies in the north reinforced the Arab Islamic identity and therefore the north-south dichotomy. Corrupt, oppressive, and alien, the Turco-Egyptian administration was deeply resented by the Muslim north and widely viewed as a government of infidels.

The situation exploded in 1881 when Muhammad Ahmed b. Abdullah, soon to be known as the Mahdi, mobilized the Sudanese people against the Turks, and met with wide-ranging support that cut across even the north-south dividing line. Initially armed with only spears and swords, the Mahdists won battle after battle, becoming increasingly confident in the process, until they succeeded in miraculously overthrowing the regime in 1885. General Gordon, the British soldier in the service of the Turco-Egyptian administration as governor-general, was killed as Khartoum fell, and the Sudan became independent.

Although the Mahdi died shortly afterwards, his successor, the Khalifa Abdullahi, held power in a centralized state for thirteen years. In the south this was a period of continuing incursions from the north. Although the Mahdists, like the Turks before them, never succeeded in controlling the south, the whole nineteenth century is remembered by the Dinka as "the time when the world was spoiled," when the world as they knew it was destroyed.

The Anglo-Egyptian conquest of 1896–1898 ironically restored the Sudan to a colonial status but brought relief to the peoples of both north and south. The condominium, as it became known, was a unique colonial device. The Sudan Government, under a British governor-general, was answerable not to the co-domini, Egypt and Britain, but to the British alone, and not to the Colonial Office in London but to the Foreign Office. No settlers were allowed in the Sudan, nor were special privileges reserved for Europeans or Egyptians. A civil service was recruited, mainly from Oxford and Cambridge graduates with backgrounds in the English public schools. The Sudan Political Service became an elite corps consisting of what Lord Cromer, the architect of the system, stipulated as "active young men, endowed with good health, high character and fair abilities, not the mediocre by-products of the race, but the flower of those who are turned out from our schools and colleges."

Concerned lest the mistakes of the Turco-Egyptian administration be repeated, the British recognized and respected the Arab Islamic sensibilities of the north. On the other hand, they viewed the south as pagan and primitive, requiring at most only protection and tutelage. While Christian missionaries were excluded from the north, in the south they were encouraged to play a civilizing role in spheres of influence defined to avoid denominational rivalry and conflict. While the medium of instruction in northern schools was Arabic, with English at the secondary level, teaching in the southern schools was in vernacular languages, replaced by English from the intermediate level. In southern trade the government preferred Greek merchants to northern Sudanese who, it was feared, were prone to exploit the vulnerable peoples of the south. By law, the south was deemed "closed districts," and attempts were made to regulate and restrict contacts with the north. What became known as the "Southern Policy" aimed at allowing the people of the south to evolve along their own indigenous lines, insulated and protected from the supposedly corruptive influences of modernity or the unscrupulous exploitation of the Arab north. Although members of the Political Service who ruled in the north were eventually posted to the south, too, the early administrators and many of their successors were military men with considerable autonomy, whose task was paradoxically both to put a stop to resistance and to provide paternalistic protection.

In both north and south the British adopted Indirect Rule, leaving the administration of the tribes to their chiefs under only the general supervision of the district commissioner. The number of British administrators in the Sudan in relation to the population was very small, and the tribes did not feel the constant oppressive presence of an outside ruler. And yet, through their remote controls, the British established peace, security, and a system of justice and civil order that contrasted with what had prevailed before them.

Although Britain was the first to give meaning to the unity of the Sudan as a state, the northern Sudanese condemned colonial policies as having deepened the north-south division and made it an obstacle to national unity. The southern Sudanese in turn resented the isolationist policies, however well-intentioned, that relegated them to a position of inferiority to the north. Apart from religiously-oriented missionary education, the first serious efforts by the government to promote education in the south began in the mid-1940s when the British belatedly realized that they were soon to leave; they hoped to help the south stand on its own in a united and independent Sudan. They even came to accept the need to formulate programs of accelerated development for the south.

Pressures from Egypt and the northern Sudanese forced the British out of the country before they could adequately prepare the south to catch up with the north. So wide was the gap that, when Sudanization came, of the eight hundred posts that had been occupied by the colonial powers, only four junior positions went to southerners. Fears of a possible return to "the spoiled world" of the nineteenth century, and of Arab domination, triggered in August 1955 a mutiny that was initially limited to a battalion in Equatoria but soon spread throughout the south. It was eventually contained only because of the intervention of the British governor-general who, though in the twilight of colonial rule, promised justice for the rebels.

Southern Sudanese were able to agree with the northerners on the declaration of independence on 1 January 1956, with the understanding that the southern call for a federal relationship with the north would be fully considered. That consideration was never given, and reaction in the south began to develop into a civil war that was to continue for seventeen years. When the Nimeiri regime took over in 1969, one of its declared objectives was to end the war. By 27 February 1972 the government was able to conclude with the southern movement the Addis Ababa Agreement, promptly enacted as the Southern Provinces Regional Government Act, granting the south regional autonomy within the united Sudan.

Hostilities resumed in 1983. These were triggered by a number of developments, including the decision to effect a massive transfer of troops to the north, the division of the south into three regions, the reduction of the regional powers as stipulated in the Addis Ababa Agreement and the 1972 act, and the introduction of *Sharia* as the law of the land. But underlying these immediate causes was a deeper resentment of the economic disparity between the two parts of the country. In particular dispute were the controversies over the Jonglei Canal (aimed at retrieving the waters of the swampy *Sudd* region, but which southerners believed endangered their environment for the benefit of the north and Egypt), the plan to locate in the north a refinery for southern crude oil, and the subsequent decision to construct a pipeline to pump the same oil to the Red Sea for export, to alleviate the country's mounting need for foreign currency. While this renewed violence is outside the scope of this book, it underscores the tenacity of the bitterness, animosity, and suspicion that have marked the relations between north and south for most of their remembered history. It also highlights the extent to which, once the initial business of pacification had been completed, the British colonial era was a unique interval of peace and security.

There is a wider reason for recording the history of this interval. Colonialism has been declared an indignity, a form of slavery that the world must work with determination to eliminate even if the slaves love their chains. But colonialism is part of an experience; experience nourishes the heritage of a people; and heritage provides a necessary catalyst for the resilience, confidence, and vitality needed to overcome the present and future challenges embedded in the continuing experience of mankind.

British rule in the Sudan differed from the characteristic form in other parts of the empire and in other areas of the world. Indeed, a number of contributors to this study objected quite strongly to the use of the word "colonialism" to describe what they considered a unique arrangement. This was particularly true of British respondents. One wrote: "Before answering any questions, I would point out that the word 'colonialism' is incorrectly used in connection with the Sudan. The Sudan was not run from Whitehall nor were settlers allowed. The whole object of British recruitment to the Sudan Government was to lead the country to independence—which was not the early object in the colonies. The words 'colony' and 'colonial,' as defined by the Oxford English Dictionary, do not apply to the Sudan and I don't think they should be used."

Another pointed out that "steps were taken, at an early date, to prevent possession of land passing to foreigners. British actions, seventy-five and more years ago, in Egypt and the Sudan were certainly examples of imperialism, but at least I can say with truth that we did not practice colonialism in the Sudan." Another remarked that he "would have liked to see the word 'colonialism' removed from [the] title. . . . The Sudan was *not* a colony in either the specific or any general sense. By historical chance it developed a new form of dependence, very different from any developed in the usual colonial empire context (and greatly superior in my view to any such). It is this difference, I speculate, that will make the 'Sudan Experience' increasingly important to historians and practical philosophers, if only as an example of what *could* be done, but never *was* done except in the Sudan." A number of contributors went so far as to say that the British officials in the Sudan and the British military men who were seconded to the Sudan Defence Force had their allegiance to the Sudan and not to the British government.

British views on the nature of their rule in the Sudan are more than legalistic quibbles. There is an unmistakable judgment of value about what they were doing and a genuine sense of discomfort about the moral connotations of the word "colonialism" when viewed in the context of the idealism which guided British officials in the Sudan. One wrote in a covering letter to his replies: "[You] will appreciate that my Sudan service as a young enthusiastic man was an important, and in some ways, in retrospect, the most important part of my life. Certainly it was the period when I felt most directly involved in 'serving humanity' (as opposed to merely earning a living) and furthering the ideals of my youth." Another wrote: "So many people have asked me why the men in the British Sudan Political and Civil services, and the Sudan Defence Force, were such happy people; to which I always make the reply that we had the honour and joy to serve (for we did regard our rule in the Sudan as service), the finest people in Africa, were they the Arabs in the north or the Nilotic people in the south. Their response to our presence and our efforts to serve them made life for us extremely happy."

All of this, of course, is vitally important to appreciating the nature of the Anglo-Egyptian administration in the Sudan and its relationship with the people of the country. But colonialism has come to connote foreign rule whether or not it is accompanied by foreign settlers. In that sense, there is no escaping the fact that condominium rule in the Sudan was indeed colonial and was rejected as such. Foreign rule would not have been any less objectionable under another name!

The Anglo-Egyptian Sudan was, however, a unique colonial variant with distinctively positive features. In particular, the rivalry of the co-domini provided a system of checks and balances between the ruling powers that proved to be ultimately in the interest of the Sudanese. It also generated a dynamic process that was conducive to a degree of amicability in the relations between the rulers and the ruled and helped to pave the way for a relatively harmonious march toward independence. In that sense, the Sudan's experience was a rather exceptional example of what is possible in terms of human values, not only in the colonial context but also in situations of interracial and cross-cultural interaction.

There are a variety of reasons for making this book largely a collection of excerpts from tape-recorded and written questionnaires. The Sudanese, despite modern literary education, are part of an oral tradition in which the spoken word is still far easier than the written. Despite the inaccuracies of oral information, it has certain advantages. Instead of freezing an experience in records, oral accounts given years later reflect not only the memory of events, but also the perspective of reflection over a period of time. Oral sources thus assimilate the facts and continue an intrinsic relevance to oral history that adds dimensions to what otherwise would have been isolated "facts" about experience. In that sense, there can be no adequate substitute for an updated version of an individual's experience. Oral sources of knowledge have been denigrated at a time when they constitute the main source of knowledge for many peoples of the world.

This project has had a long gestation period. The idea was conceived in the 1960s and data collection began in 1973. For practical reasons, all the Sudanese material came out of tape-recorded interviews, while the British material, with four exceptions, was largely the product of written responses: K. D. D. Henderson, D. C. Carden, G. W. Bell, and R. Hodgkin also responded on tape. Except for Henderson, who was interviewed in 1973, most of the British responses were collected between 1978 and 1981. Muhammad Ahmed Abu Sinn was interviewed in 1981, but the rest of the northern interviews were conducted within a period of several months in 1973, both in the Sudan and elsewhere. Except for Santino Deng, who was interviewed in 1973, the southern interviews took place in 1981.

The standard questionnaire used to elicit information in this volume covered a wide spectrum of colonial experience. Paraphrased, the themes of the questions include preconceptions, predispositions, and recruitment; the journey to the Sudan, first impressions, and expectations about the work to be undertaken; initial contacts with Sudanese at work; the dynamics of the stratification between rulers and ruled; cultivation of close relations over time; comparing exclusive social situations with mixed company; the position of British wives in the Sudan; sexual liaisons across the racial line; alleged homosexual practices by the British; the extent to which work compensated for lack of amenities; how the nature of the British mission in the Sudan was viewed; attitudes of racial superiority or equality; comparing the Sudanese among themselves and with other nationalities in Africa; changes in attitude toward each other; the nationalist movement; the achievement of independence; the circumstances of departure; continuation of relationships after independence; a critical assessment of each side in terms of likes and dislikes; and an appraisal of the experience in retrospect.

In presenting their views on these themes we have tried to keep a pledge made to the contributors not to impose a thesis or analysis that might risk distorting their own perspectives on the subject. We let them speak for themselves. But there was a humanistic theme in the framework of investigation which, though gentle in its flow, provides a conceptual basis for appreciating the vast commentary elicited from the contributors. There are a number of conclusions, interpretations, and even matters of fact with which we happen to disagree, but a critical edition of the collected material would have seemed to be an end in itself, whereas our purpose is to provide the perspectives of others. We see the value of this work, if any, not as an oral history of the condominium, but as a source for the study of that history, unvarnished and unfettered.

Notwithstanding our desire to present the views of principal British and Sudanese actors, it is appropriate to draw attention to some limitations on this collection of those views. First, it is important to note that most of our contributors experienced colonial rule in the Sudan only from the 1920s, at the earliest, and some only in the 1940s or even 1950s. Thus their generalizations should not be taken as applicable to the whole span of the condominium. Second, despite the candor evident in many accounts, a concern to protect the reputation of friends, colleagues, institutions and, indeed, oneself is obvious from time to time. This explains some of the contradictions in testimony, especially among British respondents. Third, we must take note of the unrepresentative character of our contributors. British respondents were mainly retired members of the Sudan Political Service, which was itself largely drawn from a particular class. Their responses are in many cases reflective of the "official mind," but not necessarily representative of even a prevailing *British* view. Similarly, on the Sudanese side, all the respondents were prominent men, mainly tribal chiefs and government officials. They were themselves, therefore, members of an elite, not representatives of the mass of Sudanese. Their experiences were not those of a Gezira tenant, a Fur peasant, or a Nuer cattleman.

To an extent, this may explain both the wide areas of agreement and some causes for resentment between "rulers" and ruled, for the British had been not only servants of a foreign regime but also protectors or supporters, props or creators of some Sudanese respondents. Some Sudanese gained from their experience of colonial rule and may have felt a degree of pressure or ambivalence after the colonial period because of that experience. Indeed, many of those interviewed were literally the successors of the British at and after independence. Whatever value this may give their testimony, it cannot be said to be typical of the Sudanese experience, and should not be seen as merely disinterested commentary. A telling example of this may be seen in the wistfulness shared by the British and Sudanese tribal leaders for the good old days of Indirect Rule, before upstart politicians, modern education, and nationalist politics upset their world.

The central point in the theme we have discerned is a striking tension and contradiction in the ideas, attitudes, and behavior patterns of the interacting parties on both sides. This was in a sense inherent in the paradoxical nature of the system. Ideals of service to the people were postulated which guided British behavior and ensured a relatively high degree of conformity to humane principles. At the same time, the assumptions of racial and cultural superiority underlying the rule of one nation over others generated patterns of thought and behavior which ran counter to the postulated ideals. The result was a complex network of ambivalent sentiments and cross-currents that were both exalting and condemnatory, depending on the specific issues in question. Mutual appreciation and admiration, which provided a sound foundation for cross-fertilization, went side by side with a recognition of unbridgeable gaps imposed by the very nature of foreign rule. At best, they established and maintained a certain distance even among those who regarded themselves as close friends; and at worst, they brought to the surface the underlying assumptions of racial and cultural stratification on which the system was based.

Throughout the book these contradictions emerge, submerge, and resurface with differing degrees of recognition and emphasis. Sometimes they are overlooked, sometimes underestimated, and sometimes exaggerated. They are less obvious in the British, pronounced in the northern Sudanese, and most striking among the southerners. On balance, a certain equilibrium between positives and negatives was maintained which, considering the unpalatability of foreign rule, leaves the Sudanese experience a remarkable story of victory for the human factor.

PART 1

THE RULERS:
The British and the Sudan

1

Pre-Conceptions and Early Contacts

While most British contributors to this study maintain that they had no ideas about the Sudan and the Sudanese before joining the government service, there is no question that many were predisposed positively toward the country because of what they had heard about its people.[1] A surprising number cited Kipling's poem "Fuzzy-Wuzzy" as a source for their conception of the Sudanese, especially as "first class fighting men." "About all I had heard," confessed A. W. M. Disney, who came to the Sudan in 1927, "was that they broke a British square at the battle of Tamai." This, according to K. D. D. Henderson, had "completely eclipsed any tradition of the Sudanese as being the chaps who were defeated at the battle of Omdurman." Otherwise, the overwhelming impression is of total ignorance about the Sudan.

A number of respondents had gained favorable impressions of the Sudan and its inhabitants from relatives, friends, and academic advisers who had served in the country or learned about it. P. P. Howell reports that acquaintances with experience in the Sudan "spoke of the Sudanese with respect and affection." Gawain Bell had heard that the Sudanese "were brave and resilient, with a tremendous sense of humor." Members of the Political Service who were on leave in England had described the Sudanese to D. C. Carden as great fighting men, as well as being possessed of a tremendous sense of humor. Carden recalled having been attracted by the enormous enthusiasm for the people and the country evinced by R. V. Savile,[2] a former governor of Darfur and friend of his parents. W. H. Farquharson-Lang's father was a friend of Sir Reginald Wingate,[3] the governor-general of the Sudan from 1899 to 1916: "I met Wingate frequently in his own home," Farquharson-Lang wrote, "and he told me much about the Sudan and the

13

Sudanese for whom he held the highest regard." A. D. Dodds-Parker had an uncle, Wise Bey, who had served in the Camel Corps in 1901 and in Berber and Gedaref until 1910, and who had spoken to him very highly of the Sudan. "From those years till today, I never heard anything but praise for the Sudan!"

With an air of ancestral pride, J. F. S. Phillips considered himself virtually to have been born with the Sudan in his blood. Gordon Pasha was his mother's great-uncle, and General Sir Herbert Stewart, mortally wounded at al-Qubba[4] in the unsuccessful attempt to rescue Gordon, was likewise related on his father's side. Before going to the Sudan he had "heard a lot about the Sudanese.... What I had heard was inevitably paternalistic, referring to the qualities of courage, loyalty, pride, and a 'sense of humor like ours.' Those who did govern them, the British, both liked and admired them."

The reputation of the Sudan and the Sudanese, combined with a host of individual considerations, influenced the decision of the respondents to apply for service in the Sudan. Although there was no competitive examination, they unanimously recall that standards for selection were very high. Gawain Bell recalled Lord Cromer's description of the sort of men who were to be looked for: "You remember . . . : 'active young men endowed with good health, of high character and fair abilities: not the mediocre by-products of the race, but the flower of those turned out from our schools and colleges.'"[5] In retrospect, respondents believed that financial and other terms of service were only secondary considerations: "We were taught that our first duty in life was service to others," L. M. Buchanan wrote, while T. R. H. Owen professed a youthful "interest in people, not money or mechanics or trade." Like most of the others, he recalled "feeling that the British have something worth giving, for the development and progress of the world, economically and politically."

Several former officials remembered a boyhood inclination toward the Indian Civil Service but a later preference for the Sudan Political Service. Carden had been raised in India, the son of a clergyman who had spent twenty-five years there: "As a boy my ambition was to become Resident, Kashmir." But at Oxford in 1940–41 Carden realized that he was a generation too late, that India would become independent soon after the war. He therefore "changed direction toward the only other political service" which, he said, was regarded as an "elite."

K. D. D. Henderson had also been "brought up with the idea of going into the Indian Civil Service," and had "read an awful lot about India as a boy." He claimed that in his last term at school "a man came round from the India Office, soliciting . . . people to go into the Indian Civil Service; and I decided that there must be something seriously wrong with it, because otherwise he wouldn't have to do that. So I decided that I would go for . . . what I suppose in those days you would call the next best thing." Yet Henderson remarked that "the Sudan Political Service had a very high reputation in England. . . . When I arrived at Oxford, men whom I very much respected were trying to get into it." He acknowledged also "the mundane considerations of the Sudan service. A service which gave you [three months] leave every year obviously had advantages." William McDowall's father, then in the Indian Civil Service, warned that India would soon be independent, so he too applied for the Sudan. Indeed, Phillips went so far as to assert that it was "more difficult to enter the Sudan Service than the Indian, since the physical as well as the intellectual qualifications were looked for."

A number of respondents reported motives that would later prove useful in meeting the challenges of the Sudan. Henderson said that he was attracted to the country because he felt the need was greatest there. "It seemed to me," he said, "that in 1895 practically all of Africa was in a comparatively peaceful condition except the Sudan which was, as I understood things, groaning under the rule of the Khalifa al-Mahdi [the successor of the Mahdi]. I therefore decided that that was the place to try and get in." Robin Hodgkin, the teacher, was influenced by a conversation in 1939 with Christopher Cox,[6] who told him "something about the changes that he and other educational and government colleagues were planning for the Sudan's developing education," to which Hodgkin himself was later to make a major contribution. Jean Pierre Greenlaw, the artist, hoped to "advance hand and eye training in schools" in the Sudan; he also admitted to a simple desire to see the world.

The attraction of what Owen termed "adventure and wild life" normally connotes a stereotype of Africa which had little, if anything, to do with reality. In the context of British rule in the vast, sparsely-populated Sudan, however, some tendency in that direction was useful for what could otherwise have been an assignment of severe hardship in remote areas, involving a population far removed from the British cultural experience. R. C. Wakefield recalled applying for a surveying position in the Sudan largely because of the open air life of Africa in general. Bell remembered rejecting work in the City, the professions, and the army as too restricted and too narrow, and chose the Sudan Political Service instead.

In keeping with this emphasis on the practical rather than the purely intellectual, the training for those selected to enter the political service, at least during Bell's time, 1931, had centered on the study of Arabic. But "this was classical Arabic, principally written," he explained, and like many he would find the spoken language "extremely difficult to follow and indeed to link in any way with what we had been learning of the classical language." The courses at Oxford also included "lectures on a variety of subjects concerned with service in Africa: colonial history, criminal and civil law, tropical agriculture, tropical hygiene . . . ; and we were perhaps rather surprisingly or sensibly encouraged to go to the Radcliffe Infirmary . . . to attend and watch surgical operations. It was thought to be a good idea that we should be used to the sight of blood and severed limbs!"

The experience of the first journey to the Sudan, initial impressions of the land and its people, and the perception of the mission just undertaken still evoked vivid recollections. A pervasive theme is the contrast between the shocking conditions of life and the virtues the British saw in the people. The usual route was overland to Marseilles or Italy, by sea to Port Said, through the Suez Canal, down the Red Sea to Port Sudan, and by rail to Khartoum. Many who took this route remembered rough weather, small, crowded ships, and a generally uncomfortable sea passage. "The only good feature of the voyage," Disney wrote, "was that it gave one a chance to get to know one's new colleagues quite well." During World War II even this asset became a liability, as the journey involved circumnavigating Africa. J. G. Mavrogordato recalled his wartime journey to the Sudan: "About fifty British Sudan Government officials travelled in a Liberty ship, crammed six to a cabin designed for one or two. The blackout meant that one was after dusk confined to a small, smoke-filled lounge, uncongenial to a nonsmoker.

The ship was in slow convoy and took some five weeks to Port Sudan. A member of the crew died on board from meningitis."

Although those who arrived at Port Sudan in winter found the climate pleasant, most first impressions were unfavorable. John Winder reached Port Sudan on a Sunday: "No one came to meet us. . . . Port Sudan seemed largely under a film of dust." Farquharson-Lang, who arrived on 31 August 1931, recalled that "at that time of year my first impression was the intense heat and humidity of the corrugated iron customs shed on the quay." Winder found more than the climate disheartening: "Eventually we left Port Sudan for Khartoum by rail in the evening. . . . We saw nothing of the country until next morning between Haya and Atbara. Found it pretty bleak." Many others commented on the desolation of the countryside. L. M. Buchanan found it "barren, empty, and depressing." Farquharson-Lang confessed to being "somewhat bewildered on that train journey from Port Sudan to Khartoum—the country seemed so vast and so featureless." Greenlaw was appalled by the "aridity and lack of features." "The picture in my memory," Owen wrote, "is of a flaming sunset, endless telegraph poles, and a vulture sitting on each pole!" P. P. Bowcock wrote that "it seemed difficult to believe people could exist in such an arid and inhospitable country, which made the Hadendewa and the other nomads seen from the train even more fascinating. . . . As for the British, I was first amazed that in such heat they could apparently work and organise their lives quite normally, and even play tennis and football."

The second overland route to the Sudan led from Port Said to Cairo, then by rail to Shellal, river steamer to Wadi Halfa, and finally by rail to Khartoum. This route, and especially the Sudanese leg of it, was particularly favored. Indeed, Maurice Lush asserted that "the journey by Sudan Government steamer or train was the most comfortable journey to be taken anywhere in Africa."

Whether they took the Red Sea route or the overland route from Egypt, former officials believed that even then their positive impressions of the Sudanese more than compensated for the climate and bleakness of the desert. George Bredin wrote: "In spite of the forbidding landscape through which I travelled, I felt at once the strange fascination of the Sudan, and like so many of my countrymen, found here an attraction and an interest which I have never lost." Bowcock was "chiefly impressed [by the] courtesy, dignity and cleanliness" of the Sudanese. Bredin too was "impressed at once by the cleanliness and good order of the steamer and railways and the cheerfulness and courtesy of the Sudanese whom I encountered on the journey." "Like others who have travelled to the Sudan" by the rail-steamer-rail route, said Phillips, "I was deeply impressed by the contrast between the noise, dirt and vociferous posturing of passengers in Egypt, and the quiet, cleanliness, and dignified courtesy encountered as soon as we embarked on the Sudan Railways Nile steamer at Shellal." Similarly, W. C. McDowall wrote: "My initial impressions of the country and the people were [of] the orderliness and quiet efficiency and the friendliness and good manners of the people; which was in stark contrast with the dirt, disease, begging and 'backshish' which we had experienced in Egypt at that time. I formed an immediate liking for individual Sudanese whom I met."

Once they arrived in the Sudan, young recruits were eager to begin the task for which they had come. But, perhaps surprisingly, that task was not clearly defined. As H. A. Nicholson put it, "We were all excited and keen to arrive and get involved in our work, [but] at this time obviously we had a very vague idea of what this would be." Howell remembered only that "the nature of my 'mission' was not clearly defined in my mind." A. B. Theobald "had no idea what to expect." Therein, for Owen, lay "the secret of the Sudan's fascination—everything had . . . to be found out by experience!"

Many former officials recalled that their object from the start was to prepare the Sudan for ultimate independence. This goal, while sincere, was not, of course, urgently pursued at a time when independence was seen as realizable only in the distant future. Thus, preparation for independence is variously interpreted, and the idea gained immediacy only during and after the Second World War. F. D. McJannet recalled "part of the governor-general's [Sir Stewart Symes's] address to us newly-arrived probationers in 1937: 'Remember that when the Sudanese ask in future for their independence, we should have trained them to the stage where we can, with confidence, hand over the country to them.'" But Bell viewed his role as administering a country at a "fairly early stage of development. A great deal needed to be done in the way of building up . . . the departments of government, improving the agriculture of the country, improving the education, and so forth. . . . There is not a job . . . that one didn't see that one would be likely to be required to do, from first aid or dealing with accidents, right away down to writing one's monthly reports on the way in which the district was going along."

"I think I understood that [my mission] was to take part in the government of the country," J. W. Kenrick wrote, "and that entailed playing a part in the maintenance of peace, the administration of justice, and the development of education, agriculture and economic affairs, with the ultimate aim of helping the nation to achieve a higher standard of living and political independence. The last was conceived in Western democratic terms." Dodds-Parker's "mission," as he understood it, was similarly conceived along European lines: "I believed my 'mission' was to help the Sudanese enjoy some of the things which I had enjoyed under a system of parliamentary democracy, with free enterprise capitalism. This would take some years, as it had taken Britain 700 years." Farquharson-Lang, a teacher, wrote: "Soon after my appointment [in 1931] I came to realise that there was something special in the duties I was performing. I was training the professional pioneers of a new nation and guiding them both inside and outside the classroom to assume responsibility in the government of their country." Bredin's remembered objective was less idealistic, but involved practical goals for the Sudan. "At that early stage I probably regarded myself as undertaking a career rather than a mission. With the example of India before me, I felt that my duty would consist largely of the maintenance of justice, law, and order in an efficient and even-handed administration."

John Phillips presented a balanced summary of how he viewed his role: "The nature of my mission (when I thought about it amid all the new and exciting distractions of the journey) I envisaged as combining the pleasure of meeting the physical and mental challenge posed by the Sudan and its climate (young men welcome a challenge) with the opportunity of carrying on what others had begun, in bringing orderly administration and a better life for peoples whom I believed to need more of both; in short, a constructive job. If that sounds priggish," he continued, "you can add that in contrast with 1945 Britain, I felt that I was going to a land and a job where I would have responsibility, call my soul my own, and pay no income tax!" Dodds-Parker also contrasted life in the Sudan and Britain during the depression: "My first impression, leaving Britain in the economic crisis of 1931, was that despite locusts, we were all better off in Kordofan (necessary food, warmth, and lack of tension) than in Britain."

To the question of whether their first post in the Sudan put them into close touch with the Sudanese, many responded with "Yes, very close touch," or, as Disney put it, "continuous daily touch." But it is clear that the meaning of "close touch" in the colonial context concerned the performance of official duty rather than personal contact, even though a degree of overlap was sometimes inevitable.

As new arrivals—very young men, in most cases, with little or no spoken Arabic—many were soon sent to remote areas and left alone to fend for themselves. They adapted and, judging from their own accounts, very well indeed, if only in the course of official duties. As Dodds-Parker explained, "A district officer spent most of his time on trek. I reckon I rode about 10,000 miles on a camel and mule and horses, very much more by truck—no touring cars! In the Fung I was literally 250 miles from the nearest Englishman." This naturally involved close touch with subordinates and with the local people, the Sudanese themselves.

Bell, whose first post was Gedaref in the eastern Sudan, gave a vivid description of the training new administrative officers underwent. "I learned to ride a camel. I learned to understand the way in which one toured in the Sudan: starting early in the morning, of course; resting during the heat of the day, and then moving on in the afternoon to some other village where one would spend the night." Carden (whose first job in the Sudan was training recruits for the Eastern Arab Corps, which entailed only limited "close contact" with the Sudanese) received his first administrative assignment as an assistant district commissioner in Kordofan. "I arrived in Bara on a Thursday in June," he recalled. "It had begun raining heavily and the *kharif* (the rainy season) had begun. The district was preoccupied with a locust campaign. The district commissioner told me to get ready to leave for the west of the district on the succeeding Monday, adding that he did not want to see me again until October.... I spent nine-tenths or more of my time on trek and then I rarely saw anyone except Sudanese. How rarely? Perhaps during ten days in a year."[7]

In their experience on the spot, most former political officers acknowledge the support and advice of Sudanese subordinates. Theobald, though a teacher by profession, was once briefly seconded for administrative duties. He wrote: "During my first summer, when I did not get leave in England, I was sent to Kamlin as an acting district commissioner. I knew absolutely nothing [about] the job, and I simply did what I was told to do by the Mamour, a fat, jolly man called Abd al-Razak, who was like a father to me." After service in Berber in the Nomad-Beja administration, Buchanan was transferred to Tokar on the Red Sea coast. One of the few redeeming aspects of the assignment was his relationship with the leaders of the Beni Amer, "always kindly, forthright, and courteous to a young alien Briton who was totally ignorant of them and their country."

Beyond the call of duty, the meaning of close contact in the colonial context was confusing to respondents. Some, like Bredin, qualified their answers by insisting on a more precise definition of "close touch." At his first post, Kosti on the White Nile, Bredin "was not at first in close touch, unofficially, with Sudanese." His duties, however, entailed a closer relationship: "In the office my contacts were with the Sudanese staff, and petitioners, and those involved in legal proceedings. In spite of having undergone a rigorous three months' course in 'classical' Arabic in London before departure, I had to rely for some time on the services of my Sudanese clerk as translator." T. H. B. Mynors, whose first posting was to Mongalla in 1930, also qualified his answer by distinguishing between private and official contact. "Cultural and language difficulties at that time in the south," he wrote, "made close relationships almost impossible. I was in close daily touch in my administrative duties, particularly as I soon set out to compile a grammar and dictionary of the major local language (Moru) and to record historic customs and songs; for this I made many contacts with children and a few adults. Whenever possible I used to go hunting (for meat) with the local people."

A number of former political officers initially assigned to administrative posts in Khartoum did not achieve the same level of contact with Sudanese as those who were sent immediately to the provinces. Here again, ironies of the Sudanese situation may be observed. Educated Sudanese were intellectually closer to the British, and the chances of establishing personal contact with them were better in the towns than in the countryside. Yet the overwhelming majority of the British who commented on the matter expressed an unequivocal preference for the rural population. In the towns, official functions or the manner in which they were carried out did not generally require close contact except in certain matters such as education. The presence of a large, nonofficial foreign community entailed all the responsibilities and customs of European society, from which Sudanese were largely excluded. Then, too, there was the fact, at first only dimly perceived but later uncomfortably obvious, that the educated townsman and his ways were of the future while the rural chief represented a passing, if still vital, way of life to which many British officials were themselves greatly attached. British officials in towns, therefore, often felt isolated from the local community. Even for the few Britons who worked with Sudanese or the even fewer with whom they had social contact outside the office, relations were often constrained and contrived.

A related reason for British preferences was simply the different nature of rural and town work. In the countryside there was scope for "real" administration, deciding issues, and seeing results, while in the towns a bureaucratic routine prevailed. Paul Howell was bored by his first post as assistant district commissioner in Khartoum North: "I had little direct contact of any responsibility with Sudanese," he explained, "and spent much time instructed to 'read files,' a useless and unimaginative method of training. A posting in Khartoum was atypical and unsatisfactory. One tended to be absorbed into a social life which was essentially British; and later on, lack of real contact with Sudanese made learning Arabic difficult." Owen stated that he had to wait until he was sent north from Khartoum to establish daily contact with Sudanese. Philip Bowcock, whose first assignment (in 1951) was as assistant district commissioner in Khartoum, recalled: "Being in a provincial headquarters, I was not in fact in as close touch with the Sudanese as in a district. . . . I saw more perhaps of the educated Sudanese and some of the clerks of the Mudiria, whom I used to see socially. . . . However, I had responsibility for, among other things, the prison and there was a constant stream of petitioners, so I met quite a number of ordinary people."

Wad Medani—a situation neither truly urban nor rural—was Henderson's first posting. "I was posted to Medani on December 26, 1927," he said. "The Gezira Scheme was just getting under way. . . .

The whole Gezira was the great ... development area and things were really moving. So, life there was very interesting, but of course the trouble about Medani was that you didn't get out and meet the people; you were always tied to your desk and it was in the old days of direct rule, when the district commissioner tried every tiddlywinking case.... I didn't form in Medani with any of my Sudanese colleagues a relationship such as I later formed in Kordofan with Yusuf Saad or in Darfur with Ali Abu Sinn," Henderson continued. "I didn't achieve terms of close friendship.... I made a great number of contacts, but not very close friendships ... in my first four years in the Gezira."

Those whose careers in the Political Service were chiefly during the post-World War II era, when independence began to impend, felt that they had had closer contacts with the Sudanese both officially and socially. McDowall, for example, who arrived in 1939 and who worked in the judiciary from 1946 to 1955 (from 1951 as a judge of the High Court) wrote: "I was in close contact with the Sudanese staff in the office, with the general public in my job, and socially through sports (tennis and riding) and when I visited the Sudanese Club or went to tea with Sudanese colleagues. I also had two Sudanese servants who helped me with speaking Arabic, one of whom was with me for fourteen years and was a true friend of my family. I also had a Sudanese teacher of Arabic."

A. W. Polden was sent directly to Wad Medani as a veterinary inspector. He was in close contact with Sudanese "by the nature of my profession ... particularly with stock owners." Greenlaw, whose career in the Sudan as an art instructor and educator began in 1936 (and ended with his resignation in 1951) averred that his position put him into "extremely close [contact with] a wide selection of society in all parts of the country, whose sons were being trained in Rural Education at El Dueim." Mavrogordato's position as law instructor in Gordon Memorial College (beginning in 1944) naturally involved him in close relations with his Sudanese students. "I gave weekly tea parties for them," he recalled. In the government's Legal Department "the work was mainly paperwork, ... though with the increase of Sudanization I became increasingly in touch with Sudanese officials in the various government departments requiring legal advice, representation in court, or drafting of legislation."

"Throughout the whole of my career in the Sudan," from 1931

to 1955, wrote Farquharson-Lang, "I was very fortunate in being in close contact with the Sudanese. In my early days in the Gordon College I was put in charge of a boarding house of about 80–90 boys and I got to know them very well indeed—also some of their fathers. In the Gordon College there was a staff of about ten British and thirty Sudanese. As a staff we worked in closest cooperation, but it is true that at that time in the 1930s the British staff were always heads of subjects (apart from Arabic). Relationships were always very candid but at that time the social aspect was fairly formal."[8]

During the greater part of the condominium, all British officials were senior to Sudanese, but, as a number explained, the nature of the work, the limitations they felt as foreigners, and their dependence on more knowledgeable Sudanese subordinates complicated the equation. As Mynors wrote, "There was a hierarchy . . . and until the last years Sudanese with whom I was in close contact were subordinates. But there was very much a team spirit in any district or province and as far as I was concerned I always encouraged frank dealings without question of rank." Buchanan contended that "in dealing with tribal leaders and officials we regarded them as different rather than subordinate. The concept of superiority or subordination did not arise in my mind although I was conscious, of course, of the authority, albeit limited, which we exercised over them as the local representatives of an alien government."

The question of rank was especially anomalous when it involved tribal chiefs. Bell said that in the case of *nazirs* and senior tribal notables "it was a question really of rank between one and the other. One respected the *nazir* in the same way, I suppose, as one would respect . . . somebody whose activities and responsibilities were not altogether the same as one's own, but who had very considerable powers and influence; and one got on with him generally extremely well." Dodds-Parker explained that while "all (Sudanese) were 'subordinates' . . . the senior Sudanese [chiefs], like Sayed Ahmed Omar of the Gawamaa and Sayed Muneim Mansur of the Hamar, treated us like rather backward younger sons."

Maurice Lush was even more explicit on this issue, drawing a distinction between legal and real authority: the Sudanese, he wrote, were "in rank subordinate—in experience and wisdom superior, especially in the provinces. The Sudanese leaders were my superiors. I learnt more from them of life in the Sudan and about the Sudan and Sudanese than from anyone else.... Let it be said quite clearly that 'equality' and 'subordination' between the *mufattish* (district commissioner) and the Sudanese leaders and sheikhs in the provinces were terms that did *not* arise. A sheikh might and would descend from his donkey as a mark of salutation. I would salute him as an equal mark. Because I represented the '*Hakouma*' (government) and he the '*Nas*' (people) did not spell out subordination or superiority, merely good manners on both sides."

Elaborating on the same theme, Carden drew attention to the nature of Indirect Rule in the Sudan. "The great tribal leaders were in no sense subordinate, being men who were older, wiser, and infinitely more knowledgeable, and in their way enjoying a power which was quite independent of the government and was rooted in their acceptability to the people. As a young, new Englishman, I had to depend very heavily on their goodwill and cooperation. They gave this the more readily for the British government apparatus weighing so lightly on them; there was one district commissioner and one assistant in an area as big as England and Wales [having] a population of 250,000." Carden went on: "Certainly, when one first arrived, one would have an exaggerated idea of the range of things in which one was superior to people in the district in which one was working. It was true that I arrived as somebody who had taken a longish education in Britain which had ended in a degree in Greek and Roman philosophy and history, and behind that lay years of study.... In addition to that, I had just spent the best part of a year in the British army in which I had learnt techniques. I had learnt about weapons which had evolved in our fighting with the Germans in the Second World War which was still going on. Therefore, there were ... certain fields in which one felt that perhaps one had a superior knowledge. But of course it soon became very evident that ... this knowledge, these fields were unimportant. It didn't matter if one was in Dar Kababish that one knew well how an anti-tank gun worked; it was quite irrelevant. It didn't matter that one knew about Aristophanes or Plato. The things that mattered were a knowledge of the way in which the economy of the people worked, the way in which the camels would be taken south at the beginning of the rains and west during the height of the rains and north into the Quz during the winter. It was important ... to realise how important tribal custom was, and it was very important to know that you were ignorant of this and the people with whom you were working were not. Therefore, I think that any illusions as to general superiority or inferiority simply disappeared, and instead of that one very rapidly got into a position in which one could do certain things for them and there were a very large number of things which could only be done by them for themselves; and these two came into play like two halves of a whole."

It is noteworthy that all of these references to the power relationship concern the Sudanese traditional elite, the tribal shaykhs and chiefs. When a British former official recalled relations with a Sudanese notable as brotherly, he had in mind the nomad chief, not the Khartoum *effendi*. Thus, the picture of equality is not so much inaccurate as it is incomplete, limited to those areas away from which a new Sudanese educated elite was successfully challenging British rule.

The relationship between British and Sudanese officials changed relatively rapidly, as Farquharson-Lang pointed out with reference to his twenty-five years (1931–1955) in the Sudan: "In the 1930s there were Sudanese members of staff who were all junior to me; in the 1940s there was a far greater degree of equality in status and in the 1950s—actually in 1953—a Sudanese who had been my junior in the 1930s became my chief as director of education. I can honestly say our relationship was always very good; I think we both appreciated the situation and held each other in high and cordial esteem. I hope I showed no resentment in his appointment and he certainly took no advantage of his position."

One remarkable aspect of British rule was the extent to which racial attitudes were discreet, disguised, or even unrecognized. Everyone knew they existed, for they were implicit in foreign rule, but raising the question provoked uneasy, even hostile reactions among British respondents.

Asked whether the British regarded themselves as racially superior or equal to the Sudanese, John Phillips seemed outraged: "To be 'absolutely frank,' I regard this as a bad question. . . . I regarded myself as better educated than most Sudanese as well as better educated than most British; less able to withstand physical hardships than most Sudanese, but superior in this aspect to most British; more intelligent than most Sudanese or British, but less so than some."

Theobald and Disney agreed that it is impossible to generalize.

Theobald commented that he "regarded himself as superior to some Sudanese, equal to some, and inferior to some." Disney elaborated: "In many cases—professional colleagues, tribal leaders and suchlike—I regarded myself as their equal; but to the junior official, the villager and the nomad Arab, I regarded myself as superior—in just the same way as one does in England. The deciding factor is not colour of skin or ethnic origin, but the mental level of the other person."

Gawain Bell did not share Phillips's objection to the question, describing it as "interesting" although not easy to answer. "The Sudanese and we ourselves had our own shortcomings; we had our own merits; and it's sometimes difficult, I think, in a situation of this sort, to weigh up and decide, whether one set of shortcomings as opposed to one set of merits is outweighed by the other. If, for instance, [one considers] a young market clerk or a young accountant in the office, I suppose I would have regarded myself as his superior. I had had the good fortune to have a longer, wider education than he had. I had seen a great deal more of the world. And perhaps my judgement was better formed than his was. On the other hand, you take a *ma'mur* who had had perhaps twenty-five or thirty years of service with a great deal of experience in various parts of the Sudan: there was no doubt that in some respects he was a man whose judgment I would have respected greatly, and to whom I would have gone for advice and guidance, even though he happened to be junior to me in rank. You take again a senior *nazir*. In some respects, the senior *nazir*, I suppose you might say was my own superior in that his experience with his people and his judgment in certain circumstances might have been far sounder than my own.

"What I think . . . one is bound to remember is that the Sudanese are an extremely courteous people, and they have extremely good manners. I am sure I noticed this from the very moment I got to the Sudan. On the other hand, I think that we, the British, were sometimes less courteous to them than we might have been. I think we were sometimes impatient and perhaps were more inclined to see Sudanese faults than take full account of their merits. I don't think you can say in general terms at all that we regarded ourselves as superior or necessarily 'equal to.' Each of us had merits. Each of us had shortcomings and I hope that we were appreciative of this."

The majority of respondents who recognized feelings of superiority were quick to justify or qualify them. Some spurned the word "superiority." Many admitted feeling superior only at first, until they had appreciated the nature of the country and the ways in which the Sudanese had adapted to it. Others recalled feeling superior by virtue of culture and education, but inferior in the area of social relations.

In his capacity as an enforcer of law and order, Buchanan saw himself in a "relatively altruistic relationship [and] felt no more superior or equal than does a referee of a football match." He added, however, that "one was gratified to have an accepted base of authority from which to work." It was for the same reason that Lush considered himself "as an official, superior, as a man, co-equal." Nicholson admitted that the British thought themselves "essentially superior," but that it was "in view of our official position and also because we were more highly educated, more politically mature and in a sense more civilized." Henderson elaborated with remarkable candor: "It was generally assumed that these were chaps who had been left behind in the march of progress and that your main job was to boost them along, until they caught up." He commented that while "inferior" was probably not the best word to describe the British view of the Sudanese, "the average idea was that . . . the southerners were pretty primitive [and] that the northerners were inefficient. . . . They were never able to get on with anything."

Mavrogordato based his response on professional qualifications. "Legally I considered myself as superior to the Sudanese. I had had a longer legal education . . . and had practised at the Bar in London for some years up to the beginning of the war. . . . The Sudanese started from scratch and I believe I was responsible for teaching only the second batch of Sudanese reading law. With one or two exceptions, I also considered myself technically superior to the British lawyers in the Sudan and for the same reasons. Apart from the legal qualifications, I suppose I considered myself as one of the elite, but this would be based rather on my position in the hierarchy than on race."

Farquharson-Lang testified to the powerful pride the British derived from their identity as a ruling people: "When I first went to the Sudan, with the historical background of the British Empire in mind, I suppose I regarded myself as superior." But, he added, "I quickly had to change my opinion and I rapidly came to regard the Sudanese as my equals and in some instances my superiors." Bowcock described this attitude in personal terms: "I had grown up during the war and my country had, as I saw it, stood alone and saved the world. I had won a scholarship to one of my country's two leading universities, had been a cavalry officer and was now a member of what people told me was an elite service. I was probably conceited and perhaps felt some sense of superiority to other peoples, but if so, I don't think that it was racialist or colonialist. I think I probably felt the same about, say, the Portuguese. After all, there were plenty of coloured people on an equal basis at Oxford, and in my first term the president of the union was a black West Indian. I certainly did not feel any sense of superiority when walking through swamps in the Nuer[land]. I hope that the conceit of youth was tempered by the humility and example of older colleagues in the service." The influence of time was also mentioned by Carden. "Initially my attitude was unjustifiably patronizing," he said. "But the experience of dealing with proud nomad Arabs and even prouder Nuer rubbed that off." Owen's memories were similar: "Looking back, I think that just *at first* there was some arrogance in me. That very soon cleared away. The longer one served, the more humble one became and I, for one, felt that we were in partnership with the Sudanese."

Asked whether the Sudanese viewed them as superior or equal, most British respondents merely presented their estimate of a favorable attitude, ranging from what Henderson viewed as near worship, in some instances, to a more tempered sense of respect.

Henderson stressed Sudanese politeness as a factor in the exaggerated deference the ordinary man paid to the British: "I should say by and large that the ordinary rural Sudanese treated you as though you were a divine being—unless they happened to be annoyed with you, in which case they told you something else. The Arab in general is the most skillful flatterer in the world.... One chap said to me, 'I think on the whole if you look back through the last thirty years, you will find that we have had as district commissioners in this district the pick of the Sudan Political Service. All our men have gone on to govern provinces or territories or even higher things.' Despite all one may feel in the way of knowing perfectly well the base motives which dictated that, you can't help getting a bit of a boost to your ego."

Flattery was occasionally a matter of interpretation: when he became governor of the Northern Province, Maurice Lush was told by an *umda* that his predecessor had spoken Arabic very well—"but we did not understand one word of what he said or meant. You speak Arabic very badly, but we understand exactly what you mean!" Lush also gave a more serious appraisal of the British: "*'Wallahi ana mabsout'* [By God, I am glad] cried a drunken but charming Jaali," as he reeled into Lush's office. "*'Wallahi ana mabsout* because I can come to you the *hakouma* and tell you, without fear, how *mazloum* [in need of justice] I am at the hands of the *hakouma.*'" Phillips also discerned a positive Sudanese attitude toward him: "I think that on the whole, the Sudanese who knew me regarded me personally very fairly: as a somewhat impatient and hot-tempered individual, a faithful servant of the government, who nevertheless had deep (if paternalistic) affection for the Sudanese and concern for their well-being. They recognized that I had taken the trouble to learn Arabic fairly well and that I was genuinely interested in their day-to-day problems and social life." Disney agreed: "I don't think that it is presumptuous to feel that the Sudanese appreciated my integrity and sense of justice. Some may have regarded me as a fool, but I don't think that anyone ever regarded me as a knave! I think that they recognised 'plain good intention' when they saw it and liked and respected it."

Bell summed up the extent to which the human factor in British rule eventually transcended the cleavages and hostilities of foreign domination: "When I went to be governor of Northern Nigeria some years after leaving the Sudan, I was visited by Abdalla Khalil, who at that time was prime minister, and he spent some days in Northern Nigeria talking to the Northern Nigerian politicians. And they subsequently said to me: 'You know, your prime minister said some strange things. He said to us, "For goodness sake, don't be in too much of a hurry to get rid of your British officials." And we said to him "Why?" And he said, "You will find them—although they may have been your masters in the past—you will find them very good servants." Furthermore, he said, "If you get rid of them, you will have to employ others from overseas, and they won't be of the same caliber at all."'"

Almost without exception, respondents felt that their attitudes toward the Sudanese and Sudanese attitudes toward them improved over time. V. L. Griffiths, the educator, was typical of those who attributed the change to improved personal relations. Over the years, "one thought of people more as individuals," he said. J. F. Madden spoke of the growth of "mutual confidence" in many cases. Farquharson-Lang commented that "as one got to know individuals better, one's regard and affection for them increased." G. E. R. Sandars also considered this deepening of affection as a natural process: "Inevitably, as time passed, friendship with individual Sudanese developed and I saw more of their virtues: their loyalty, their kindness, their hospitality, and so on." Phillips observed that "greater knowledge brought greater understanding of each other's motives and habits: an advance along the road to *tout comprendre, c'est tout pardonner.*" Nicholson referred to the fading of "any instinctive feeling of suspicion" and its replacement with "friendship and a feeling of trust." Hodgkin "came much more to feel [that the Sudanese] were people from whom I could learn and with whom I enjoyed doing things, [rather] than subjects or pupils. Much would depend on the individual, and I'm now talking mainly of Sudanese of considerable ability and success who worked closely with me."

Notes

1. An important study of the social background of the Political Service is J. A. Mangan, "The Education of an Elite Imperial Administration: The Sudan Political Service and the British Public School System," *International Journal of African Historical Studies* 15, no. 4 (1982): 671–99.

2. Lt. Col. R. V. Savile (1873–1947) joined the Sudan Government in 1902. He was governor of the Bahr al-Ghazal in 1908–1909, of Kordofan from 1909 to 1917, and of Darfur from 1917 to 1923.

3. Wingate was governor-general of the Sudan, 1899–1916 and high commissioner in Egypt, 1917–1919. For his governor-generalship see Gabriel Warburg, *The Sudan under Wingate* (London: Cass, 1971). For his biography see Ronald Wingate, *Wingate of the Sudan* (London: John Murray, 1955).

4. Called "Gubat" in British sources, the battle occurred near Metemma on 19 January 1885.

5. The quotation, slightly inaccurate, is from Cromer's introduction to S. Low, *Egypt in Transition,* 1913.

6. Cox was director of education from 1937 to 1939.

7. Carden means while on trek. At headquarters and during long annual leave he was, of course, in constant contact with non-Sudanese.

8. Cf. Edward Atiyah's critical account of life at the Gordon Memorial College in *An Arab Tells His Story* (London: John Murray, 1946).

2

Official and Personal Relations

Because the British ruled the Sudanese for almost sixty years, questions are raised which go beyond initial contacts and focus attention on personal and working relationships and how these evolved. It might be expected that the high regard former officials have expressed for the Sudanese must have extended beyond cordial working relations to the level of personal attachment. This is an area in which the barriers of authority, cultural differences, and racial attitudes can strongly manifest themselves, where tension is felt and contradictions are exposed. For this reason, it is a highly sensitive subject, which perhaps explains why many respondents were obviously disturbed by a question posed to them and were somewhat cryptic or evasive in their replies. The dual question asked of British former officials was, "Did you get to know any Sudanese closely? And what did it mean to be close to Sudanese?"

In his tape-recorded response, Gawain Bell began: "I am a little lost. I don't know quite how to answer that question. . . . They say a close life lived among a people as primitive as some of them were, means that in a sense one was very close to them." As Bell elaborated, it became obvious that he was thinking of working relations. "But when the question goes on to say: 'What did it mean to be close to the Sudanese?' what it means was this: One was constantly talking to them generally about problems with administration, tribal problems or difficulties that had arisen with their neighbors, or indeed dealing with their court records. And very often one was trying cases because as a district commissioner one had the powers of a first class magistrate. And there was always, of course, a certain amount of crime, and particularly violent crime; and a lot of murders took place up and down the country. So this brought one into very close touch with the Sudanese." As far as closeness beyond official contact was concerned Bell prefaced his answer tentatively: "If it means, 'Did I like the Sudanese?' the answer is emphatically yes. Certainly I did. One had one's problems from time to time. There were tribal chiefs who oppressed their people; and then they had to be dealt with by being dismissed or warned or whatever it might be. I think all I can say is, in answer to the question of 'What did it mean to be close to the Sudanese?' I would say that it meant a great deal."

H. A. Nicholson was another who queried the clarity of the question but proceeded to estimate the extent of relations: "It depends on what you mean by 'closely.' We did not live in each other's houses, but we used to play tennis and polo together and from time to time we entertained our Sudanese friends, both official and unofficial, to tea and to dinner. And if we were trekking together or met while on trek or in our own homes, we enjoyed each other's company and often discussed world affairs and general subjects in which we were interested."

R. C. Wakefield's answer was similar, but he stressed the working aspect of relations and the limits of unofficial contact. "This is a difficult one as I don't know what you mean by 'close.' I spent a great deal of time on survey work all over the country and particularly in desert work, and I was always accompanied by varying numbers of Sudanese *effendia* (officials), mechanics and labourers. We worked happily together and I have a very high appreciation of their hard work and loyalty under sometimes extremely difficult conditions. In Khartoum, apart from the odd tea party, there was very little contact with them outside the office. This was largely due to their wives not being allowed out with them and [their] not playing the sort of games we indulged in—cricket, squash, tennis, golf, etc."

Somewhat provoked, John Kenrick was even more candid in revealing the invulnerable barrier of authority between the rulers and the ruled: "I find this difficult to answer. Of course I got to know my servants and district staff well as individuals, but not on any basis of equality."

Other responses ranged very widely. Winder responded with a terse "no." Lush answered, "Frankly, no. In the provinces I never served long enough to acquire close friendships. In the secretariat and the government propinquity was not possible." Howell's "no" was unqualified: "Positively the closest relationship" he had with a

Sudanese "was with [his] Arabic teacher, Obeid Abdel Nur—but that was a working relationship." E. C. Haselden said: "I always had my own house or shared with another Englishman, and although I frequently exchanged visits with Sudanese I do not think I knew any Sudanese closely." Dodds-Parker rationalized that "the circumstances of our work in those years (1931–1939) did not allow close touch with any Sudanese or British. We were all moving around too much on trek or on transfer to allow the sort of closeness which follows from working in one place."

Other respondents sought to explain the lack of close relations by pointing to different social customs and practices as inhibiting. A. W. Ireland knew a number of Sudanese well, "but none intimately (in the sense that I was intimately friendly with a few fellow British)." In his opinion, "the Islamic views upon alcohol and women were probably the main barrier to intimacy with Sudanese." Buchanan remembered that during his early years in the rural Sudan "there was almost no social life"—either with the British or the Sudanese. "We occasionally had tea on each other's verandas and played bridge (with British) or chess (with Sudanese). The game of chess . . . opened up easier informal relationships with Sudanese who were otherwise reserved and invariably courteous with us, but naturally cautious. What seemed to me to exclude an easy social relationship with the Sudanese was the banishment of their women to the background or behind walls. I accepted this, of course, although I considered it both backward and degrading." Buchanan was particularly intolerant of one custom: "The barbaric practice of female circumcision was always an insurmountable barrier to full social relations between British and Sudanese families throughout my whole service of twenty-six years (1929–1954) in the Sudan." Alan Theobald also felt that "cultural differences" in addition to "my change of job and location every few years . . . made it difficult to become 'close' to any Sudanese as to a British friend." But Theobald was one of the very few to acknowledge a closer cultural proximity to the educated Sudanese: "It was possible to have long and deep discussions on subjects such as religion, politics, family life . . . to learn their characters and outlook on life. . . . But this applies to relatively few persons compared to the large numbers one could know in a more remote way."

T. R. H. Owen, more typically, reported: "From the nature of the work the majority (not all) of the close relationships . . . were with nazirs and other leaders. I came to value their friendship, to understand their way of life, and my own horizons were enlarged and [my] knowledge of humanity developed by the close contacts." John Phillips "got to know many Sudanese very closely—too many to mention here." But in illustrating the point he described working associations with "Bur Mohamed Ahmed, my *mamour* at Talodi, and Fadlallah Kheira Allah, the police officer there. Bur, aged about fifty, taught me more about my job and about Sudanese than I could have hoped to learn from my fellow expatriates or from written reports; I called him 'my uncle' and was very fond of him. Fadlallah was a wise old 'nugget' (as we used to call a certain type of Sudanese) from whom I learned much and for whom I also had much affection."

In the field of education, relations were easier, as summarized by Farquharson-Lang: "It was not difficult to establish a close and friendly relationship with pupils and with Sudanese staff. When I was in the School of Arts and as headmaster [at] Wadi Seidna, we used to go on expeditions together to the remoter parts of the Sudan, travelling together by lorry or camel, and there were many opportunities of long talks together and getting to know one another. These meetings were natural and uninhibited and were the basis of close friendship. After about forty years I still correspond with several Sudanese whose friendship started on these journeys."

By far the most profound analyses of the social relations between the British and the Sudanese were offered by D. C. Carden and K. D. D. Henderson. Carden explained both the ease with which it was possible to develop "frank, easy relations with Sudanese in those days" (1942–1954) and the impediments that stood in the way of such relationships. "As a young man" in the Sudan, he began, "I lived very largely in the rural areas. And the drivers and the servants who were with me were really the equivalents of my family at home. Conversations I would have with my mother or my father or my brother in England would be about the commonplace or day-to-day events. One would talk about whether the apple tree in the garden was going to come into fruit early. . . . One might say that the gate at the bottom of the drive was coming off its hinges. One might talk about a tree which needed to be brought down and cut up for firewood. My father might complain that I had done damage to some part of the house.

"These are the things that one talks about—the trivialities of day-to-day life—which are the things that one focuses on with those to whom one is close. One doesn't talk about philosophical problems with them, and so it was with my [Sudanese] cook and driver. One would talk about food or the house or the garden or the car or the fuel, the journeys one was going to make, whether one was going to get stuck. . . .

"And since these people were the salt of the earth, since my cook looked after me in illness, there evolved a closeness of relationship with these men who normally were ordinary and uneducated, but who, in reality, if they had been given the opportunity for education might have evolved into important people. . . . These were indeed the people with whom I was very close.

"It was possible," Carden went on, "and still is possible [in the Sudan] to have the most open and easy conversations with people you never met before, with whom, for example, you may fall in at a well field or with whom you may be riding camels, or with whom you may be sharing a lorry, or in whose house you may find yourself staying—people to whom you've not been introduced, people who in England you would simply pass by in silence. So, particularly in the countryside, it was easy to talk freely and happily and without inhibitions to the people you chanced upon.

"By contrast, when I later came to work in Khartoum (for the Ministry of Finance) I found it much more difficult to have an equivalent relationship with those people with whom one might work. At the end of the working day, they went home to spend time with their wives, their children, their Sudanese colleagues, and we tended to go to our houses to spend the rest of the day following our pattern of behaviour, which was different from theirs. And though it did happen, it was relatively seldom, after the office was over, that one would find some shared interest like fishing or playing tennis or watching football, all of which were genuinely shared interests which would engross one and permit an entirely uninhibited hour or two hours with someone with whom you had spent the morning in the office."

Carden's "essential" criterion for close relations was "to have a completely uncontrived and genuine common interest. It might have been that the interest was in the treatment of camels [or] in bringing a fight to an end. . . . Relationships may either be genuine, frank, uninhibited, uncontrived—and those are the only worthwhile relationships—or they may be contrived and artificial. In days gone by it was easy for the administrators, or the vets, or the agriculturists, or the engineers out in the countryside to have uncontrived, genuine relation with those Sudanese with whom they moved.... It happened to be much more difficult in Khartoum." In urban situations, "for the most part British/Sudanese occasions seemed contrived rather than spontaneous and they lacked the happy, uninhibited friendships which were struck up as one worked in isolated districts. How much nicer to drink cold camel's milk with tribesmen in the shade of a thorn tree than to eat the most expensive cakes in a garden in Khartoum!"

Carden's post-colonial relations with people in the capital, when he returned as his country's ambassador, were different. "Now I am interested in Zimbabwe and so are they. Now I am interested in the history of the Mahdiya and so are they. Now I am interested in the complex issues which centre on the Palestinians, and so are they. Now I am interested in the whole range of economic problems which confront the Sudan, and so are they. This means to say that whereas thirty years ago, I might have taken tea with someone and had to search and he had to search for subjects in which we both had a strong, genuine interest, now there are far too many subjects for one to be able to cover."

"I have no doubt at all that those people who were at the top of the government, people like Sir Douglas Newbold,[1] had absolutely genuine, uninhibited, deeply interesting conversations with those Sudanese who had political aspirations," Carden said. "And this is on the record from the letters which ... Newbold exchanged with political leaders of that time.... And there was another group of people in Khartoum who could have the same sort of relations and these were the educationists—people like [G. C. Scott].[2] Scott was deeply interested in and personally deeply involved with the student body. And I haven't the faintest doubt that he would not spend his afternoons playing tennis with three other Englishmen— not a bit. He probably would spend his afternoon trying to unravel some problems for some student whom he had been teaching. Now in this, of course, his position was identical with that of the district commissioner who was sitting under a tree 250 miles west of Khartoum. There could be genuine, sincere, frank relationships in the town, but they were enjoyed by a much smaller percentage of the people."

Referring back to his personal experience, Carden explained that it had been much easier for him to form close friendships with Sudanese when he was unmarried. "I mean, as a bachelor one had nothing to hide!" But the real limitation to making friendships with the Sudanese, according to Carden, "was imposed by one's mental energy. One was working in a new language. All one's thought processes were therefore more of an effort and it is true that after one had spent five hours talking to a group of Nuer, one would be very tired. At that time of day one wants to go to sleep and recover. And the only snag was that they might not let you. They couldn't see, or anyway they didn't see, why you should want to stop talking until sundown when it was time to go to their *luaks.*"

Henderson gave details of his relations with Sudanese in each of his posts after the initial assignment to Medani. From there he was transferred to Nahud, where he established a "permanent friendship" with Yusuf Abu Saad, the *ma'mur* of the Baggara. "He was an extraordinary chap," Henderson said. Their friendship was built on mutual respect and a degree of distance. "I was a Christian, he was a Muslim; our arrangements were quite separate.... When on trek together, we would work together; we would separate to our respective tents and eat lunch; we would work together in the afternoon; in the evening we would retire to our respective tents to have our respective evening meals. Yusuf then used to get into his *jallabiya* and nine times out of ten he would send a chap over and say, 'Come over and have a cup of coffee.' But we never made any attempt to ... amalgamate ourselves because we recognized that we were different; our religious backgrounds were different. Our customs were different. He liked to eat stuff that would have burned out my insides and he regarded the kind of thing I ate as being almost unbelievably frightful. And so we didn't bother."

Henderson believed that the "reciprocal hospitality" which later entered into British-Sudanese relations "caused a great deal of discomfort." The notion that "people must feed together [was] not a matter of natural function, but almost a policy.... One or the other of them didn't enjoy the meal.... To go and have dinner with Sayyid Muhammad Khalifa Sharif and try to eat your way through thirteen courses—only the English of the Regency period could have done it.... A meal with Sayyid Muhammad really was a bit of a bind.... Sayyid Abd al-Rahman [Al-Mahdi][3] got to know better that the English stomach was of a limited capacity. If you dined with Sayyid Abd al-Rahman you were pretty sure to have a reasonable meal.

"Otherwise, a great deal of anguish . . . was caused amongst other things, by the fact that sometimes people didn't know whose business it was to tell when the party had come to an end. And I sat wearily until I realized that the host was wishing desperately that one of the guests would say, 'Well, don't you think that perhaps we should call it a night?' . . . It was at this stage that it was necessary for Griffiths[4] to bring out a book called *Sudan Courtesy Customs*,[5] so that the English would have some idea what the hell they were doing or not doing. In the earlier days you lived in compartments, but it didn't affect your social contact."

Henderson developed close working relations with Daud Abd al-Latif who, although a government official, was involved in the independence movement. Henderson told an anecdote to "illustrate the extraordinary personal relationship" between them. "There was a stage when Daud was working with me and I was supposed to be whatever I was, director of Public Security, I think. There was some talk of a big demonstration by the Ashigga Party. . . .[6] Daud came in with a bunch of vernacular press under his arm, as usual, in the morning. I said, 'Well, now what about this Ashigga demonstration?' He said, 'There won't be one!' And I said, 'How do you know?' And he said, 'Well, Yahya al-Fadli is in Cairo and somebody else is somewhere else and in the absence of those two, I am really running the party myself!'"

On another occasion, many years later, "Daud was over in London . . . and we were having lunch together. He said, 'Oh, by the way, I never told you about that! The day [your sister-in-law] was getting married [in Khartoum] they were going to have a monstrous demonstration. . . . I had to go over and explain to them that [the police] would ring you up and you would be called away from the wedding. And so they cancelled the whole thing.'"

The extent to which British and Sudanese were successful in bridging gaps may be judged, in certain respects, by comparing relations within the national groups with relations between them. As a rule, Nicholson explained, the British "met together frequently to play games or join[ed] each other in our respective homes or in the club—if there was one—to have a drink and/or dine together. . . . We talked about our private affairs and our children and what we planned to do when we went on leave. We also discussed world affairs and the political situation in Britain. Between us and the Sudanese there were not so many common interests, although we met them, for example, at the Cultural Centre in Khartoum for discussions and lectures, and some of us played cards or chess with them." John Winder placed more responsibility on British class barriers: "Meeting socially is not a thing the British find easy. They are said to be snobbish, and they probably are. They like to associate with people 'out of the same drawer' as themselves. In Port Sudan and in Khartoum there were clubs restricted to senior officials and the division between senior and junior officials was even more marked in Atbara. Having this attitude of exclusiveness militated against easy social intercourse with Sudanese. This did not mean any lack of respect or even affection. Though they might like to have Sudanese in their houses, they would be slow to invite countrymen with very different social backgrounds. I think it is important to understand this."

Circumspection was, for K. D. D. Henderson, the key to the difference in social relations among Britons and between them and the Sudanese. When he was the only Englishman in Nahud during the rainy season, Henderson said, there were long stretches of time that were best spent talking with someone. After a day's paperwork, "I used to go down to the Nahud Nadi al-Salaam [Peace Club]. . . . I knew perfectly well that although everybody was very polite and liked to see me there and so forth, they wouldn't really set their head down and start enjoying themselves until I had gone home. I always, therefore, took off after drinking a cup of coffee or something, after dark went back to my house, and was confronted with an entire evening. Now you reach a stage in which you can neither write nor read any more . . . where there is nothing left to do but to go to bed at nine and perhaps wake up and find . . . it is only twelve o'clock and you happen to have the whole night ahead of you. Now, none of that happens if you have got somebody of your own kind there whom you can sit with at night and—having got rid of whatever shop you talk (which, of course, was always the danger, that you could simply talk, talk, talk Nahud District)—you could sit back and start talking about something else and forget the whole thing. That was the closeness. . . . It was helped by the fact that we were very much drawn from the same class of English society. We thought the same way, we talked the same way, we had the same background, we probably had the same form of education. . . . Most of us read classics[7]; we had a slight difference between Oxford and Cambridge—it didn't amount to anything. . . . Now with your Sudanese contacts, until you got to know a chap as well as I got to know Yusuf Saad or Ali Abu Sinn, which was pretty intimately, you always had to have at the back of your mind the need for being careful of what you said." Henderson made an analogy with the way he would treat a clergyman visiting his home: "You usually try and adapt your conversation, or in some way to talk so that you aren't treading on one of his corns."

With the Sudanese, Henderson found himself limited by insufficient Arabic. "If a man was non-English speaking, and Yusuf was, one couldn't talk to him a great deal about matters of philosophy and so forth because one hadn't got the vocabulary. . . . You could talk about herd tax or the various points of camels or . . . anything that came into the law courts or . . . police affairs. But when you were confronted as I was for the first time when I went to Kosti . . . with dining with a man who wanted to discuss Christian theology . . . you found you were lamentably lacking in the words, the language."

Henderson related an incident which illustrates the sensitiveness of cultural differences, especially regarding religion. "Sayyid Abd al-Rahman al-Mahdi . . . was a very well-read chap. And Mr. Hancock[8] . . . rather ill-advisedly became involved with him on discussing about the Prophet's rules for drunkenness. Mr. Hancock was a very, very violently rigid sort of anti-drink man. We were talking actually about the status of women in Islam and Sayyid Abd al-Rahman said, 'Well, the Prophet was a chap who went along quietly stage by stage.' He said, 'Take drunkenness. He started off by saying, "You shouldn't say your prayers when you are drunk." And then he went and said it wasn't a very good thing to drink at all.' And Mr. Hancock took him up on this and said, 'Well, he was wrong in condoning drunkenness at all.' And Sayyid Abd al-Rahman looked at him and said, 'Well, it wasn't *our* Prophet who turned water into wine!' I thought he won on that one."

Sir Gawain Bell stated that "social mixing was, generally speaking, confined to tea parties, dinner occasionally, and occasions in the officials' club, when there was some party for some particular occasion or some official being transferred; and they were giving him a tea party to send him off. Speeches would be exchanged, and so on: it was fairly formal, this. When the British met over dinner, naturally the atmosphere was rather more relaxed because they spoke, in more senses than one, the same language. They had the same sort of cultural background, they had probably known each other for quite some considerable time.... And so there was a difference."

According to George Bredin, it was the Sudanese who made the adjustment in mixed situations: "I have always admired the capacity of the Sudanese to adapt themselves to the customs of their hosts. I believe that this facility makes Sudanese more at ease with British hosts than vice versa." Even in educational and cultural circles, the image of the rulers was safeguarded in front of the ruled; the British felt it necessary to protect one another in mixed company. According to V. L. Griffiths, "possibly the most significant fact was that in socially mixed situations, the British were likely to avoid any criticism of fellow British in front of the Sudanese." Another contributor admitted that even today he would not want to be quoted in disagreement with his ex-colleagues!

Many respondents stressed the role of women in the overall social equation. "I think in general an all-Sudanese or all-British occasion was easier than a mixed party, particularly if wives were involved," William McDowall said. "Large mixed social gatherings were likely to be more difficult, especially if senior officials or politicians were present, than smaller gatherings of four to six people who knew each other well and could talk freely. The younger men (British and Sudanese) were less inhibited than their seniors in this respect." Maurice Lush distinguished between small private gatherings and larger or public social events. The latter "only occasionally brought out the humour and good companionship which every Sudanese possesses; good manners prevented them. These qualities always emerged in private but seldom in public or social parties. One often wondered how the Sudanese would 'pillory' a British party."

On the issue of wives, Jean-Pierre Greenlaw noted that the social occasions at which they were present were not very different from social functions anywhere: "More decorum on the part of men—Sudanese and British—though the Sudanese *always* behaved with complete ease and perfect manners." Greenlaw also noted that the situation worsened "when short-term contract wives [sic] from a different social background began to arrive in greater numbers.

Their relationship with the servants was noticeably worse. The subject is very complex and involved—but I was impressed by the high degree of mutual respect and understanding of roles and behaviour expected by all, irrespective of colour, sex and rank."

The absence of Sudanese women, rather than the presence of British women, was regarded by many respondents as the main barrier to British-Sudanese socializing. As Kenrick illustrated: "An Omdurman notable would invite me to a meal with my wife. She would be expected to sit alone with me with perhaps a dozen men. After the meal she would be taken into another room to meet the women of the household." Nicholson also observed that "social mixing was difficult because the Sudanese wives would not come out with their husbands. On occasion some of my Sudanese friends came out to a meal in my house where my wife and I entertained them, but they could not bring their wives . . . which was understandable but unfortunate." D. C. Carden carried the point to its logical conclusion: "An Englishman in those days simply couldn't be taken into the heart of a Sudanese family, in the sense that he simply couldn't reach the stage at which he could ever meet the womenfolk. This, I believe, must have put a considerable brake on the . . . business because in his own home country that would be the way in which he would really get to know people apart from any working relationship."

Not surprisingly, the customary rigidity of town-life was unmatched in the provinces, as seen in Henderson's account: in Nahud he had a "very great friend" in Abd al-Rahim Abu Daqal,[9] who had been a "terrific character" during the Mahdia. "He was one of what we used to call the Slatin *nazirs* . . . put into power by Slatin Pasha. . . .[10] But his son Muhammad was like an elephant; he was the most enormous, terrific man. He must have weighed about twenty-five stone. When I used to go there—a place called Ayal Bakheit—we used to sit in the court all morning and in the afternoons he had a very engaging custom of inviting you to his inner home. There the old man used to sit on a groaning *angareb* [bed] and you sat on an adjacent *angareb*. And his various wives and daughters and his pet baboon, which was called Bakheit, used to come and play around. One sat there all through the heat of the afternoon gossiping, a thing I remember always as being utterly delightful, although it was a place set in a sea of *haskaneet* [thorny grass] and sand."

The position of British women in the Sudan shared in the ambivalence which characterized Anglo-Sudanese relations. On the one hand, there is ample testimony to a remarkable adjustment made by the wives. On the other hand, social and cultural constraints and the racial hierarchy implicit in colonial rule were powerful barriers to deep involvement in Sudanese society. There is a wide variety of viewpoints about the role of the British wives. Some contributors cited political reasons for their stated views, others stressed the hard conditions of work, some emphasized cultural constraints on the wives, while others noted their positive contribution.

K. D. D. Henderson described the early policy of the government to discourage young British officials from marrying or bringing their wives to the Sudan. "I was married in my last year at Nahud. I was a bachelor until 1935. I did nine years as a bachelor. Of course, you weren't allowed to get married then. For the first five years there was a ban on marriage, the most extraordinary rules. The governors were absolutely arbitrary. Baily Pasha[11] made a rule that no Englishman, no expatriate DC, if you prefer that, was allowed to have his wife in the country at all, except for some extraordinarily limited period of sixty days a year or something. It was considered in the old belief of men like Baily and Dupuis that they distracted a man's attention from his work, and Dupuis was very, very strong on it, you see. He said, 'If you must have that sort of thing, then you can go and get a Baggara girl; get a Baggara girl to come to you and improve your Arabic.' Of course, what he didn't realize was that if you had a Baggara girl, of all people on earth, you might improve your Arabic, but it would be the absolutely intolerable position for a district commissioner because of the dark side." For Henderson, the "dark side" was that the district commissioner would compromise his position as an impartial administrator.[12]

Respondents agree that relations with local women were extremely rare. But here, too, the complications of the colonial context pertained. Being unmarried, or if married not bringing wives to the Sudan and maintaining a distance from native women, all combined to create new cross-cultural problems because the Sudanese found it incomprehensible that a man of the district commissioner's age and responsibility should remain unattached.

Henderson encountered this attitude. "The Missiriya al-Zarug once got worried about my bachelordom. We had a meeting of the court once in the rains and it petered out. It was one of those lovely days in the early rains when the entire place is turning green and the animals are grazing and there is a nice grey sky and there was a gentle rain into little puddles. . . . We sat there drinking coffee, and they all went into a huddle in the corner of the court. . . . And after a bit [a *shaykh*] turned around and . . . stroked his beard and said, 'Do you mind if we ask you something rather personal?' And I said, 'No.' And he said, 'Well, we think you ought to get married. We don't think it is right for a man of your age not to be married. It is very unsuitable, sort of undesirable. What we have decided is that we understand that you marry for life, and therefore it is only natural that you aren't going to go rushing in and marry the first woman you clap your eyes on. We well understand that all these years you have been looking about; you still are. But all right, marry a Missiri girl, and hand over [cattle as bridewealth]; and then, when the time comes that you want to marry one of your own women, you can divorce her. Anybody would be very happy to marry her and you will get back your cattle; they will give you back your cattle.'

"And I said, 'Well, first of all, what about the children?' 'Oh,' they said, 'well, they could be brought up as interpreters; they will be great children.' So I said, 'Now, well, look gentlemen. What are we going to do next winter while we are in al-Lagawa?' They thought for a bit and then said, 'Oh, you mean making the boundary with the Homr and the Tombar.' I said, 'Yes.' And I said, 'Supposing I come down to make those boundaries bringing with me my Missiri wife. What sort of credit am I going to be given for giving an unbiased judgement by the Homr and the Tombar?' And they said, 'Well, that is perfectly true.' I must say that at one stage in the proceedings they said, 'You can take your choice of any of our girls.' And I thought how wonderful it would be to say, 'Rightho, parade them on Tuesday,' and walk down the line and say, 'Out, wait over there,' and knock them down to six. However, they said, 'All right, all right. No, we quite agree, perhaps you cannot have a Missiri girl, but why not have a girl from the river?' I said, 'Well, that is perfectly simple: because no respectable girl from the river would marry me." And they said, 'Oh, well, we could arrange one.' And I said, 'Yes, well, thank you very much. . . . '
But anyway I ended up saying, 'Well, it is a matter of religion in a

way. One doesn't do that in my country.' Which perhaps made things a bit difficult for some of my colleagues who unknown to me were indulging in some of these practices—but not DCs."

Mrs. Henderson (who attended the interview with her husband) interjected: "I think you should also remember that they [Baily and Dupuis] had a certain amount of reason, because Charles Dupuis was governing a province [Darfur] which was very difficult to get in and out of. And if women or children got ill there, the husband would have had to get them somehow down that terrible road.... What about the leg that got broken on the lorry on the way home from school from El Obeid? I mean injuries were probable and people were a long, long way from proper medicine, weren't [they]? And terribly difficult to get ... no aeroplanes. Once there were aeroplanes, the whole picture changed."

"I think this was a good rule," said Gawain Bell about the ban on wives. "It was important that a young man learning his job should be free of any sort of encumbrance, should be free to move about the country at short notice, travel long distances, make exhausting journeys; and I think that to have a wife and possibly even a child with him at that early stage would have been a disadvantage. So I think rightly this rule was introduced. And with regard to British officers of the Sudan Defence Force: they were not allowed to marry. If they wished to get married they had to put in their resignations. Some of the very senior officers in Khartoum did in fact have wives, but I don't think there were ... wives in any of the corps stations—that is to say El Fasher, El Obeid, Kassala, Shendi, and so on. I think they were all unmarried officers."

"It depended very much on the wife, how she fitted into the situation and her husband's work," Bell observed about wives in general. "There were a number of ladies who were certainly interested in the countryside and the people, who learned a certain amount of Arabic. There were quite a number who were good artists and did a good deal of sketching and drawing and so on. There were some who collected flowers and shrubs and things of that sort. And as far as it was possible—this applied to my own wife, after all—whenever one was on tour, one's wife ... would ask permission to call on the family of the *omda* or *shaykh* in the village ... and make some sort of contact—superficial, certainly, but at least a friendly gesture toward the ladies of the village or the encampment. There were wives who travelled with their husbands when they were on trek. And when they were in the station, of course, they made themselves responsible for running the house and arranging the meals, and if there was entertainment to be done, that was their responsibility."

"Life in general was much more difficult in the Sudan for expatriate wives than for their husbands, particularly in remote or lonely posts," John Phillips said. "Husbands had their jobs to do: wives were left for long periods to their own devices in a climate which for much of the year was not conducive to much activity. Some adapted well, finding various ways of helping their husbands by getting to know Sudanese and, in a few cases, Arabic or another local language. In the larger towns some could themselves find jobs. A few were temperamentally or physically unsuited to be in the Sudan at all, but I think most coped pretty well."

John Kenrick expressed the generally-held view that the role of British women largely depended "on whether the British wife had learnt Arabic. Those wives who were not able to speak it met . . . in each other's houses or at the clubs. On the other hand, those who could speak Arabic took an interest in the people they met when on trek with their husbands, or took a leadership role in women's affairs, as for example my wife did with Girl Guides in Omdurman and Khartoum."

"British wives varied," said D. C. Carden. "Some made marvelous companions for their husbands, being ready to smile at any trial, tribulation, illness, or separation. Others became embittered. . . . The life that we led, particularly if we were living in the countryside, was very different to that of a family in England. For example, one might well need to spend twenty days out of every month on trek. This meant leaving the house. It meant camping. It meant perhaps illness. It certainly meant very real complications if a wife had children. All these things a wife would take in her stride if she was devoted to her husband. Indeed, the mere fact that they were difficult perhaps added to the satisfaction that she derived from overcoming them for the sake of the man to whom she was devoted. . . . But say she really wasn't devoted to him: might she then not come to think that this way of life was not worth the candle? And then you might indeed have a situation in which the husband, very much enjoying this type of life, wished to go on with it; the wife very much not enjoying it, might want to stop it: and then the wife would be embittered."

Maurice Lush, however, gave unqualified praise to the British wives. "I was married in 1930. I can say without hesitation that British wives fitted into the administration, and every situation, most admirably—without them the administration would have suffered severely. Make no doubt about it: the presence and the infiltration of the British wives into the lives of the Sudanese families made a tremendous influence for good in the Sudan, which the men alone could never have achieved."

Robin Hodgkin warned against generalizations but called attention again to the dichotomy in British attitudes toward the remote areas and the towns: "I think that most British officials who were married in out-stations carried their wives with them in regard to progressive policies and in all that happened as the country moved toward independence. There were exceptions, of course. I think there was a tendency for some wives, who were not closely involved with educated Sudanese or technical Sudanese, to develop a somewhat more conservative attitude, partly because their horizon tended to be limited to catering and small-town talk. I do think this applied more to those couples who lived in cities, however, than to those who were making a rather more challenging life in the country."

Others drew the same distinction between town and country, always, paradoxically, favoring the latter, which was culturally more foreign and physically more difficult for British ladies. Greenlaw believed that "most wives in the provinces fitted in remarkably well and many actively helped their husbands, accompanying them on vigourous treks and undertaking local work with [Sudanese] women—in schools, hospitals, in small-group entertainment, or classes in homes. Some—younger ones—took time to adjust; a few could not—but they were a few. In towns where this kind of work was not so easy, women kept more to themselves and to 'good works' amongst the white community—church work, etc. With them, social contacts were less harmonious: too little to do." John Winder observed that "in Port Sudan and Khartoum, and equally in Malakal . . . the British wives had little to do with the Sudanese. In the districts—outside Malakal—the wives often played a more important part and saw a good deal of the people."

The situation of educators, according to William Farquharson-Lang, was particularly favorable for the involvement of British wives: "We were very fortunate insofar as all wives shared so much in all professional interests. At a boarding school or in the school of arts, our wives got to know many of the students. We entertained them, played games with them and so on; and with the staff, my wife ran a club for the British and the Sudanese wives and their children; and the New Year party was a remarkable event of the season. I can honestly say I never saw any racial feelings among the members of my staff or their wives. I think I was very lucky in that respect—British families were on first name terms with Sudanese families and relationships were very cordial."

Although the role of British women was complicated, it was clearly less so than the relations between British officials and Sudanese women. To disentangle political, racial, cultural, official, and personal factors in describing those relations is difficult and illustrative of the limits imposed by the colonial context. A substantial number of respondents stated unequivocally that they had not been aware of such relationships. A. W. Ireland was definite: "To my knowledge, there were no such relationships at all and the matter of how they were viewed did not arise, either privately or publicly." Similarly, F. D. McJannet stated: "As far as my limited knowledge goes, there were no such relationships during the time of British rule." Douglas Dodds-Parker was even more categorical: "If anyone even winked at one of those delightful Baggara girls, he was sent back to Britain. None did go back to my knowledge."

Contradicting these denials, a number of respondents acknowledged that there had been or could have been love affairs between British officials and Sudanese women, but stressed that they were very rare, discreet, and viewed with disfavor or, at best, ignored. "I know of isolated cases," Bredin said, "in which British officers married Sudanese girls with local customary ritual. Less formal relationships no doubt existed. Liaisons of either kind were generally frowned on in the Political Service." According to Nicholson, "there was a certain amount of what one might call temporary concubinage between bachelors and local native women in outlying parts of the country, especially where officials living lonely lives . . . had very little, if any, social life. This was tolerated, provided it was not too blatant."

These relationships were discreet liaisons outside marriage. Recognized marriages were even more exceptional, or, according to Maurice Lush, out of the question: "I heard of—did not know—one small group in another province which was said to indulge in orgiastic parties. For the rest (I am writing of the Political Service), on the whole the idea of taking a Sudanese girl to wed was simply not in tune with and in fact repellent to the position of the *mufettish* [district commissioner] and his people."

A number of respondents properly distinguished between the period up to 1924, during which British officials were discouraged from marrying or bringing their wives to the Sudan, and the subsequent period after the policy was reversed. Then, in Buchanan's words, "more British wives joined their husbands for the first time in relatively isolated stations—for example, in Darfur. Until then, a few British DCs had taken Sudanese mistresses who lived in the background, but this was not a common practice—most of us remained celibate." The dividing line, according to Gawain Bell, was the First World War: before then "there were no motor cars, ... distances were vast, men were cut off and lonely for long periods of time. There were a number of man-woman relationships, very limited. ... I heard of two, and indeed in the Nuba Mountains there was a child who was the product of a British-Sudanese relationship. Between the wars, I think I knew of only one case."

Addressing himself to the later period, Henderson explained that even informal liaisons were extremely rare and were viewed with disfavor. "Earlier on it varied in inverse proportion to distance. In the old days, in Darfur, when you didn't get off on leave very often and you were a long way from anywhere, I think it was pretty common. I know there were one or two. ... The awful warning to my generation was a fellow who ... got involved with a daughter or niece or something of a local *omda* of some kind, who brought pressure to bear on him and in a way blackmailed him. He was a very promising young man, but his career was finished. He ended up simply as a personal assistant to the governor of the Blue Nile Province. ... Normally, he would have been governing a province himself." Even despite this warning, there were tempting moments: "The only time I was ever, as it were, physically attracted or tempted by a Baggara girl, and the Baggara girls didn't conceal their charms, was after a long, the longest spell for me anyway, without leave. I can well remember the occasion with the girl. She was involved in some case. And her story was that the Nuba from one of the hills attacked her and they were going to cut off her breasts until she was rescued or something or other. Well, she was always turning up. And it was always necessary to tell me exactly what they were going to do, removing anything that she happened to be wearing above the waist and giving me a demonstration of what they were going to do. And I remember her turning up once. It was a thing which left me completely cold until one time when I had been out and she turned up about the fourth occasion. I suddenly looked at her as a woman for the first time. She spotted it. She looked at me and sort of raised an eyebrow and all of a sudden the interview came to an end. But honestly, I have been surprised to learn since I retired that A or B whom I knew had been so involved.

"I think it would be a surprise for many people who are living in the 1980s in the United Kingdom if they could know just how few British, who were isolated in the Sudan during and after the war, *did* seek out sexual relationships with Sudanese or with others outside marriage. Most of the people I know or knew best were either in the Education Service or in the Political Service, and what I say probably applies more correctly to those two than to the others, though in general the same applies. First of all, there were relatively few instances where isolated British officials had affairs with Sudanese. In 1940 I had the good fortune to travel very widely, in Darfur and Kordofan, staying with DCs and other British officials. I suppose I must have got to know something like twenty. Most of these were isolated, and their wives were at home, or they were not yet married."

The situation in the Three Towns was the focus of Farquharson-Lang's comments. "Most of the British officials were married. There were a few bachelors, likewise a few unmarried British girls working as nurses, teachers, and so on, and there were certainly close friendships between the unattached. But in the Three Towns I never heard of any close or lasting friendship outside marriage between British and Sudanese. It is true that some British bachelors in Khartoum infrequently visited the establishment of a certain Madame Zeinab who would provide attractive Sudanese girls for their entertainment. The authorities in Khartoum discreetly shut their eyes to what was a very natural outlet for virile young bachelors."

A variety of reasons were given for why "both officially and privately," to use Bell's words, these relationships "were viewed with disfavor." For one thing, "it was not thought at all right that a British official and particularly a British administrative official, a member of [the] Sudan Political Service, should have any sort of relation with Sudanese women. It put him in a very vulnerable position, quite apart from the fact that it was regarded as morally wrong." And, according to Bredin, "It was clearly undesirable that an officer with such authority should have a relationship of this kind with one particular family in the district." Henderson's self-restraint was based on similar considerations: "Knowing the whole of the northern Sudan setup in which every girl would have sisters, cousins, aunts, and brothers, all people in need of jobs, the lady would say: 'Couldn't you get my chap made a sub-*ma'mur*?' Or: 'My cousin George is working in the post office and has been done out of his promotion.' I thought, 'No, I cannot involve myself in that sort of thing.'"

The extent to which "proper conduct" was upheld had much to do with conditions of service and the attitudes of both sides. The overwhelming view of respondents was that annual leave enabled them to endure the hardship of loneliness. According to Maurice Lush: "The Sudan Government determined from the outset of the condominium that life would be hard and generally lonely for British officials, and that loneliness, lack of female society and comfort would be hard to bear. It was therefore decided that for expatriates, annual leave of three months should be granted. This wise provision, which was interrupted only by the two wars, did a great deal to maintain a level of sexual behaviour which was on the whole normal."

The attitude of the Sudanese was also significant: the rarity of mixed relationships probably owed much to the fact that "Sudanese girls were carefully guarded. . . . At least in the Muslim north," Phillips said, "it was generally socially unacceptable for Sudanese girls of marriageable age to meet potential husbands who were not themselves Muslims." Others also drew attention to differences between attitudes in the Muslim north and those of non-Muslim southern Sudanese and, to a certain extent, the Muslim population of the western Sudan. Jean-Pierre Greenlaw wrote of the rarity of British-Sudanese love affairs before World War II, "except for isolated areas in the south where it was not unknown for district officers to take a southern Sudanese wife. It was not encouraged. In the north it was unknown and discouraged by Sudanese as much as the British." Owen, who had had extensive experience in both north and south, also reported: "The only ones I know of were in the south, where the Bimbashis generally kept a woman (partly as a means of getting intelligence from the Suk!). There were one or two 'coloured' children about, sons of officers with a Sudanese mother, but very few indeed." Henderson, too, remarked that intermarriage "was much commoner in the south, of course. There was Jack Poole who married a Dinka girl. I always remember a story about being in the chief's court there in Gogrial or somewhere, and a young Dinka coming in and being very respectful to all concerned, including all the chiefs who were present. And as he walked out he slapped Jack Poole on the shoulder. Jack Poole said to Monywir Rehan or whoever the chap was, 'Who is that fellow?' And he said, 'Don't you know your own brother-in-law?'" While Poole's case seems to have been accepted locally, it remained an anomaly as we shall see in the accounts of southern Sudanese themselves.

Several contributors indicate that while Islam prohibited the marriage of a Muslim girl and a non-Muslim man, attitudes in the western Sudan were more liberal. "In two instances known to me," John Phillips wrote, "British district commissioners, both in the Nuba Mountains, married Sudanese girls by local custom. One was Major Deane,[13] in the 1920s, who eventually returned to England [in 1930] and married an Englishwoman, leaving his Sudanese wife and his two sons well provided for by local standards of the day. (Douglas Newbold, then governor of Kordofan, took a personal interest in their education and welfare.) The other was Oswald Bentley,[14] who resigned in 1921 after five years in the Nuba Mountains. I do not know what arrangements he may have made for his dependents. Ian Gillespie, a veterinary officer in Darfur, also left a half-Sudanese son, Yusuf, who appeared to be flourishing in Khartoum during my ambassadorship (1973–1977), but I know no details of this affair."

As is apparent in British accounts, these relationships and marriages were hardly ever formally recognized. The British never took their Sudanese wives or children to England. According to Carden, this was primarily for cultural rather than racial or other reasons: "Of course, it would have been difficult if the women had been taken home to England or Scotland. They would have been like fish out of water. It is an entirely different matter for a Sudanese now to go to England and meet and marry a girl there, in the sense that the cultural gap between them would be smaller."

"How did the Sudanese men view the British women?" Henderson's answer was equivocal: "Well, that you will have to ask them about. You see, I simply don't know because they were far too polite to indicate in any way what their view on that was. I always assumed they regarded them as being a very unattractive bunch of women, but I may be quite wrong. You see, that chap who said to me about Bint Beila, how wonderfully beautiful she was: that if she lay down on her side you could roll a watermelon through the arch of her waist; his idea of pulchritude and mine were so different. I always sort of considered that they regarded our women as being not really in the same category.... I don't know. They would never let on.

"Governor Baily told me that right at the end of his career [in 1933] the chief merchant said to him one day, 'You know, we know each other very well; do you mind if I ask you a personal question?' And he said, 'What?' And the merchant said: 'One thing that absolutely staggers us ... is why you English have never brought your wives out to this country since the war.' That was the '14–18 war. And Baily said: 'Never brought our wives! Whatever do you mean?' The chap said, 'Well, you haven't brought out your wives.' And Baily said, 'You were having tea in my house last week.' 'Oh, yes,' he said, 'indeed I was. And nobody could possibly ask for a more charming hostess. And we all in this town greatly appreciate the work she has done for the hospital and midwives,' and whatever it was that Mrs. Baily occupied herself with. But, he said, 'We know what an Englishman's wife looks like. She wears a blouse up to there and she wears a skirt down to there. Not one of them has been out here since 1914.' He then realized that for fourteen years they had all assumed that all the Englishmen's wives were in fact their mistresses because they wore short skirts, weren't respectable. But they never let on. How could you expect me to be able to tell you what they thought of ours?"

Times changed, and so did mutual views. In the accounts of British respondents there is general agreement that in the last years of the condominium era, male-female relationships between British and Sudanese increasingly relaxed, particularly with regard to marriages of Sudanese men and British women. T. H. B. Mynors wrote that "with the change in culture and education, mixed marriages were increasingly accepted without difficulty." Others were less certain about attitudes toward these marriages and their prospects for success. Griffiths noted that "there were a few intermarriages during my period (1929–1950), but they usually occurred in

England when Sudanese were on courses. I think that while they were generally accepted by the British community, many people thought them doubtfully wise because of the many differences in family customs." McDowall felt that the reception given these marriages was even cooler: "In those days [1939–1947] mixed marriages were frowned on by most British and, I suspect, most Sudanese." In Greenlaw's opinion, these "Sudanese-British marriages . . . were not always successful, but there were some notable exceptions where British wives of Sudanese contributed socially to their husbands' careers." Theobald also noted that "some of these mixed marriages were notably successful, but rather frequently they broke down in a few years." In Bowcock's recollections, "when a Sudanese brought a British bride back from his studies in Britain there was usually some apprehension as to how she would fit into the Muslim family pattern, particularly with her mother-in-law. However, I remember there was one older couple who seemed very happy and were entertained everywhere. I cannot remember their name but she was Scottish." "Where the man had adopted a Western style of life, we would exchange entertainment," Kenrick said, but "where the man's family still followed a Sudanese style of life, the wife tended to do the same and disappear."

John Phillips indicated that while there has been a considerable shift in favor of mixed marriages between the Sudanese and the British, no generalization can be justified concerning their acceptance or prospects for success. To illustrate, he recalled the British reaction to one proposed marriage: "I well remember, when I was district commissioner, Southern Gezira at Wad Medani in 1951–1952, hearing the story about a meeting at the Sudan Gezira Board at Barakat, at the same time when Mekki Abbas, recently appointed deputy manager SGB, was about to marry Dr. Elmer Davidson. A rather pompous, colour-conscious British senior member of the board asked the manager (Mr. Raby, who had recently succeeded Mr. Gaitskell), 'What is the policy of the Sudan Gezira Board in the matter of the proposed marriage of Mekki Effendi Abbas and Dr. Davidson?' To which Mr. Raby's reply was, 'The policy of the Sudan Gezira Board in this, as in other matters, is to mind its own bloody business.'"

Presumably because of their isolation and the absence or discouragement of relationships between British men and Sudanese women, there is a popular assumption in the Sudan that homosexuality was prevalent among the British. Indeed, it is generally believed that homosexuality as such was a colonial import previously unknown to the Sudanese. Virtually all contributors, however, emphatically denied any knowledge of homosexual practices among the British in the Sudan. Most responses were curt but to the point. "I never heard of any and would say it was most unlikely to have happened," John Winder wrote. Paul Howell did not "recall ever hearing such tendencies even discussed in connection with colleagues."

Several respondents offered possible reasons for a complete absence of homosexuality. Farquharson-Lang observed that "British officials were very carefully chosen, and I am sure a known homosexual would not [have] been appointed." Carden agreed: "In that era, homosexuality was so despised that anyone with the slightest reputation for it would have failed to obtain a job. In addition, homosexuality had an effeminate connotation. And service in the Sudan called for robustness and resilience." Theobald offered the opinion that "the rigours of the climate and most jobs, coupled with the free way of living, were likely to lessen any sexual pressure of that sort." Bell drew attention to the generous leave granted the administrators: "There was really no reason why anything rather abnormal of this sort should develop, simply in view of isolation. No, the answer is no."

A few had heard rumors of homosexual liaisons or incidents involving British colleagues, but these rumors were usually secondhand and vague, and those who mentioned them stressed their isolated nature. McDowall, for instance, wrote, "I know of only one *alleged* case—I cannot be sure that it was true. Homosexuality was very much frowned on by the British in those days." Henderson, too, had heard of only one case, and that was related to him after he retired. It involved an officer who had allegedly kept a Sudanese "fancy boy." Henderson learned of this from the widow of the officer's successor, who disclosed that her husband had always borne a grudge against his predecessor, because his own administration had been marked by attempts at blackmail by the boy's mother.

Henderson stressed the sublimation of homosexual tendencies, indeed of all sexual urges, by the British in the Sudan: "You see, one of the things that is unbelievable to this generation—unbelievable, I think, to my own son—is that we were celibate but not homosexual. . . . I don't say that it was universal but I do know that amongst half a dozen men who were my particular friends at Oxford, we led a celibate life . . . and not only were we not homosexuals, but any suggestion of homosexuals revolted us. And yet we contrived, as I suppose a Roman Catholic priest contrives, to get along without it." In the Sudan, he said, "there were chaps who were mildly homosexual in the sense that they preferred the company of men to the company of women and were rather frightened of women. Our most distinguished man, Douglas Newbold, was such a man. Douglas Newbold was in no conceivable sense of the word a homosexual, but . . . if you said to him that your wife was on leave, his eyes would light up and he would say, 'Ah, when is she going? On Monday? Come to dinner on Tuesday.' He liked the company of men and . . . [especially] of young men . . . ; it stimulated him. He was not in any manner of speaking homosexual, but he did like, and preferred, male company. There were plenty of others like him."

Robin Hodgkin corroborated Henderson's views on a number of points. "Many people in the 1980s," he said, "would find [it] difficult to understand [that] the number of homosexual relationships between British officials when they were isolated from womenfolk was, amongst the people I know, practically nonexistent." In Khartoum he had suspected that one or two Englishmen were practicing homosexuals, "but I never inquired very closely." He could state with certainty, however, that "all the people that I knew well—well enough that we would have shared such knowledge—were not in any way practising homosexuals." Hodgkin went on to say, "I can remember one colleague, an extremely good schoolmaster, who was known to be quite fond of his pupils, and to develop such affection rather more strongly than most of us, but I'm quite certain that he had no actively erotic relationships with any of his pupils or with any other British.

"What contemporary British intellectuals fail to understand when talking about these questions is that we lived a fairly full life in many ways, but we were to some extent 'guarded' by taboos. It is fashionable nowadays to speak of 'taboos' as though they were something undesirable which one had to escape or stop. This may sometimes be true. But what modern sociologists and social scientists totally fail to realize is that taboos such as those on incest, but also on homosexual behaviour and even on sex outside marriage, had an exceptionally strong influence in making a disciplined and dedicated society capable of resisting.

"The three British for whom I had the greatest admiration and from whom I learned the most were all bachelors and probably all homosexuals in a nonactive way. That is to say, I think they had found it difficult to form a relationship with a woman before the war, during that short period of leave, and had got accustomed to the idea that they were bachelors. And, as a result of this, they probably did have quite strong feelings of attraction to men. . . . These three people, whom I deeply honour . . . were Douglas Newbold, who became civil secretary; Cuthbert Scott, who was my first headmaster (a man who, though not a vociferous Christian—in fact he would sometimes say he wasn't a Christian—was nevertheless a person of saintly dedication and of greatness); [and] Griffiths, who founded Bakht-e-Ruda, was also a very great man in his way and he funnelled most of his great gifts—intellectual, imaginative, and brotherly—into the development of his great Institute of Education. I remember slight undercover accusations being made at one stage that perhaps he was an active homosexual, but I do not believe this to be the case, and it would have been quite out of character."

Newbold was "criticized by his contemporaries because he was rather inclined to have young assistant district commissioners or teachers like myself to stay at his house. I lived with him during the early years of the war for about three months as a guest, and it was a tremendously educational time. He would sometimes speak a little bit indiscreetly about what was happening in the war, but he entirely trusted me—and similarly, he would trust young assistant district commissioners, who might spend three or four months with him as his guests. This was really a wonderful education and one learned a great deal about the philosophy of a highly gifted administrator. It was very civilizing. He taught us a great deal about the Sudan and he taught us how to love it.

"To my knowledge there was never . . . any erotic element in these relationships. Nevertheless, I can quite understand that some older district commissioners or governors might have felt that this was indiscreet. I think this is another interesting example of the way in which a modern biographer would probably suggest there was 'no smoke without fire,' but in fact the relationship was honorable and correct."

Notes

1. Sir Douglas Newbold (1894–1945) served in the Sudan from 1920 (from 1939 as civil secretary) until his death. Enormously influential and respected by British and Sudanese alike, he made a deep impression in the development of Sudanese politics. See K. D. D. Henderson, *The Making of the Modern Sudan: The Life and Letters of Sir Douglas Newbold, K.B.E., of the Sudan Political Service*, 2d ed. (Westport, Conn.: Greenwood Publishers, 1974).

2. George Cuthbert Scott served in the Sudan from 1922 until 1946: as warden of the Gordon Memorial College from 1937 to 1943 and as vice-principal, from 1944 to 1946.

3. Sayyid Abd al-Rahman al-Mahdi (1885–1959), son of Muhammad Ahmed, the Mahdi, leader of the Ansar and patron of the Umma party.

4. V. L. Griffiths was the founding head of the Institute of Education at Bakht al-Ruda. For his work see his *An Experiment in Education: An Account of the Attempts to Improve the Lower Stages of Boys' Education in the Moslem Anglo-Egyptian Sudan, 1930–1950* (London: Longman, 1953).

5. Coauthored by Abdel Rahman Ali Taha and published by the Sudan Government in 1936.

6. Literally "full brothers," the first Sudanese political party, it called for the "Unity of the Nile Valley," that is, political union of the Sudan and Egypt.

7. Cf. Mangan, "The Education of an Elite Imperial Administration"; and A. H. M. Kirk-Greene, *The Sudan Political Service: A Preliminary Profile* (London: Oxford University Press, 1982).

8. G. M. Hancock served from 1925 until 1950. He was deputy civil secretary 1945–1946 and governor of Kassala 1946–1950.

9. Abd al-Rahim Abu Daqal (ca. 1859–1933), *nazir* of the Gharaysiya branch of the Hamar tribe. Cf. Richard Hill, *A Biographical Dictionary of the Sudan*, 2d ed. (London: Cass Publishers, 1957), 15.

10. Sir Rudolf von Slatin (1857–1932). An Austrian official of the Turco-Egyptian regime and sometime prisoner of the Khalifa Abdallahi, he served as inspector-general in the Sudan Government from 1900 to 1914. His personal influence was often brought to bear in the appointment of Sudanese. For his biography see Richard Hill, *Slatin Pasha* (London: Oxford University Press, 1965).

11. R. E. H. Baily served from 1909 to 1933, as governor of Kassala from 1926.

12. As a young district commissioner, Henderson fully supported the government's policy on the matter of wives. See M. W. Daly, *Empire on the Nile: The Anglo-Egyptian Sudan, 1898–1934* (Cambridge: Cambridge University Press, 1986), 357.

13. L. A. Deane served in the Nuba Mountains from 1918 until his retirement in 1930.

14. Bentley served from 1905 to 1926, as governor of the Fung Province from 1921 to 1924, and as governor of Dongola from 1924 to 1926.

3

Working Conditions and Attitudes

British respondents were unanimous that interest in, and liking for, their work largely compensated for the "lack of amenities" and relative absence of opportunities to mix socially. McDowall wrote that "for most of the British the Sudan was a hot, trying and unhealthy country compared with Britain. There were long separations from wife, children and family.... Yet most of the British men enjoyed their lives there, for two main reasons: (a) they loved their work because they felt it was worthwhile; and (b) they liked the Sudanese." "When I was in Talodi," Bell said, "especially during the rains, there were periods when for at least two months I had no social life at all. There were occasions [during] that length of time when I met no other European, and it never really worried me at all. I was constantly in town; one's work was full of interest and activity; one was very tired at the end of the day; and one probably went to sleep at about eight o'clock at night because one was getting up at five in the morning."

"I would have been miserable to see my youth slipping away in such discomfort and isolation had it not been for the fascination of the work and the sense that it was worthwhile," Bowcock explained. "The job gave responsibility at a very early age and enabled one to achieve much more than one could have in any other field of activity until one's forties or fifties." Sandars agreed that "the sense of responsibility ... compensated for many discomforts." He added: "We were fired with an almost missionary zeal in the performance of our work." Griffiths felt that he "was very lucky in having a job [as an educational administrator] with creative opportunities far in excess of those in any job I might have got at home." He found himself "too busy to worry" about any lack of amenities or social contact. For McJannet, the work was "all-embracing and absorbing." The lack of European luxuries had been a shock at first to John Phillips: "I found the going a bit rough during my first months at Talodi in the hot season, with no refrigerator—and of course no electricity. But I was young, robust and unmarried, and as often on trek ... either with horses or mules—even bulls—or on foot, as I was in the Merkaz." And, according to Robin Hodgkin, despite "a somewhat Spartan and isolated existence ... it should be said that in many ways our life was relatively comfortable, if one were to compare it during the war with people on active service."

Several respondents drew attention to the outside interests which filled any spare time. "I think it should be remembered," Farquharson-Lang wrote, "that British officials spent the best part of their lives (age 23 to 48) in the Sudan.... The British ... at that age have the peculiar facility of finding entertainment for themselves, sometimes intellectual (like the study of Arabic or anthropology) or physical (like horsemanship or gardening or shooting)." Owen commented similarly: "There were so many *hobbies* to keep one happy—local history, languages, hunting, forest knowledge, archaeology, climbing mountains (where they exist!) and so on. I always encouraged my district commissioners to take up hobbies." And according to Theobald, "The interest was enormous at almost all times—human factors, natural history (birds, animals, scenery, etc.), local and national political situations, the genuine feeling that one was somehow contributing to the betterment and 'progress' of the land. In my early years my spare time was spent in linguistic and cultural studies and research. In later years, I devoted much time to the development of organised football competition. These are but examples of how interest filled one's day." Indeed, Theobald "was not conscious of a lack of amenities and lack of opportunities to mix socially in Khartoum. I loved my work and enjoyed my social life."

"Taking one year overall," Dodds-Parker observed, "one had as much social life during one's leave as one needed." Carden recalled that "people worked without a break from the day upon which they returned from leave until the day upon which they went on leave the succeeding year.... But the leaves were long. Eighty days in England—and that was the period for morale. I was prepared to put everything into the nine months' work and not worry too much about rest and comfort." The incentive provided by the lengthy leave was absent elsewhere: "I noticed the contrast in northern Rhodesia. The climate was much better and the tour was two and a half or three years. The result was rather less enthusiasm for the job." Farquharson-Lang concluded that the annual leave was a valuable period in which "our intellectual batteries could be recharged."

Given the idealism which British ex-officials remember as informing their work, it is not surprising that a substantial majority of respondents claim that their overriding purpose was to guide the people; a fair number affirmed that part of their task was protecting the Sudanese. Only a few admitted an element of dominion in their idea of the British mission, and several adamantly denied it.

The educator, Griffiths, saw his mission as one of guidance: "Essentially, I believe this to be the right attitude toward education." Hodgkin agreed that "the predominant motive among educationalists was to guide. . . . But I don't think 'to guide' really quite covers what we were learning to do during the later and more material part of our service. . . . I'm quite sure that we also realised that there was an element of what would not be called, in contemporary jargon, '[being] there to help in the process of consciencization'; that is, of making . . . our pupils, our colleagues , and ourselves more deeply conscious of the problems in which we were involved. This is not the same as guiding—it is a subtle concept, but it is one we were certainly experiencing in the more effective and imaginative joint enterprises in which we were involved, in places like Bakht-e-Ruda or in the development of a project like the Gezira. But there [at the Gezira Scheme] my impression was [that] there was only a small minority of people like Arthur Gaitskell, rather than the main body of officials, who entered deeply into this 'consciousness' with the Sudanese that he was working with."

Hodgkin submitted another example of "this kind of educative process" at work: "Newbold and Griffiths and one or two others, during the later years of the war, conceived of the idea of having a new kind of cross-cultural conference—rather on the lines of what they now call a workshop in the United States—in which Sudanese and British officials and teachers would come together to discuss important problems. Thus was born the Erkowit Study Camp. This was an innovation of quite spectacular success and importance. I think there were about four of them altogether. We would go up to the hill station in Erkowit for about ten days or a fortnight. The personnel would be roughly half British and [half] Sudanese—perhaps forty people altogether—and we would get down to serious work on problems such as, I remember one year, socialism. I think another one was on planning. And we would work in small groups, and there would be hard study and consultation of literary material—books and magazines that would be especially provided or borrowed from the University College in Khartoum. And during this time, as well as having a lot of fun and entertainment and some quite strenuous walking in the mountains, we would spend most of our time doing serious study and would finish by writing a substantial report."

Although it provides the best examples of the guiding role, education was not without inherent difficulties, even conflicts, since it required "a gradual adaptation to Western influence," in Greenlaw's words. "'One step ahead of the Sudanese' was our aim. It proved too slow and the Sudanese rejected it for more rapid development." Ironically, Sudanese opposition was initially an obstacle to education. "In most parts of the northern Sudan, education was not popular," Henderson asserted. "Education for women was absolutely taboo.... Right at the end, one had this problem of lack of demand from the rural areas and lack of facilities in the town.... Shortly after Ali Abu Sinn went to Zalingei, I was coming from El Dafei, and he asked me to pick up a couple of school girls in the village, and bring them in at the beginning of the term to the Zalingei school, which I duly did. And when we halted for people to spend a penny or whatever it was, the little girls ran away to the bush; and they were recaptured only with great difficulty after a long time and were brought weeping back. And then I discovered that they had been nominated on a roster, and Ali Abu Sinn reckoned that there must be some girls from each area sent in to school to learn, whether they wanted or not.... I turned around and drove back to the village.... I couldn't bear to take two weeping little girls."

Bell, who also saw the British role as guiding, was concerned with material progress. "We were there to improve the product of the country, whether it be in agriculture or ... cattle breeding or ... the conservation of water supplies or production of extra water, [or] well-digging." Kenrick held a similar view. "I must confess that in the first year or two I thought I knew what was best for the people of the district. They should grow cotton or coffee, make roads or dig wells because it would be good for them. But I soon realised that if I wished to leave anything viable behind me when I left, it would not be a project which I had forced the people to undertake, but one which they themselves undertook of their own free will because they were convinced of the benefits. . . . It was therefore a question of example, persuasion, education, and trial."

Several former political officers claimed that guidance consisted of preparing the Sudanese for eventual independence. "The more efficiently we did the guiding," Bell reflected, "the sooner would the Sudan, in the natural course of things, say: 'Thank you very much: we reckon that we have learnt as much as we want to learn from you, and we think it is time for you to go home.'" Henderson said that the mission of the British had been to do their best "to make a viable state of the Sudan." He recalled asking the governor of the Blue Nile Province "very early in my career . . . 'What are we aiming at? Are we aiming at a sort of British India or . . . at a sort of confederation of maharajas? . . . What do we hope to do? When we hand over power to the Sudanese, do we hand it over to a council of princes based on native administration or do we hand it over to a modern sort of state like is now . . . coming up in India?' 'Oh,' he said, 'you shouldn't worry about that, my boy. It is a hundred years before you need think of that!' One did feel a sense of the most tremendous time. He said, 'It will work itself out.'"

Farquharson-Lang made the important observation that during his time (1931–1955) "there was a marked change of attitude toward our mission in the Sudan. In the early days the British were there to rule, as . . . in other parts of the Empire. Gradually, and perhaps more rapidly during the war, there was a change of attitude and our mission became one of partnership. After the war, the Labour government in the U.K. decided the Sudan should get its independence and the governor-general was told to instruct the British officials to train the Sudanese to take over. Independence came more quickly than Mr. Attlee . . . had anticipated, but that was our motive during the last eight years of British rule in the Sudan."

The question of autonomy or even independence for the southern Sudan had been regarded similarly, according to Henderson. "'Give them a chance! Give them a chance!' . . . That was what everybody always said about the south. 'Some time around 1980 they will be in a position to decide whether they are going to throw in their lot with the north or not.' The whole thing accelerated and it is impossible now for people to realize quite what a long-term view people took in the old days." The fate of the south particularly concerned British administrators there, such as Howell. "I was not anti-northern in outlook," he maintained, "but I was much concerned with the lack of development in the south and the illogic of a minority policy without much more development or effort invested in the south. I did not think, either, that the northern Sudanese had the knowledge or sense of mission to assume my role in the south."

Protection, then, from the British perspective, often involved what Sandars called protecting the Sudanese from themselves. Bell viewed his routine duties in this light: "When you are responsible for the administration of justice and good order in your district, you are there to protect the people. You are to protect them from violence. If there is a tribal fight, it's your job to go there and stop it or prevent it from happening again." Phillips spoke of "protection ... of poorer, more primitive and more vulnerable people from exploitation. I have particularly in mind the exploitation of Nuba by 'Gellaba,'[1] though I have to admit that the Gellaba were also a civilizing influence in some respects." McDowall, who served almost exclusively in the south, put protection "in a limited context only, to protect them from exploitation, e.g., by moneylenders and sometimes by unscrupulous traders and shopkeepers." Mynors's perspective on the south evolved: "Although in my early years I objected to what I thought [was] exploitation of the south by the north, in later years I objected to any continuation of keeping them apart."

Few former British officials admit to "domination" of the Sudanese as inherent in their role. Owen said paternalistically that "to dominate" entered his concept of mission only "when it was temporarily necessary to guide." For Nicholson "there was no question of domination except that the government had to govern and ensure that the laws were observed and peace ensured against any threats from within or without." Howell conceded that "a certain arrogance had been present in the minds of the British in thinking one knew best.... One was, of course, sometimes exasperated by Sudanese lack of enterprise, inaction, inefficiency—and one was arrogantly concerned that there should be no injustice or corruption among subordinate officials or tribal authorities."[2] This, however, fell far short, in Howell's estimation, of a "sense of domination." Mynors wrote that a desire to dominate existed "only insofar as [it] might be desirable for attaining what seemed to me to be the right ends." Phillips admitted that "domination inevitably [occurred] because without authority (and visible authority at that) one would not be accorded the respect needed to maintain the peace and public order in which alone progress could be maintained." Only Hodgkin, the educator, conceded that "there may have been in the background of a good many people's minds a notion that it was pleasant to dominate, but I don't think this was often talked about or made explicit. I would say it was rather a hangover which could still be found in some parts of the administration as an inexplicit element amongst the less able and dedicated members of the expatriate staff." Mynors's view was that the Sudanese could not, in any case, have found the British yoke to be a heavy one: "Although the British may have been said to 'rule,' the fact was that we could only act in general with the consensus of the local people since—outside the Three Towns, at any rate—there was no realistic way of enforcing that 'rule.'"

Some viewed their mission as limited by specific duties. The surveyor, Wakefield, for example, reported that when he was recruited (1929) he was told that the general aim of British rule was "to help the economic development of the country and to lead the Sudan to independence, the original object of the pacification having more or less been achieved. With this end in view, the Survey Department combined its functions of building up the survey structure of the country, upon which all the maps required for land registration are based, [with] running its own school which specialized in survey work.... Our whole object was to Sudanize posts as soon as qualified people became available."[3]

As to how the Sudanese may have viewed the British mission, the majority of respondents refrained from generalizing, distinguishing instead between intellectuals and traditional leaders, northerners and southerners, and between the early days and the post-World War II period. "A politically ambitious young educated man regarded the British as imperialists," Disney said. "A tribal leader appreciated the support of his authority and general backing that he got from the British officials with whom he came in contact. The *'zol sakit'* [the ordinary man] looked upon the British as just another band of Turks who, on the whole, were a more decent lot!" Phillips agreed that Sudanese views of the British role varied "with the status of the Sudanese concerned. Rural Sudanese, and particularly the traditional leaders such as *sheikhs* and *nazirs* and *meks* . . . regarded us on the whole very favourably as fair-minded benefactors, dispensers of justice, keepers of the peace, providers of medical and educational facilities: above all as men having authority and exercising it impartially. Senior Sudanese officials, and educated Sudanese in general, were more critical; while giving us credit for impartiality in dealings with individuals, they naturally regarded us as agents of a foreign government, to whose interest we would give priority in the event of conflict. A number also tended to feel that we were keeping them out of better-paid jobs which they would like to have. Although we were, I think, scrupulous in our respect for Muslim susceptibilities, there was among both rural and urban northern Sudanese some resentment at being ruled by *kufar* (infidels); this did not often manifest itself in personal relationships, but it was undoubtedly there."

Bowcock, whose term of service began only in 1951, noted differences between the northern and southern Sudanese views of the British mission. "In the north the Sudanese were friendly but quite critical. Independence was just over the horizon and there were already Sudanese ministers. The vernacular press . . . was vitriolic without any regard for the truth. In the Upper Nile, on the other hand, the relationship with the Nilotics was still in a honeymoon period. Though strongly independent, of course, they were prepared to concede that we had brought . . . them many advantages, though it seems little enough now, and were very ready to cooperate." Carden, working among the Nuer, believed they regarded him as a "useful innovation in their society. Without a British district commissioner to act as referee in their fights there was no apparent reason why the fights should ever end. And certainly they collaborated readily with me. One indication is that I had only thirty-six policemen for 180,000 Nuer. Another is that their chiefs told me that I was too soft in sentencing people who refused to return cattle, and then they virtually fixed a schedule of prison sentences that I would enforce both for the nonreturn of cattle and for participating in fights in which people were killed. Six months for being present. One year for wounding someone. Four years for killing someone."

A great many respondents thought that the British were valued more highly in the early years, "when," to quote Sandars, "the memories of the Khalifa's regime were still fresh." As Owen observed, "In 1926 people still remembered the Mahdiya and its horrors. They accepted and even appreciated the security, the law and order, the stability brought by the British." Nicholson agreed: "In the early days I think the majority of them were contented with the government, which gave them a security of life and prosperity which they had not enjoyed either under the old Turco-Egyptian government or during the Mahdiya, as several of the old men in the north told me. And in the south, of course, we put a stop to the practice of slavery." Bell recalled an old man's telling him: "'Oh, goodness me. I remember the Mahdiya, and how everybody was fighting everybody else. And today you could get a goat and you could tie a bag of *shattah* around its neck, and you could set it off from El Fasher; and it would arrive safely at Kassala and nobody would have killed it." That was a flattering thing to say, and I like to think that there was a certain measure of truth in it."

As political consciousness deepened, the British had recognized that opinion among the intelligentsia was turning against them. Farquharson-Lang claimed that the "vast majority" of Sudanese striving for independence understood that the British shared their aspirations, but "most thought we went too slowly, a few thought much too slowly. . . . Mekki Abbas once said to me, 'Your administration was efficient. Your education was sound, your law was just, but, by God, you were slow!'" Mavrogordato and Greenlaw both distinguished between the Sudanese reaction to them as individuals and as professionals. "When I was advocate-general and as such responsible for government litigation and prosecutions," Mavrogordato said, "I hope and indeed believe that I enjoyed the reputation of being fair-minded and not oppressive, giving the subject the benefit of the doubt when he was in conflict with the government in civil or criminal proceedings." Greenlaw, commenting that "art and Islam are uneasy partners," said that some found his mission difficult to understand, but that his students were "grateful and eager to learn. . . . There were few critics except in matters of detail."

McDowall summarized Sudanese attitudes toward the British in these words: "Some of the older Sudanese who remembered the past possibly gave the British some credit for their achievements. The younger, educated Sudanese thought that we were too dominating and too slow in handing over the reins of power to them. I think the great majority of the Sudanese people, especially those living outside the larger towns, were either sympathetic or did not think about our 'mission' so long as they had a roof over their heads, enough to eat and drink, and reasonable security and freedom to lead their own lives in peace."

As independence approached, indirect rule became increasingly discredited, and the British realized that the educated elite and not the chiefs would inherit the reins of power. Thus, they reluctantly accepted that it was with the elite and not the tribal leaders that they should deal. Although most British officials probably recognized this shift as inevitable, they generally continued to feel more comfortable with the chiefs and their rural subjects who seemed appreciative of the British contribution, while suspicion and distaste for the educated class increased with the harassments of nationalism and the independence movement. Henderson characterized the stages in his relationship with the Sudanese in this way: "I [first] had a filial affection, but as I got older, of course, I graduated from the filial to the fraternal and ultimately, to a certain extent, to the paternal. I mean, I ran the School of Administration for a year and the fellows who were there then, I always regarded in a paternal way when I met them after [and] I don't remember any difference in attitude generally. I mean, it seemed to me that they were the same lot of chaps when I went back there in 1964 as they were when I went down there in 1926."

Notes

1. *Jallaba:* northern Sudanese peddlers.
2. Howell's sarcasm masks the fact that the abuse of tribal powers was condoned by British officials determined to make a success of Indirect rule. See Daly, *Empire on the Nile*, 360–79.
3. Subordinate surveying duties were in fact among the earliest Sudanized, beginning as early as 1903. See Daly, *Empire on the Nile*, 243–45.

4

Nationalism and Independence

Although its roots lie in the immediate post-World War I period, Sudanese nationalism reached maturity only during and after the Second World War. Therefore, many of the British contributors to this study were not only eyewitnesses, but were participants in the politics of nationalism. Several, such as Gawain Bell and J. W. Kenrick, occupied central posts during the crucial stage of the movement in the late 1940s and early 1950s. The period was one of hectic activity and debilitating uncertainty for British officials. The suddenness with which they were confronted by modern nationalism found them unprepared, both personally and institutionally. The conviction that too much too soon was a recipe for political disaster was widespread among them, and there was great frustration, even grief, at what seemed the headstrong precipitateness of the Sudanese nationalist leaders. In retrospect, British ex-officials have moderated their views. It must be remembered, however, that Sudanese nationalism implied a rejection of the British sense of mission and involved, in its confrontation with the Sudan Government, not merely a disagreement over timing but the survival or passing of an era.

Regarding the British "mission," we have noted the frequent reference to preparing the Sudan for independence. Disney, for example, claimed that he "always knew, from the first, that [we] would eventually leave. . . . It was the 'object of the exercise.'" It is important to qualify this assertion in two ways. First, the general acceptance of this object came very late: it was certainly not the guiding principle during the inter-war period. Second, the lack of urgency in pursuing the object implied its realization only in a vague and distant future. Thus, the practical difference between an indefinite continuation of colonial rule and an intended end to it was small. As late as the mid-1940s, British officials saw the optimal date for self-government as at least a generation away, and even then the possibility of a continuing British role was not excluded.

The origins of the Sudanese nationalist movement may be traced to the early 1920s. Influenced by events in Egypt and elsewhere, a small number of educated Sudanese began to question the assumptions on which foreign rule was largely based. There were several discernible strands of opinion, including responsible, modern elements who accepted the need for British guidance on the road to self-government, but most attention was paid to a more outspoken, ostensibly pro-Egyptian group. In 1924, as the relations of the co-domini, Egypt and Britain, deteriorated, anti-British demonstrations were organized in the Sudan by the White Flag League led by Ali Abd al-Latif, an ex-officer. The November 1924 assassination in Cairo of the governor-general of the Sudan, Sir Lee Stack, led to the evacuation from the Sudan of all Egyptian troops. While this was under way, Sudanese units refused the orders of their British officers and were forcefully put down with heavy loss of life.

Following these cathartic events there was a period of reaction, as the Sudan Government sought to eliminate the threat of future nationalist trouble by closely controlling the scope and even the size of the educated class. Quiet prevailed until 1936 when, after long negotiations in which the Sudanese had no voice, a new Anglo-Egyptian treaty reaffirmed the condominium status of the Sudan. Deeply offended by this paternalism, educated Sudanese organized themselves in the Graduates' General Congress, founded in 1938. In 1942 the Congress submitted a memorandum to the government, demanding, among other things, independence for the Sudan immediately after the war. The dismissive reply of the civil secretary, Sir Douglas Newbold,[1] to the congress is considered a watershed by some: "It is a great mystery to most of us, that reply of Newbold's," Henderson said. "[Sir James] Robertson covers the point in his book. He says it 'seems inconceivable that that man could have written that letter'[2]; I personally don't think [Newbold] did write it. . . . I think it was the secretary [who] was responsible."

Whoever wrote it, the letter neglected a tenet of British rule: attention to Sudanese pride and dignity. According to Henderson, "the only thing that was necessary to do on that congress letter was to stall. Well, I mean, to start by saying: 'We don't admit you have a right to speak for the people of the Sudan. However, you do represent the educated classes in the Sudan who are, after all, the most vocal section of the population. And, therefore, we reckon that you deserve a reply to your queries. We think that some of your suggestions are reasonable enough and some of them are not so reasonable. In normal circumstances, we would suggest a round-table conference, but until Rommel is out of North Africa, we don't feel that we can possibly devote ourselves to this subject. But we thank you for your letter. At the earliest possible opportunity we will discuss this.'[3] That was the answer to give, but they didn't. They more or less said, 'This is no bloody business of yours.'" Henderson therefore claims that 1942 was the "dividing line. Most of the intelligent British people saw the writing on the wall."

Rather than speculating on what would have been an appropriate reply to the congress's letter, several respondents expressed anger that the issue should have been pressed at a time when the British were confronting Nazi Germany. Bredin was Newbold's deputy at the time, and "could well remember my indignation that the question of independence should be raised so strongly by them at a time of grave crisis, when it could not fail to embarrass an administration deeply involved in the civilised world's struggle against the evils of Nazism." Bell agreed. "I think that we British felt that the activities of the graduates during the war, when we were very hard pressed, and when they claimed to speak for the whole of the Sudan (which they certainly didn't) was something that we—I am not saying altogether disapproved of—but we didn't think that it was right to give it the weight and influence and the consideration that the graduates felt that they should be given. They were a tiny, tiny minority; they represented essentially the Three Towns and I think that their claim to speak for the whole of the Sudan as they did wasn't justified."

The Graduates' Congress was unable to maintain a united front, and split along sectarian lines. The Umma party, patronized by Sayyid Abd al-Rahman al-Mahdi and deriving most of its support from the Mahdists, championed "the Sudan for the Sudanese," while many of the adherents to the Khatmiyya leader, Sayyid Ali al-Mirghani, called for the "Unity of the Nile Valley" or union with Egypt as a means of ejecting the British. The expressed willingness of the Umma to cooperate with the British was an asset and a liability to both, while the adamant refusal of the unionists to participate in government-instituted reforms solidified its reputation as the anti-colonial party. It is L. M. Buchanan's contention that these parties lacked political maturity and were not taken seriously by the majority of Sudanese. "The issue of national independence was hardly regarded by tribal leaders as a practical possibility while senior officials tended, on the contrary, to press nationalism but to avoid the realities of a political transfer of power." He said that "political parties based on social programmes of development and democracy had hardly emerged, even by the early fifties when self-rule was imminent." In Buchanan's view, nationalist sentiment "outside Khartoum . . . seemed artificial, as the main groupings continued to be basically tribal. The principal focus and thrust of politics were reflected in religious leaders and tribal loyalties, in particular the Khatmiya/Mahdist confrontation."

Responding to this sectarianism, dissatisfied young people began to coalesce around ideological parties. Donaghy observed a change among many of his students, from support of Mahdist or Mirghanist claims "to the appearance of the Communist influence (and money) after 1950." The Sudanese Communist party was actually formed in the mid-1940s, as was the Muslim Brotherhood in the Sudan. Farquharson-Lang "knew very well Abdel Khalig Mahgoub, the Communist leader who was executed in 1971.[4] He had been a student of mine and was one of the most brilliant that passed through my hands, and at that time one of the most charming."

Farquharson-Lang also "knew intimately the leaders of the Ashigga and Umma parties and indeed played a small but very discreet part in advising on the setting up of the Umma party." He also knew the leader of the unionist Ashigga, Ismail al-Azhari: "When he was politically most active [he] was on my staff in the Omdurman Secondary School, and it was my unhappy duty to dismiss him from government service for repeatedly neglecting his teaching duties. . . . Azhari eventually became Prime Minister, and the night before I left the Sudan in 1955, he very kindly invited my wife and myself to drinks at his house. Over a whiskey and soda, he raised his glass and said, 'Let bygones be bygones.'"

"Inevitable" and "desirable" are words often used by the British to describe the achievement of independence. Wakefield remembered his fear that the "timing, which was so unfortunately forced on the country by outside pressures, and which stirred up Sudanese emotions, would lead, as it did, to . . . the unfortunate introduction of corruptive influences from the north."

Several officials formed negative views of the nationalist movement despite their later-expressed sympathy with its objectives. "Believing as I did that the British administration of the Sudan was eminently for the good of its people, who were not yet qualified for self-government, I regarded attempts to bring it to an end as seditious rather than patriotic," Bredin said. Winder's objection was milder but unequivocal: "Harassing us . . . tended to annoy." Buchanan claimed to have favored the movement "while the Nationalists were prepared to give us credit for working toward their independence." But he found that "the Sudanese then seemed unable or unwilling to believe that the British did not at heart wish or intend to control the Sudan as long as possible in their own interests, and they were reluctant to accept that the tendency of the British not to move faster in a declared policy of de-control was dictated by the impracticalities of the situation (for example, lack of education and social cohesion) rather than by latent imperialism." Phillips commented that "many of the manifestations of nationalism, particularly of the more violent demonstrations in the towns, seemed to me at the time to be unnecessary, like breaking down an open door." He suggested that "those who instigated the demonstrations may have felt that to have been granted independence peacefully was inglorious—not to have fought for it would have made them feel deprived."

Among the most powerful reasons for British caution regarding independence was the fear that the Sudan would come under the domination of the despised Egyptians. The British worked to cultivate those nationalists who were, in Greenlaw's words, "pro-Sudan for the Sudanese and anti-Egypt." According to Henderson, "one was almost automatically opposed to the pro-Egyptian party. . . . [James Robertson] said that frankly the thing is that we may have been wrong, but we regarded the whole Egyptian setup from top to bottom as hopelessly corrupt,[5] and we did not want to see that filtering into the Sudan, and we would have done anything. . . . Well, there is a passage in that book of mine about Douglas Newbold in which he quotes the Bible: Egypt staggering in its vomit like a drunken man. It's a quotation otherwise vile, but the anti-Egyptian feeling among the British in the Sudan was very high indeed."

The British who had served for a lengthy period in the south were particularly concerned with another type of domination: the potential power of the Muslim north over the south. Howell recalled his belief that "a policy of separation rather than the encouragement of integration was a recipe for difficulty." He was "opposed to northern domination of the south which, neglected in terms of what nowadays is termed development, was not ready to take up a position on equal terms." His preoccupation consequently was with "economic development which had to go side-by-side with other forms—education, social services and so on." When independence became a reality, Howell "considered the constitutional measures of protection for the south as being quite inadequate and believed that it was necessary to have a federal constitution under which the south would have had its own assembly and its own civil service so that British officers could have stayed on if they were wanted."

Carden, who "liked the countryside and saw very little of the politicians," was a close friend of the southern nationalist, Buth Diu. "He besought me not to leave and sought my advice on how condominium government could be dissuaded from leaving before the south had caught up with the north. I felt that the only means of dissuasion would be for the Nuer to go en masse into Malakal and there kill a lot of people. Such an event would have been world news. But I could not say [such] a thing and remained silent."

"The northern Sudanese were keen on independence," Winder said; "the southerners [were] frightened of our leaving." McDowall reported that "many southerners, chiefs and other educated people expressed to me their grave fears for the south if the Sudan became independent without adequate safeguards for the south and its people." Polden felt "very sad for the southern Sudanese," and Winder was "very anxious about the south and felt too that I was letting down people like Buth Diu." Kenrick voiced his fear that "the more primitive people of the south and the Nuba Mountains, and the peasants of the northern Sudan [might] suffer from the absence of impartiality and lack of self-interest in the administration of justice which we, as foreigners, were able to provide." Mynors expressed concern that "progress for the 'backward' rural population might suffer in a mainly urban political movement." Bredin had a similar concern that "the more primitive, and much more numerous country population would not get a square deal from the more sophisticated minority and 'politicians' in the towns." His predictions for the south were more dire. He said that "when our controlling hand was lifted, the age-long mistrust and hostility between north and south would produce a conflagration."

"With regard to . . . the departure of the British, in the south I think the atmosphere was distressing," Gawain Bell said. "The northern Sudanese, the Egyptians in particular, were very suspicious of the British officers in the south. Quite unjustly so, I think. I think they really believed that perhaps [the British] were working toward an attempt to cut the south off from the north. This, of course, was not so. . . . The activities of certain Egyptians who toured the south, who I'm quite certain distributed money here and there and influenced southern leaders by the use of inducements . . . led to an unhappy situation in the south. And the southern administrative officers who had served many, many years in the south were extremely unhappy at the way in which things had gone. They thought that we had let down the south. And to a certain extent we had. . . .

"Being the last senior British official in the political service to leave, I was provided with a special train from Khartoum to Port Sudan. I received a very courteous letter from the prime minister, who then was Ismail al-Azhari, with whom I had worked comparatively happily for fifteen, eighteen months. And the courtesies were paid. At Port Sudan, I was surprised with a guard [of] honor. It was quite right."

Some respondents transcended the fears, tensions, and hostility of the period to give a rational and sympathetic analysis of the situation. "There was nothing unusual in the Sudan nationalist movement," Farquharson-Lang said. "It followed a very natural and moderate pattern. Sometimes a little noisy and sometimes a little frightening if you were caught in the middle of a demonstration in Omdurman, as I was, but it passed without major incident and almost without casualty—perhaps a tribute to the moderation and good sense of both the Sudanese and the British.

"As headmaster of a boarding school [Wadi Seidna] of 500 boys at this time [1945–1950], I had to deal with several demonstrations. One learnt by experience to play cool at such incidents, and although at times they looked aggressive, no one was hurt and no property was damaged. Impatience at the slowness of granting Sudan independence was expressed in demonstrations, and impatience was natural. While in the earlier years, British rule was too slow and overly cautious, the last years of the British rule progressed fairly swiftly. On hindsight, the speed with which the Sudan got its independence was probably about right."

Generally, working relations between the British and Sudanese remained civil. British contributors reported that Sudanese colleagues kept their opinions to themselves. Bredin said that "although the subject was referred to from time to time, I cannot recollect having discussed it at length with individual Sudanese.... With their unfailing sensitivity, the Sudanese were perhaps alive to my conservative attitude to the issues." McJannet commented that while there was among Sudanese civil servants an "undoubted and understandable sympathy for the nationalist aspirations [of their countrymen], perfect correctness was observed" in professional relations. Some respondents suggested that the Sudanese were reticent about independence because they did not consider it an issue. Wakefield reported that his successor in office was "completely apolitical." And according to Haselden, "none of the Sudanese with whom I worked regarded independence for the Sudan as an urgent matter or had clear ideas on what they should aim at." Yet Carden spoke of the independence movement's "bedevilling" some personal relations in the late 1940s and early 1950s. "We had jobs which we loved," he said. When the political process "quite rightly [began to lead toward] stepping into our jobs, [relationships with the people who were] going to extrude [you became] a bit difficult."

Some contributors remember feeling that the manner of their departure, almost an expulsion, was distasteful and unfair. Some contributors had retired before independence and in some cases had entered into new careers. But of those who stayed until the end, only Polden left "looking forward to the more professionally satisfying prospects of work in England," where he was in the process of buying a partnership in a veterinary establishment. For many, "there were great regrets at leaving a wonderful and challenging career among the Sudanese," to use McJannet's words. McDowall had "had to accept the inevitable, but felt sorry to be leaving the Sudan in mid-career."

"We felt sad," Bell confessed. "I think all of us felt sad ... that it was necessary, within a period of three years, for officers who had genuinely devoted the greater part of their lives to the Sudan, who had the welfare of the Sudan very much at heart; that they should be called upon to go within so short a period.... We didn't like the idea. We didn't think that it was right."

As in so many other areas, British respondents discerned a distinction between the towns and the rural areas regarding the nationalist movement. "In the tribal areas, with which I was in the closest touch," Sandars wrote, "the feeling was one of apprehension at the prospect of being ruled by intelligentsia in Khartoum." "As you would expect," Owen wrote, "the intelligentsia were all for independence while *sheikhs* and tribesmen mistrusted it, as being likely to lead back to chaos, and to endanger their interests." Timing continued to be the main issue. Bowcock commented that most of his Sudanese associates would have agreed with his choice of 1960 as the appropriate year for independence in the north, "give or take a few years.... The south needed at least another fifteen years after the north." Bell, however, reported that Sudanese in official positions "generally voiced the opinion that obviously the Sudan had to be independent sooner or later. They would prefer it to be sooner.... In all territories that were under colonial administration," he continued, "you will find that the administrators say: 'Independence is coming too soon; we want another ten years. We want another twenty years. The people aren't ready for it'.... The same situation arises in a family, after all, doesn't it? A father thinks that his children are not quite ready, perhaps, to stand on their own feet. It would be better if they remained under the parental roof ... for another year or two years.... It's human nature."

Although a number of contributors admitted the belief that independence had come too soon, few discerned in the country's alleged unpreparedness the result of the policies they had pursued. "Our essential task was to train the Sudanese to take over control of their own land," Nicholson said. "But there were difficulties, not only because there were not enough people sufficiently educated to run a modern administration for some years ahead, but there was also the problem of the south, where we felt very strongly that the people were even less able to play their full part in government, and that we could not leave them at the mercy of what to them was another foreign government until we were reasonably satisfied that they could stand up for themselves and play an effective part in the administration." Henderson recalls a conversation with Newbold in which they decided that the optimum time for the transfer of power was "[first] when you have got enough chaps trained, naturally, to take over the administration [and also] when the demand for independence is no longer confined to the coffeehouses and has spread to the rural population." Henderson felt that independence came about five years too soon. Buchanan claimed to have "envisaged [from 1928 onwards] that the British would leave the Sudan as rulers as soon as the development of the Sudanese ... and of the Sudan ... could justify self-rule—perhaps in two generations or fifty years."

"In 1954, by any standards of good government, I myself did not regard independence for the Sudan as realistic," Buchanan said. "We had not in my view completed the task of fitting the Sudanese to rule themselves," Phillips explained. "We had, so to speak, put up the walls of the house, and perhaps its doors and windows, but the roof was incomplete." "We could not help feeling sad that the standards of administration which we had achieved should be let down," Owen commented. The dominant feeling was expressed by Bowcock in a paraphrase of Cecil Rhodes: "So much to do and so little time to do it."

It was the Second World War that had forced the British to recognize how imminent their departure was. "The war . . . brought the country into close contact with the outside world," Sandars commented, "and it became clear that we should not be given the time to advance the Sudanese to the point at which we, rightly or wrongly, thought they could take over from us." Owen credited Newbold during the later years of the war with pressing the realization upon the British "that independence must be very soon." Nevertheless, according to Carden, "it is surely true that about six years before independence it was expected that independence would come, say, after fifteen years; but with every year that passed, independence drew rapidly, very rapidly, closer and closer."

As hinted in connection with the south, many British did not consider their departure a necessary corollary of independence. McDowall was disturbed by the effect of the "speed of Sudanization on the Sudan Political Service, the police and the army, which seemed to leave too large a gap in the maintenance of law and order." Henderson had hoped that the Sudan, like Nigeria, would keep British civil servants: "I have always thought that the enormous mistake the northerners in the Sudan made was in insisting on getting rid of everybody under that Sudanization Committee. . . . I must confess I never thought it would happen."

Henderson remembered being asked by James Lawrence, a young district commissioner who arrived in Darfur in 1949, about career prospects. Henderson had warned that he did not stand much of a chance of appointment to a high position. "I reckon you may have perhaps another ten years to run before independence. But I see no earthly reason why ... you shouldn't go on being a district commissioner for another ten years under the independent Sudan."

Almost without exception, the British were unhappy about leaving the Sudan, however inevitable many regarded it. The natural sadness at the close of what was for many a rewarding period during the best years of their lives often combined with disappointment at the abrupt setback in their careers. Most prominent in British memories, however, is fear that the independent Sudan faced a dangerous future. A number of respondents expressed concern that the basic political institutions of the country might prove inadequate. Ironically, the traditional systems, which the British had reinforced and promoted, were later criticized by them as evidence of a backwardness and immaturity incompatible with independence. "I was doubtful whether the Sudan would or indeed could operate a democratic government on the European model," Nicholson said. With more candor, Mynors felt that the government structure was "unimaginative, unprofessional, unprogressive—too much rooted in the past and in tribalism, too isolated from world developments."

Another worry of the British was that, in Bredin's words, "the infiltration of Egyptian influence and standards of government, against which we had tried to protect the Sudan, would gather speed to the detriment of the administration." Phillips had feared that "Egypt would not allow the Sudan to be truly independent." "My only real qualm was whether they would be able to keep the Egyptians out," said Disney. Dodds-Parker concluded that Sudanese affairs "had become inextricably mixed up with Anglo-Egyptian relations."

Technical officials were free to stay in the independent Sudan, but in Disney's recollection, "the politicians made it clear, in their speeches, that they would not be welcomed.... Many who could have stayed—and done valuable work for the country—took the line, 'Well, if that's how they feel about me, I am off.' In the commercial firms, I do not think that there was any attempt to force the firms to Sudanize all their jobs at once and remove the

British, but there was a tendency for the men to feel a sense of insecurity and to be unwilling to renew contracts." Under the temporary constitution, British judges were also permitted to stay. McDowall, however, recalled that the chief justice, William Lindsay, supported by all British judges of the high court, "felt it would be wrong for us to stay unless the Sudan Government under Prime Minister Azhari was prepared to state publicly that they wanted us to stay. This the government was unwilling to do; so we all resigned. The chief justice and I were the last to leave, in April 1955."

The ambivalence of the British about their departure is reflected in the words of Dodds-Parker, who represented Her Majesty's Government at the Independence Day ceremony on 1 January 1956: "As far as I was concerned, and all who cherished the welfare of the Sudan, it was a very happy occasion, although one realised only too well that many problems remained." Phillips remembered "numerous parties [which] were given in our honour and attempts made to press gifts upon us (which we were not allowed to accept). Our many friends expressed what I believe were genuine regrets and not mere polite expressions, and at no time did we encounter any hostility." According to Kenrick, "Nothing could have been more generous or moving than the manner in which the Sudanese said farewell to the British officials as they left. In my own case, one of the last to go, my wife and I were entertained for days on end during our last week with a round of parties and invitations to meals. When we took the train at Khartoum, there was a large crowd of our friends at the station to see us off, and another crowd was at Khartoum North station where the train stopped."

The emotional nature of the departure sometimes punctured British reserve. Mrs. Henderson reminded her husband of the occasion on which he said good-bye "to the man who was your greatest friend, Sudanese friend. You both went off in different directions in tears to the edge of his district. We stopped under a tree and everybody had a good cry." Henderson himself was quite open about his feelings. "As for one's personal leaving of the country, it was absolutely undiluted hell, of course. The last thing on earth one wanted to do was to retire.... Time and again I stood at the airport at Fashir to see military gentlemen with whiskers, tears streaming down their moustaches as they took off."

As always, there were crossing currents. The behavior of some

Sudanese politicians and colleagues eager to be rid of their colonial masters was remembered by many contributors. Winder recalled: "I had some trouble with the Sudanese who had been designated as my successor, who expected us to remove ourselves much faster than it was physically possible for us to do.... The trouble was settled by the prime minister, and my proposed successor was removed." Although Howell stated that in general "the British left with affectionate regret and on the best of terms with the Sudanese," the circumstances of his own departure left something to be desired: "I personally was on leave when I received a telegram recalling me and giving me a date for compulsory retirement. In fact, when I was going back I was sent for by the prime minister, Ismail El Azhari, who told me that he wanted me to stay on, provided it was understood that I did not go to the south or to the west. I refused this offer, but agreed to stay on until my report on southern development was complete. (This, of course, was based on only five months' field work—the three-year program intended was scrapped.) I had to get out of Malakal and worked in Khartoum for two or three months and then for three months in London."

At the local level in the south, reaction to the British departure was said to have been drastically different: Bowcock recalled that "the departure was harrowing. My wife and I came back from leave and I was given two months' notice. During that time I had to hand over the district to my northern Sudanese successor. He was a good and competent man, though I think a little wooden.

"I called all the chiefs to Fanjak to explain what was happening and to introduce the new district commissioner to them. I really did try to make the best possible case but it was hopeless. One after another of the chiefs got up and spoke on the following lines: 'We have always welcomed you Bilrial, Pernyang and other Turks [British] who have come to show us many good things. We thought that we had made you happy with us but now it seems that you are offended and going back to your country. If you must go, you must, but it is not at our wish. As for this Gellaba, we know that you say that he has been trained in the school of administration so he will carry the *hakuma* [government] on as before. We will give him a trial, but we do not really believe it. We can easily go back to the way of life which we had before you came.'"

Notes

1. Newbold's letter stated that "by the very act of submitting the memorandum . . . and by its wording, the Congress has . . . forfeited the confidence of government"; and that it was "the duty and business of the Sudan Government alone . . . to decide the pace" at which increased Sudanese participation would be allowed. Newbold further stated that the Congress should "realise clearly once and for all that the government must and will insist that the Congress confine itself to the internal and domestic affairs of the Sudan and renounce any claim . . . to be the mouth-piece of the whole country." The full text is published in Henderson, *The Making of the Modern Sudan* 542–43.
2. In fact, Robertson says that it was "most unlike Newbold." See his *Transition in Africa: From Direct Rule to Independence* (London: C. Hurst, 1974), 83.
3. Henderson paraphrased Robertson, ibid.
4. Abd al-Khaliq Mahjub, long-time secretary-general of the Sudanese Communist party, was among those executed by the Nimeiri regime in 1971 for an alleged role in the abortive coup of Hashim al-Ata.
5. In *Transition in Africa*, 161–62.

5

Post-Colonial Contacts and Perspectives

One unquestionable test of the human factor in British rule is the extent to which ties survived the passing of time. Twenty-six of thirty British contributors maintained contact with the Sudanese in some way following their return to Britain. A number corresponded. Some have returned to the Sudan, either in a working capacity or on private visits.

Many contributors enjoyed opportunities to discuss their experiences and current affairs in the Sudan. Polden kept in touch "only through old Sudan Service friends [who had] either had correspondence with the Sudan or ... been back there." Bredin hosted regular reunions at Pembroke College, Oxford, inviting "all the Sudanese residents," their families, and many British former colleagues in the neighbourhood. Many attended the meetings of the Anglo-Sudanese Association, which brings together British and Sudanese in London. The Sudanese ambassador often attends such gatherings. A tradition has also been established whereby British pensioners of the Sudan Government are invited to tea at the embassy every year after their annual meeting.

When young Sudanese were included in such social events, Bell often found gaps in their knowledge of the condominium period. "I've always been astonished and surprised by some of the questions they ask me.... 'You were an administrative officer in the Sudan, were you?' 'Yes,' I say, 'I was.' 'What did you do?' they say. And when I begin to explain to them the manifold jobs that fell to our lot as administrative officers, it always seems to me to surprise them very much indeed." Bell was concerned that young Sudanese he encountered were unaware of "how very lightly the Sudan was administered: that immense country, a million square miles. Population of what? Nine million, ten million? A total administrative staff of perhaps 120 British in the field: rather less, a hundred, perhaps. Ma'murs, sub-ma'murs ... what, another hundred? Sudanese police officers: what, one per province? No. Three per province, perhaps. And a total police force, I think I'm right in saying, of six thousand all locally enlisted men."

Several contributors had had extensive professional involvement with the Sudan as representatives of the British government or in business. Others have visited privately. Greenlaw, who left the Sudan under the unusual circumstance of conscientious objection to colonialism, observed that he had "perhaps more Sudanese friends today than British." Virtually all of those who returned found their visits memorable and were entertained by former colleagues and friends as well as in some cases by the government.

Most contributors maintained that they were not surprised at the distinguished and powerful positions attained by former colleagues, students, and friends. Some failed to foresee certain trends in Sudanese society: the involvement of any southerners in the top echelon of government, for example, or the presence of women in public life. Their respect for the people did not lessen British awareness of the problems the Sudanese have been called upon to solve. "I was always confident that the best Sudanese would prove themselves competent to hold the highest posts," Disney asserted. As managing director of the Blue Nile Brewery, he found it "good to meet men, whom one had known as schoolmasters and such, functioning with dignity and ability: for example, as ambassador in London. One complete surprise was meeting here a man whom I had known many years before as a quite 'ordinary' clerk, who had gone to one of the 'Oil Sheikhships' and started several very successful business enterprises, from which he had gained considerable wealth." Phillips remembered that "a number of former Sudanese colleagues in the administrative, medical, and police services became ambassadors. This did not surprise me: all were men of ability who spoke excellent English." Indeed, according to Dodds-Parker, "Many have held the highest offices successfully, as their British colleagues foretold."

The educators in particular saw nothing surprising in the success of former students and colleagues. Donaghy wrote: "I have been delighted but not surprised at the positions in world affairs achieved by some of my friends: that is, as United Nations diplomats, as ambassadors, and as university teachers." Farquharson-Lang commented on the success his students had made: "When we returned to the Sudan in 1977, we were received by the president, Jaafar Mohamed Nimeiri. I had not met him since I knew him as the captain of the Hantoub football team, the great rivals of my school, Wadi Seidna. Half of the cabinet were from Wadi Seidna and many of them were my former pupils. One of my former pupils was a member of the Council of the World Bank, another a much esteemed member of the United Nations, another the Sudan ambassador in London—to name but a few. Some have taken first class degrees in British and other universities, and some I know have distinguished themselves in the field of medicine."

Henderson differed from most British contributors in that he "thought going back ... that we had grossly underestimated the ability of our Sudanese colleagues. I thought we had no idea of how well they were going to run the administrative side." But he explained that the new relationship of British and Sudanese, with many Sudanese occupying positions of influence superior to those of their mentors, had not destroyed the bonds of friendship. Henderson mentioned Daud Abd al-Latif, "this splendid comedian. You see, Daud was an absolute classic chap. [When Daud was] removed from Juba to Khartoum because he was supposed to be too pro-southern as governor, [he] met somebody in the streets of Khartoum who said to him, 'What are you doing here, Daud? I thought you were in Juba.' And Daud replied, 'My post has been Sudanized!' When I was collecting material for that last book of mine, I sat with him on the veranda of the Grand Hotel and I laughed until the tears streamed down my cheeks with his stories."

Upon his return in the 1970s, Dodds-Parker found "progress in the affairs of the south," while Winder was "happy to hear that an Anuak, a Shilluk and a Nuer [had] risen to the most senior post" in the Upper Nile Province. "Akout Atem was my police clerk," Carden remembered, "I have met with him again as a southern regional minister. But as a young man he was exceptionally able and I then recommended him for the fastest promotion. I regarded such people as him and Buth Diu as able men by any standards. So it comes as no surprise to see Nilotics in particular being star performers now—this is no soft soap."

Bell considered the change in the status of Sudanese women

"remarkable in a generation," with many more now involved in public life. "They were voting, in offices and departments of governments and so forth, and they obviously had a far greater influence, I would have thought, than they ever had in an earlier generation. When I went to the Sudan, it was with the greatest difficulty that we used to try and persuade people of influence— *omdas, nazirs,* officials and so on—to send their daughters to school.... They thought it was quite unnecessary to have a girl educated."[1]

Phillips was "a little surprised to find so many former Sudanese Army officers achieving high political and administrative rank.... I had personally known virtually no Sudanese military men during my service in the Sudan—none of it spent in the Three Towns." He added that perhaps he should not have been surprised, "if one takes into account the tendency in so many emergent countries for the military to intervene in politics."

On the issue of development, Howell remarked that progress "was not unexpected, but nor was the lack of progress. The Sudan displayed and continues to display all the difficulties of finance, technical know-how, administrative and human failings which face those concerned with the development process. It has its fair share of seemingly insoluble problems in this context." McDowall ventured "to add a critical note and bring to notice a weakness for which the British as much as the Sudanese are to blame.... It seems that the middle range of the professions, administration, and technology are not giving sufficient support to the top posts, and that a failure to achieve excellence may be due more to the weakness of the backup services rather than the top echelon. I think the British administration can be blamed for attaching insufficient importance to technical education. Perhaps the Sudan administration can be blamed for sacrificing quality to quantity in education."

Henderson appeared to have reached a mixed but nostalgic appraisal when he returned to the Sudan in 1963. "I went to Medani and Managil, the new Managil development scheme, which interested me because we had nearly done it. If it hadn't been for the world recession, we were going to do that Managil scheme in 1929–1930; and I had been appointed to be the sort of DC [in] Managil to do the administrative side of the land allotment and all the compensation. I went to Managil and, of course, it was humming with activity. But the town itself was exactly the same.... I asked after an old local government accountant called Ahmed Abdalla, who went and electrified me in the year 1927 by refusing to transfer onto the central government roster because he wanted to go on living in Managil. He was still there as Uncle Ahmed and he now headed the local government accounts section. They went away and fetched him and then we came and fell on each other's neck over the breakfast table.... Everything to me seemed to be the same. I went to Darfur, and I mean, somebody had built a cinema, and they built a railway to Nyala, but people were the same: they looked the same and they smiled the same way." Henderson concluded by remarking, "Now, you see that's my criterion. When you drive through a country, do the people grin and wave as you go by? If they do that, then there is nothing wrong."

Contributors were asked whether after a period of years or upon returning to the Sudan, they had noticed any change in the Sudanese attitude toward the British. Nicholson responded, "No, they appeared to me to be still the same friendly people with whom I had lived and worked." "I have found and still find the Sudanese an extremely friendly, generous and likable people with a delightful sense of humour," Farquharson-Lang remarked. Disney, while warning that generalities are of "doubtful value," commented that "one thing was always clear and that was the continuing friendliness of everyone I met." "If anything," said Howell, "relations were even more friendly than pre-independence. For me it was like going home.... Of course, there were varying temperatures in political relationships with the British over this period, but personal relations were universally close and friendly."

Phillips's analysis of Sudanese attitudes toward the British during and after the independence movement was more ambivalent, perhaps patronizing, though probably quite accurate: "History has involved us in the Sudan whether we like it or not. Beneath all the frustrations of Anglo-Sudanese relations since independence, there has flowed a current of mutual liking and respect.... The vicissitudes of the years between should not surprise or deter us, in the light of what has happened elsewhere in relations between developing countries and their former rulers. For an emergent nation, not to have a glorious past is to feel deprived; a need is felt for glories and miseries, and there is a temptation to bring them about by violence. Independence achieved, there follows a suspicious chip-on-the-shoulder period when the representatives of the former rulers are put ostentatiously into the rear rank of foreigners, and new and exciting friends are courted. Eventually, when it is seen that, in Julius Nyerere's words, 'with independence the mangoes grow no faster,' disillusion sets in with some nostalgia." With time the Sudanese developed, in Phillips's estimation, "a more balanced appreciation of the merits and demerits of the condominium period than they had in the first heady days of independence."

Comparisons of the Sudanese before and after independence suggest that the present-day relationship is more mature and healthier as the inhibitions and constraints of the colonial regime have disappeared. Griffiths noticed a less reserved attitude among the Sudanese. "In the early days of my career in the Sudan, there was a degree of servility," Farquharson-Lang agreed. "This has now gone and the Sudanese regard the British as equals, but this change has in no way lessened their consideration, their politeness, and their very good manners." Bredin offered this summary: "Whereas during the days of the condominium we were tolerated (and perhaps respected) as rulers, now we are welcomed, indeed warmly welcomed, as friends."

To explain the lack of bitterness in relations between Sudanese and British despite the tensions of colonialism and independence, Henderson told a story about a critical phase of the nationalist movement. In 1946 he found himself in the midst of an immense demonstration against the Bevin-Sidki protocol.[2] Ten thousand Sudanese marched through the streets of Khartoum and rallied around the statue of Kitchener, where a petition was read which Henderson was subsequently to deliver to the governor-general. Shaykh Ahmed Uthman al-Qadi, a member of the Advisory Council, "read out this long [statement] saying the British had betrayed the whole of the Sudanese, and the foreign secretary had perjured himself, and the governor-general had let them down, and the British were all so-and-so's and everything else. He read it awhile. Then he handed it to me and said, 'Nothing personal, of course.' Well, that was the Sudan. It was never anything personal." Illustrating the point further, Henderson asked, "What could you do with a chap who wrote violent attacks on you and walked into your office the day after? And when you said, 'I am surprised to see you here,' he said, 'Why?' and I said, 'Well, I thought you must be rather contaminating yourself walking into the office of a chap like me!' And he looked at me and said, 'Oh, you mean my article in the *suk* yesterday or whatever the paper was, *Rai al-Aam* or something?' And I said, 'Yes.' 'Oh,' he said, 'Don't believe what you read in the newspapers!'"

Mavrogordato illustrated the people's "absence of malice, resentment or grudge-bearing" with a similar personal reference. "I was once responsible for getting a railway rabble-rouser a six-month prison sentence for his anti-government activities. On my subsequent visits to the Sudan, he used to greet me effusively if he met me in the street, as if I were a long-lost friend. There was no ulterior motive, as by then I was merely a tourist." Mavrogordato noted also that "the same is true of politicians, who bore no ill will to the British officials, whom they had opposed before independence."

There is a remarkable blend of pride and modesty in the British evaluation of their role in the Sudan. Contributors acknowledged the record with satisfaction, conceding only that it was not perfect. No one apologized for the old regime. Allowing for circumstances of history as well as for the constraints, both human and financial, under which they worked, the British felt that they had played a valuable part in the Sudan's evolution toward maturity. They were convinced that no other foreigners could have done better or as well.

Certain premises are fundamental to this perspective. First, the British argued simply that imperialism was not confined to them but was characteristic to the age. Would the Sudanese have preferred some other rulers? A similar line of argument compared life under British rule to daily existence during the Turkish and Mahdist periods. Bell explained, "The Turkiya—I don't think that was a very happy time for the Sudan. The circumstances of the *khalifa*'s rule: internal strife, famine, the reduction of the population—estimated from perhaps two million to three-quarters of a million. Whereas when the British administration was established in 1899, assuming the population was, let us say, a million at most: well, when we left, what was it? Eight? Nine? I should have thought that was a sign of peace and prosperity and the fairly favorable social circumstances.[3]

"We must remember, too, that at the beginning of this century, Europe was expanding into Africa—the Germans, the French, the Italians—would the Sudan have done better to have had the Italians there? What about German rule? Would they have been happier, perhaps, under German rule? Or had the Egyptians been able to manage it, had the Egyptians been able to reconquer the Sudan by force of arms on their own, would they have preferred perhaps an Egyptian administration? I would have thought not."

A. W. Ireland, a staunch defender of colonialism, acknowledged that the Sudanese experience "may have been a bit of a freak in the general 'colonial context.' Certainly I feel no call to apologise for that regime and my association with it. At that time, and in that general context, it was in my view historically the best such arrangement the world has known or probably will ever know.... The reasons are complex. An important element was certainly the Foreign Office rather than the Colonial Office link with the U.K. I, and much more importantly the 'political service,' regarded ourselves as serving the Sudan and the Sudanese, not the U.K. or the Empire, and could so conduct ourselves. The U.K. government was administratively remote and the Sudan Service was able to get on as it thought best for the Sudan.... Another important element was the 'selection' of the British staff along the lines which can be mocked (that is, 'country of Blacks ruled by Blues') but was in practice most effective and advantageous to the Sudan. I myself noticed the difference postwar and when working in other parts of the Empire.... Also of importance, no doubt, was the absence of ready 'development' prospects attractive to large scale 'commercial' interest. (For example, in West Africa political control followed belatedly in the wake of 'commercial' interests, leading to a very different setup from that in the Sudan.) ... Of great importance also, of course, was that in the north, at least, there existed a well-established and mature 'civilization.' I have often speculated that an alien professional administration, not subject to local sectional pressures and largely free of corruption temptation, may have merits beyond the 'colonial' context."

"It is true," Buchanan wrote, "that in pursuance of their policies the British were able to be singleminded on behalf of the Sudanese partly because the Sudan was not a colony (in its original sense) and there was never any question of colonization as in Kenya or Rhodesia; partly because valuable commodities and exports were virtually limited to cotton, and there were no minerals or oil; and lastly, the harsh climate inhibited any settlement by other Europeans for their own profit and development."

Howell, whose observation is representative, compared British rule in the Sudan to British rule in other parts of the world and found it superior. "Standards and quality of professional competence were, of course, outstanding in India, but one gets the information that relationships were less close. In African colonies generalizations were not possible (for example, the circumstances of colonies with British settler interest and those without) but the Sudan Service seemed to me much superior compared with, for example, that in East Africa.... There were far less administrative and other British officials in relation to population in the Sudan than in the African colonies. I think this led to closer uniting social relationships, and it also (with annual leave) meant that responsibility was passed down the line to subordinate Sudanese more freely." Howell concluded that "if British rule in the Sudan was successful in this kind of context, much was due to the character of the Sudanese themselves."

D. C. Carden believed that "broadly speaking, the relationships between the Sudanese people and the British people in the colonial era were, for the most part, happy. I know I'm on firm ground when I say that very many English people look upon themselves as having been exceedingly fortunate if they spent their working lives with the Sudanese. And it certainly wasn't because of the climate or the country. It was because of the people. And I simply do not believe that the administrative machine could have operated efficiently or indeed, operated at all if there had not been a very wide measure of mutual goodwill, because the British administrative machine was so slender.... It is true that we were rulers, but it is also true, whether it seems incredible or not, that we ruled very largely by consent. And, of course, when that measure of consent expired, we left."

Another basis for the positive British evaluation is the argument that a foreign element is an important—some would say essential—part of the development process. "I hold no brief for imperialism," Owen said, "but it has always seemed to me that no country which is politically and economically backward can survive and advance without going through the imperial stage. It is a necessary part of history." Phillips made the same assertion while ambassador in Khartoum: "Given the enormous disparity in development at the end of the nineteenth century between the rich industrial countries of Europe and the poorer, undeveloped, rural countries of much of Africa and Asia, a period of colonialism, of imperialism, or whatever you like to call the subordination of one country to another, can, despite the humiliation of being subordinate to foreigners, be an effective means of bringing an underdeveloped country more quickly into the twentieth century. Just as Lenin said that war is the midwife of revolution, so imperialism can be an efficient midwife of progress. If you compare the state a few years ago of certain countries which had never been under foreign domination (Afghanistan, Yemen, Oman) with many of those which have, you will understand what I mean." While Phillips claimed that "there are those who would prefer to remain backward and free rather than undergo a period of subordination to anyone," Carden concluded that his glowing assessment "in no way invalidates the truth of the dictum that rule by aliens is unpalatable, however well-intentioned or efficient they may be."

A distaste for colonialism in general but appreciation of its role in the Sudan's experience was most pronounced in Hodgkin's response. "I'm glad that we have got out of the period of imperialism," he said. "In itself, it was part of a dominant, dominating pattern of western over eastern or southern countries which I think had in it a good deal of evil." He felt, however, that the era of imperialism "reflected good qualities about Britain which we are now tending to lose." In particular, the doctrine was redeemed by "certain good individuals and certain interesting cross-cultural happenings which took place.... So, I'm anti-imperial, glad it's finished, but also proud to [have played] a part in a fascinating and rich bit of history in which ... Arabian, African, and British strands have been tightly woven together."

The British felt that they had established in the Sudan the infrastructure of a modern state. "In 1898 they took a country full of insecurity, barbarism, bankruptcy, and blood," Owen wrote, "and in less than sixty years they handed over a country civilized, economically viable, politically conscious, and at least in theory united. I doubt if this has been surpassed anywhere in the history of the world." Less grandly, McDowall wrote that "in the context of the time, we created an efficient, honest, and effective government. We honestly tried to work for the welfare of the Sudanese. We established peace, law, and order after a period of disturbance and insecurity. This enabled the British and the Sudanese together to start building a stable system of administration, good communications (considering the size of the country and limited finance), and local government institutions suitable to Sudanese needs at the time." Kenrick affirmed that "British rule during the period of condominium government brought, in the space of fifty years, orderly government, material progress, education and medical care, and development of social and political institutions. The Sudanese were also brought into close contact with Western Europe and enabled to stand on their own feet in the face of the West when independence came." Finally, he added, "the process of throwing off the 'parental yoke' was handled in such a way that the mutual affection" felt by the British and the Sudanese "was not soured, but remained."

Carden paid special tribute to the role played toward the end by several senior British administrators: "A deeply felt thing was admiration for those people who were at the top of the service, who inspired the service, and who went to great trouble to influence the thinking and attitude of the people at the bottom, the people who were new.... When I first arrived, I stayed with Sir James and Lady Robertson. He was not the head of the service then, Sir Douglas Newbold was. But, nevertheless, he was one of the most senior people of all. And for seven or eight days, they went out of their way ... to enable one to accumulate the necessary stores—camping equipment, clothes, cooking things, sheets—that were the essentials of life; and in addition, in casual conversation, to give an insight into the type of life one was going to lead, and to give an insight into the things that you ought to do and the things that you ought not to do both for your health and, in addition to that, for the success of your work...

"Newbold ... died in Khartoum. He was in the hospital for maybe a week; he was in great pain. And fortuitously I happened to be in Khartoum hospital, ill at the same time. He, hearing that I was in a ward two or three doors away from him, penned a letter which was as scholarly, and as wise, and as encouraging as anyone could write when he was at the top of his form and not distracted by anything.... It was such acts as that by people at the top of the service which did a great deal to sustain the spirit which pervaded the service."

"What was the essence of the spirit?" Carden posed this question to himself. "I believe that it was our job to learn as much as we could about the areas in which we were going to work, to learn as much as we could about the needs, the wishes of the people, to hold the leaders of the people in the district in high esteem.

Somebody like Sir Douglas Newbold would have endless stories of great *sheikhs*, leaders with whom he had worked. And, certainly, his presentation of these people would always be shot through with admiration.... So I'm sure, in thinking of those who were in the political service, it is right to think of a service which had a job to which its members were dedicated, and very gladly and happily dedicated; and a service which was pervaded by the influence of such men as Newbold; and a service which was lucky in the sense that each member in it had a finite and not very difficult job, and one in whose achievement there was a great deal of satisfaction."

A major criticism of the regime has always been the varying rates of development in north and south. "The British administration moved too slowly in the process of educating and training the Sudanese to take over the administration, particularly in the south," Mavrogordato conceded. Howell's censure was stronger: "One of the biggest [British] errors was to have a Southern Policy which not only led to a scandalous lack of investment in development and education in the south, but was really incompatible with the aims of a unitary state. This was, ultimately, a burden which had to be carried by the northern Sudanese no less than the southern." But, Howell said, "it is nonetheless difficult to see how the British could have adopted a policy of total integration without running the risk of adversely affecting southern interest." The same point was made by Disney, who wrote that British slowness in developing the south "must be viewed against the background of all the evils of exploitation of the south by the north—especially in the matter of the slave trade of the previous century, which probably made us 'over-protective.'"[4]

Bell's speculations on the "whole problem of north and south" reflected an appreciation of the dilemma faced by the British and a conviction that the regional conflict that has befallen the Sudan since independence might have been averted. "Now, the Sudan Government was in a difficult position here. I think what they hoped to do was to keep the south isolated to a certain extent, but gradually to build up the economic drive of the south. Educate the southerners so that they came onto a level with the northerners in this respect, until the two could merge and integrate in the normal course of events. [Unfortunately], there wasn't time to do this. The north wasn't a rich country by any means, but it received a far larger share of the government budget in terms of projects, development than the south did." Without commenting on the government's abdication of responsibility for southern education, Bell said that "there was a feeling on the part of the missionaries, and it was naturally a very strong one, that it was wrong to throw the south open to the influence of northern Islamic missions. The great majority of British serving in the south were, of course, Christian, too, and I suppose by and large they may have felt a little more sympathy with the idea that the south might in due course become a Christian country rather than a Muslim country.

"But the fact is that the government failed to solve the problem. And I think it failed to solve the problem because it didn't appreciate early enough that independence would come as soon as it did. What ought to have been done, I think, was that in the twenties there should have been much more cultural, educational, and administrative interchange between the north and the south. Not that I am saying that necessarily the south should have become a completely Islamic area. I think that the missions should have had their opportunity; but this is only a personal feeling. If the Sudan were going to become a really united country, then I think steps should have been taken to integrate the two parts of the country which, after all, geographically, were not a unit. But steps should have been taken to try and integrate the two far more closely together."

Bell felt that history has two choices in assessing British rule in the Sudan. One is the judgement of the former prime minister, Ismail al-Azhari, who said at independence: "Throughout those years, colonization sat heavily upon the land . . . tyrannizing over its population, destroying its peculiarities, and spreading hatred and separation between its people in order to acquire a long stay." For the opposite view, Bell quoted Odette Keun's *A Foreigner Looks at the British Sudan:*[5] "Whatever vanishes, the realities remain indelibly written in the collective consciousness of mankind: and neither triumph nor defeat, nor past, nor future, can erase their marks. The realities here are that while the English governed the Sudan, they released slaves, and suppressed slavery. They increased prosperity, gave education, protected the weak and the outraged, defended and taught strength and courage to those who were else the predestined victims of chiefs and priests, fought disease, and postponed death. So long as our species endures, these things will enter into the composition of its spirit, and form part of the heritage.

There is ultimately no other significance to human endeavour, and no other reward." But as Sudanese contributors to this study indicate, there are other options from which history may choose.

Notes

1. Interestingly, the great pioneer of girls' education in the Sudan was a locally-educated Sudanese, Babikr Bedri. His *Memoirs of Babikr Bedri* (vol. 1, London: Oxford University Press, 1969; vol. 2, London: Ithaca, 1980) are an important source for the study of this development.
2. A draft Anglo-Egyptian agreement recognizing the sovereignty of the Egyptian crown in the Sudan. Intense Sudanese and British opposition led to its abandonment.
3. The population of the Sudan at the time of the Anglo-Egyptian conquest was the subject of much British propaganda. Estimates are at best conjectural. See Daly, *Empire on the Nile*, 18–21.
4. Reference to the nineteenth-century slave trade may be seen as indicating embarrassment at the lack of more positive achievements of British rule in the south. See Holt and Daly, *A History of the Sudan*, 153.
5. London: 1930.

PART 2

THROUGH THE EYES OF THE RULED:

The Northern View

1

Early Contacts

The northern Sudanese reaction to the British passed through three phases: ferocious primary resistance to the imposition of foreign rule; a period of general collaboration during which smoldering resentment and mistrust were outweighed by recognition of accumulating benefits; and the post-World War II period of growing nationalism that led to independence. Throughout, the human factor was important. Personal experiences were significant in determining the Sudanese view of the whole colonial period. It is important that, as the principal actors pass from the scene, historical writing takes account of this human dimension, for without it the developments of the period are less easily intelligible. It is useful to remember, too, that we are dealing here, as in the case of the British, with the views of notables, leaders of the people, not with those of the man in the street or in the field: although ruled by the British, they were yet members of the Sudanese elite whose experiences and perceptions cannot be said to have been typical of the Sudanese as a whole.

Before their first encounters with individual British officials, Sudanese had, as boys, regarded them with a mixture of superstition, awe, fear, respect, and admiration. By reputation they were known as the new "Turks," according to Babo Nimir of the Missiriyya, "just as tough as those Turks who had been here before the Mahdiya," although more aloof and less inclined to wanton violence than the old Turks. Even among those who had grown up in fairly close contact with the British—such as Muhammad Ahmed Abu Ranat, whose father regularly received British officials at home, and Muhammad Ahmed Abu Sinn, who served tea to British visitors to his father, the *nazir*—there was little familiarity. From these meetings the young Abu Sinn gained an early impression of the foreigners as hard workers. But "the people used to fear them. Although they felt they would have justice done in everything they raised to them, they were afraid."

Many had vivid memories of their first encounter with the British. Daud Abd al-Latif recalled how, at the age of six or seven, he was brought before the district commissioner, sitting at the high table of the judge. Daud had witnessed a theft in his father's shop and had been called to testify against the accused. "I was a small child, about two feet tall, trying to answer a person the others treated nearly as a god," he recalled. Fearing a beating, the young boy burst into tears, an experience that left him mistrustful of the British for years to come.

Daud's childhood experience was not unique. Yusuf Bedri vividly recalled a similar encounter at the age of twelve which became so imprinted on his mind that subsequent years of congenial relations with British officials could not entirely erase it. On his way to school in Rufaa he was confronted by the district commissioner, J. N. Richardson.[1] "I was wearing European shoes, not *marcoub*, the locally produced shoes.... He said, 'Why are you wearing these?' I replied, 'Well,' and gave a sheepish answer.... I said, 'These were given to me by my brother who bought them from a shop.' He sent me back in a furious temper to change my shoes and put on my *marcoub*, the native shoes. By the time I got back to school, I found the whole school paraded and Mr. Richardson was inspecting the shoes of the pupils. Every boy wearing European shoes was sent home to change into Sudanese shoes."

By contrast, two chiefs, Zubayr Ahmed al-Malik and Babo Nimir, who by virtue of their fathers' positions were in closer contact with the government, developed early opinions of individual Britons they met as "very reasonable, good people." Babo Nimir had been favorably impressed by his first meeting with a district commissioner, one Mr. Crawford. Taken by his elderly grandmother to meet this official, the twelve-year-old Babo Nimir shocked her by shaking hands with him rather than giving the traditional greeting of lowering his head slightly and offering his shoulders for the elder to touch. "'What are you doing!' she exclaimed. 'Why don't you bend your shoulders for your father?' 'No, no,' Crawford replied. 'A man greets a man with his hands; he doesn't greet with his shoulders.'"

Sharply-defined childhood portraits of the British became

blurred, if not altered, by closer association with them at school and the Gordon Memorial College. Zubayr Ahmed al-Malik remembered a spirit of cooperation, particularly in sports. "We did not have anything against them. We were in fact quite happy with them," he said. Sorror Ramley observed that it was very common for friendships to develop between senior students and teachers: "They took their relationship outside the classroom into social circles." Even more impressively, the student-teacher relationship was honored after the schooling was complete: in 1931, when the students at the Gordon College struck over graduates' wages, the warden, D. H. Hibbert,[2] went to Wad Ramley accompanied by the district commissioner "and talked to me as a [former] student of his." This was Sorror's first consultation with the British "on something which concerned the country."

Jamal Muhammad Ahmed remembered "Billy" Williams,[3] warden of the Gordon College, as "kindly, devoted to games . . . a father figure to everybody in the college." The tutor of Jamal's house at the college, A. B. Theobald, was recalled as a stern taskmaster but with a strong personal interest in each boy and his academic progress. Later, after Jamal and his classmates had graduated, they "used to go back to him as young teachers, young clerks, young bookkeepers, and so on [and found him] a very different man altogether from that disciplinarian character we used to know at the college."

Close personal interest in individual students at the Gordon College reflected the public school and university tradition of which British officials were themselves products. This was epitomized during the wardenship of N. R. Udal. "The relations between Mr. Udal and the students were really intimate," Yusuf Bedri recalled. "He used to go around the hostels. You could feel his presence at every moment. It was not a feeling of fear but of sympathy and paternal relations. . . . I felt so much for him that when I met him during his visit to the Sudan in 1952—I was then principal of the school and Mr. Udal must have been in his seventies—I kissed his hand when I saluted him, a sign of Sudanese respect; that is, you exaggerate in showing your feelings of deep respect and gratitude. What I did is not normally done by Sudanese to the British, but it shows the human influence of Mr. Udal on his students." Yusuf Bedri continued: "The life in the college was really a model which every graduate felt he must adopt. Of those of us who went through the Gordon College, nobody can deny that he has been influenced very much by the atmosphere of the college and by the cultural impact of the British tutors, which came in quite smoothly. . . . A few arrogant reactions on the part of some tutors . . . were, perhaps, not meant the way they appeared."

For some, the experience of Gordon College was not entirely positive. Muhammad Abu Ranat described a "relationship of distance" with his British instructors. Muhammad Ahmed Abu Sinn observed that while many tutors "were very keen on the welfare of the students, [some] were stiff, hard. They used to lash the students and to make them labor." Daud Abd al-Latif's relations with British teachers were not good. He regarded the tutor of English language and literature as "oppressive and conceited," determined to enforce a degree of discipline which Daud considered unacceptable. Earlier feelings of enmity toward the British were reinforced by his reading of leftist publications critical of colonialism; Daud had fallen under the influence of a Greek bookseller who "pushed me by giving me Karl Marx." In 1936, when Italy occupied Abyssinia, Daud's hostility toward Britain was so strong that he considered learning Italian "to help the Italians enter the Sudan. We hoped the Italians would come, fight the English, and send them away from the Sudan." Daud's tutor remained ignorant of his pupil's reading material: "I never told him anything, nor did I discuss my readings with him. All he was concerned with was whether I wrote my English well." The more leftist literature Daud read, the more his English improved.

Despite this anti-British sentiment, Daud Abd al-Latif felt that his British teachers had not been particularly hard on him. "On the contrary, some of them, one or two among them, were very sympathetic with me because I was the top of my class, and usually tutors like clever boys." Daud was nonetheless dismissed from the Gordon College at the time of the 1931 students' strike, when the police, according to Daud, determined that he had been among the instigators. When he finally became a government employee, he was sent to a remote district as a warning to behave himself, despite (or because of) his expressed desire to remain in Khartoum.

Daud spent the next seven years working as a bookkeeper in al-Damer and Wadi Halfa. Unknown to him at the time, it was precisely an independent spirit that set him apart from his contemporaries and ironically revealed the qualities of leadership which adversaries respected. At Wadi Halfa he came abruptly to the attention of the district commissioner, T. G. G. Carless, who once shouted at an old Sudanese accountant, "Damn your father!" When other Sudanese in the office remained silent, Daud marched up to Carless and told him, "According to the ways of our people, and according to the customs anywhere in the world, what you did was wrong." The district commissioner, bemused that "a small boy like this . . . in Scale J, is the one who should tell me that I am wrong," apologized to the old man and thanked Daud, urging him to speak out at any further evidence of impropriety.

Six months after this episode, Carless offered Daud a place in the special training course for sub-*ma'murs*. Daud declined, saying that enrollment would make him an "informant of the British." Remarkably, Carless then arranged for Daud to study the cultivation of date trees in Brazil, a plan more agreeable to him. The Munich crisis intervened, however, preventing Sudanese travel abroad, and Daud applied for the sub-*ma'mur* course after all. He was rejected because he was too short, despite the examiners' acknowledgment that he was the brightest candidate before them. Daud complained to Carless that the board must have been interviewing for porters "rather than selecting sub-*ma'murs* for the administration!" Carless showed Daud's letter of complaint to Newbold, the civil secretary, who thereafter took a personal interest in the case. Daud was accepted into the course the following year without an interview.

Yusuf Bedri's first experience of a British superior was quite unpleasant. After taking a degree in pharmacy at the American University in Beirut, he had returned to join the Sudan Medical Service and was, by his own admission, "a swollen-headed young man with lots of ideas and self-conceit. I thought I must do something in the arrangement of the [Wad Medani] hospital pharmacy and the way medicines were dispensed, that sort of thing. There were certain things—I do not want to blow my own trumpet and call them innovations—which I thought I was going to bring about. I was checked up by the senior medical inspector [F. H. Goss].[4] He took me into his office and said, 'Why did you do this, Yusuf?' And I said, 'I used my discretion.' And he banged his desk, saying, 'I don't want discretion!'"

Like Daud Abd al-Latif in similar circumstances, Yusuf Bedri had felt indignation rather than fear, and was convinced that his superior "was a wicked man. . . . I went back to my dispensary and wrote my resignation addressed to the director, Sudan Medical Service, with a copy to him and a copy to the governor of the Blue Nile Province. . . . I don't know why I sent that copy to the governor. Dr. Goss . . . was really perturbed about it. Anyway, he made a challenge to me. He gave me his own car and asked me to go and inspect the dispensaries in the Gezira. This was in 1937. I made the tour and wrote the report." Meanwhile, his resignation reached the director of the medical service, Sir Eric Pridie,[5] who was a friend of Yusuf's father and allowed the matter to drop quietly. Yusuf still had to deal with Dr. Goss, however, who sought at every opportunity to find fault: "I must say that my relations with Dr. Goss were very severe, very tense indeed."

Zubayr Ahmed al-Malik's first encounter with a British superior also involved youthful rebelliousness. After he completed his intermediate education, his father persuaded him to join the army. Zubayr had no particular interest in the military, preferring a career as an engineer, but agreed. "In those days, they used to treat new students very roughly. . . . There was bad treatment, very bad treatment, for any undisciplined student. . . . There was too much pressure." Provoked by some minor issue, Zubayr persuaded the authorities to allow his return to the Gordon College.

Muhammad Ahmed Abu Sinn's working relations with the British began in 1935 when he had several encounters with the district commissioner, Desmond Hawkesworth.[6] "I thought of him as a very twisted man. He used to threaten the *shaykhs* indirectly when he wanted to force something on them which he thought they would not like. . . . But I did my best to check him. I made him understand that such a policy would not work. It was better to be plain, and to explain how any action taken was in the interest of the people." The *nazir* recalled a particular dispute regarding the distribution of land to tenant farmers. Required to pay compensation to the landowners, the former tenants were burdened with a huge debt. Hawkesworth pressed on, regardless of Abu Sinn's opposition.

Despite disagreements with individuals, Muhammad Ahmed Abu Sinn retained considerable respect for the British: "They worked very hard; they worked very hard: irrespective of the circumstances, irrespective of the broken-down cars they might have, irrespective of the hot weather. They fulfilled their responsibilities under any circumstances." And they expected an equally wholehearted effort from the Sudanese: "If they spoke of a person as 'good,' they approved his output," he said. Abu Sinn's own dedication won the respect of administrators, who commented in reports that "Muhammad Ahmed Abu Sinn works outside the office as if he is senior to the district commissioner or in the rank of district commissioner."

Of all the Sudanese interviewed, Amin Hassoun's attitude toward the British was the least ambivalent. For his first British superior, G. W. Power, head of the personnel office of the Sudan Railways, he had nothing but admiration: "His name was just like his features—he was powerful," Amin Hassoun recalled. The bell summoning him to Power's office was, to him, "music in my ears." He valued Power's instructions and learned much from his superior's experience. At times, he said, he would awaken in the middle of the night to jot down notes on what Power had asked him to do the next day.

Jamal Muhammad Ahmed was effusive in his praise for the first Briton with whom he worked closely, Robin Hodgkin, then editorial director of the pioneering youth magazine, *Al-Sibyan*. Designed for the thousands who left school with only an elementary reading knowledge of Arabic, the publication was an astonishing success. As co-editor, Jamal developed a relationship with Hodgkin not of superior and subordinate, but of mutual respect. "I don't think I worked with a person, before or after, whom I liked so much," he declared. In particular, he praised Hodgkin's "energy, inventiveness, and vigor.... He would take an article to the printers and compose it himself; he would repair a car if a car went wrong; he would be able to spend a terrible, dreary night in awful rainy weather in the open countryside.... He was a tiny man, but with stamina—mental stamina and physical stamina. I cannot spare any praise for Robin Hodgkin—anything I say about him is less than he really deserves.

"To be close to him meant actually talking about everything openly, discussing things, and social mixing—just to go to their home as we do in the Sudan, without appointments—which I now consider a most inconvenient thing to do, but at the time it was quite a natural thing because the society was not so large as it is at the moment. Then the fact that his wife was also an educationalist made the group, so to speak, hang together. But there was much more to it than getting people together. I mean there was that personal thing."

Notes

1. Richardson served from 1919 until 1940, when he was killed in an accident at Atbara.
2. Hibbert served from 1929 until 1954, lastly as director of education, 1950–1954. He was warden of the Gordon College from 1943 to 1945.
3. C. W. Williams, later assistant director of education (1937–44) and director (1944–49).
4. Dr. F. Hennessy Goss worked in the Sudan Medical Service from 1926 to 1943. For a biographical note see H. C. Squires, *The Sudan Medical Service, An Experiment in Social Medicine* (London: Heinemann, 1958), 54.
5. Pridie served in the Sudan from 1924 until 1945. For a biographical note see Squires, 51.
6. Hawkesworth worked in the Sudan from 1927 to 1954. He was assistant civil secretary (1949–1952) and governor of Kassala Province from 1952 until his retirement.

2

Official and Personal Relations

Beyond initial encounters, closer relations developed which were fondly remembered long after the tensions and disagreements of the colonial encounter had subsided. Friendships transcended colonial barriers, bureaucracy, and cultural differences separating the northern Sudanese from the British, yet certain aspects of these could never be bridged and remained a source of tension.

In some cases, relations characterized by trust and respect remained close in a business rather than a social sense. Babo Nimir believed the district commissioners "respected me because I never told them a lie. I always told the truth, and my word was always highly regarded by them." Even when he was a child, the then district commissioner, George Bredin, respected him, Babo Nimir said. "He used to consider me a personality with a future, and never treated me as a child." This close but official relationship with the British remained throughout his career.

According to Muhammad Ahmed Abu Sinn, it was his dedication to duty and lack of self-interest that the British admired in him: "One thing that I think made the governor and the district commissioner respect me: during my time as a member of the Executive Council, I never asked a personal favor. I worked for twenty years, and I did not ask for an increase of pay. And they didn't give it to me. At that time, there was a trend among the Sudanese to initiate pump schemes. I did not ask the government for a pump scheme because I did not think it was right for a member of the Executive Council to do so. That, I think, earned me a certain personal affection or respect."

Zubayr Ahmed al-Malik ascribed British liking for him to his administrative skill, in particular to the fact that unlike his father, whom he had succeeded as chief, he did not inspire fear and envy in the people. "I was different from my father. Times had changed, and of course I had advanced with time and with education. Nobody was afraid of me.... My contact with these DCs was very close." After agreeing to move his headquarters from a remote village to Dongola because the British had wanted easier access to him, Zubayr Ahmed had few disagreements with them. One dispute, a misunderstanding over whether a pay raise for Sudanese clerks was a permanent adjustment or a temporary allowance, was resolved by a letter of apology from the district commissioner.

In some cases, friendship developed across the fine line between official and social relations. An affinity arose between Muhammad Abu Ranat and the chief justice of the Sudan, Sir William Lindsay,[1] with whom he became "great friends." Lindsay "liked me very much and we were frank with each other. We used to speak about everything.... In fact, the recommendation for me to become chief justice designate emanated from him. Some of them asked me to go with them in their social life, for example, to a party or dinner." Similarly, Ahmed Mahgoub was personally as well as officially close to J. A. Hartley,[2] assistant director of education. "He never gave me the feeling that I was in any way unequal to him, except for age and experience.... I went to his house and he came to mine.... It was quite customary for him to take me for a drink, or for me to take him for a meal. We took turns paying for meals.... So I think it was quite a close relationship, apart from the work side."

Amin Hassoun was moved by his friendship with C. R. Williams, the general manager of the Sudan Railways, and his wife. "Although there was a very big gap between me and him—I was a very junior clerk—still, by virtue of giving Arabic lessons to his wife I used to associate very much with him, very much. I would go to their house about three times a week, and I stayed with him and his wife in the garden.... He treated me very nicely, to the extent that whenever I came to enter the gate into his garden and saw them sitting in the garden, I felt as though I was going into my house. I never felt that I was coming to the general manager, Sudan Railways."

Daud Abd al-Latif had a different view about what it meant to be close to the British. Officials like Carless or Newbold looked after him. They were "concerned that I be 'contained.'" Daud recalled that Carless convinced Newbold that Daud was "politically-minded." Newbold "used to really give me a great deal of care and attention. All the young people he thought were intelligent—he would keep correspondence with them, wherever they were. If one was in Nyala and one was wherever, he would write to him and ask him how the district was going. He began to cooperate with them, just as, or even better than, he was cooperating with the English." Newbold gave Daud easy access to him, at home and in the office. He had weekly teas with Daud and his friends, lent them books, and discussed government matters with them. "He would give us the impression that we were important people."

Yusuf Bedri also made the distinction between a working relationship and a personal friendship. During the early 1950s Yusuf worked closely with the director of education, D. H. Hibbert, who, in Yusuf's opinion, was "a pretentious person. He pretended that he liked the Sudanese and wanted to associate with them. Socially, he was quite pleasant, but when you came to the reality—to business transactions—one would feel a bit of his impudence. . . . I may be a bit influenced by his behavior toward me. We were conducting quite a voluminous amount of money—a grant given by the Sudan Government to Al-Ahfad College for building and purchasing equipment. . . . I felt that he was suspecting our—I won't say honesty—but the way we were disposing of the money, to such an extent that I had to talk to him. Incidentally, he had taught me English in 1930 when I was in third year secondary school, so he was my teacher and I had some sort of respect for him. But his last behavior compelled me to be a bit insolent, to the extent that I said to him, 'Well, sir, this money has been appropriated by the Legislative Assembly and not by the Ministry of Education, and it was a grant given in the name of Shaykh Babikr Bedri, more or less a personal sort of grant.' He interrupted me quite furiously and said in Arabic—I still remember his words quite clearly—'If this man [Babikr Bedri] with his ideas doesn't die, we won't rest.'"

Yusuf Bedri admitted that his own independence of mind and determination never again to be employed by the government after resigning from the medical service "must have given me some sort of irritating attitude toward my British bosses when they compared me with the other Sudanese subordinates." There were, however, officials in the education department who dealt with Sudanese colleagues in a quite different way. Yusuf mentioned W. B. M.

Jamieson, who became assistant director of education, as an example. He and others like him "gave time to listen to arguments. You felt that they considered it as part of their responsibility, and there was always a very pleasant human relationship. For instance, [Farquharson-] Lang, whenever we got at loggerheads, he would send in a note regretting the whole thing, and he would invite you to a cup of tea or for dinner and elaborate on the problem. Jamieson would come over himself to the school [al-Ahfad] during the day and sit in your office and discuss the disagreements until you saw eye to eye. So, there was certainly a difference among the British in the way they reacted in carrying out their duties."

Most Sudanese discussion of relations concerned government officials, but British wives (as Amin Hassoun mentioned in reference to Mrs. Williams) were involved on the home front. The question of what place British women occupied in the Sudanese social context elicited a wide variety of responses from Sudanese contributors.

Perhaps both because of his family's role in the education of women and his own liberalness, Yusuf Bedri was more comfortable with British women than his Sudanese colleagues were. He was deeply impressed by their work with the Girl Guides and in raising funds for social and voluntary organizations on behalf of Sudanese women. As examples, he cited Grace Crowfoot,[3] wife of the director of education, and Mrs. Thorp, the Anglican bishop's wife, who was medical officer at the Church Missionary Society's hospital in Omdurman. They and others like them "associated themselves very freely and comfortably with so many Sudanese homes."

Some respondents greatly overstated the extent to which British wives assimilated into Sudanese society. Babo Nimir commented that British women "were very good.... They would go to the cattle camp; they would meet the children; they would meet the women; and they would talk with the women as women. They were really fully integrated. They didn't see themselves as strangers among the people." Amin Hassoun's opinion, like Babo Nimir's based solely on personal observation, was equally generalized: "I must say they fitted into the Sudanese community very comfortably and well.... [C. R. Williams's] wife used to come and visit us in the house.... [She] was very nice with my people." Muhammad Ahmed Abu Sinn said that British women "would take a full share in the duties of their husbands, and would take part in the social life—celebrations to open the schools, the awarding of prizes, and so on—in the community where they were staying."

A number of contributors were reserved or uncertain about describing the role of British women. Zubayr Ahmed al-Malik allowed that there was social mixing, but could not "really tell you that there was full integration or association." Social contact was "confined to a certain class of very educated or the very enlightened, or those holding high posts.... Among most people, there wasn't much contact." In his view, social interaction increased with time: "It occurred after people like Newbold came onto the scene. At the beginning, there was a kind of bar. They were somewhat aloof."

Daud Abd al-Latif pointed out that British wives generally remained in the Sudan for only six months of the year. "In April all the British would go back to England because they thought they could not stand the heat of May. They would stay in the Sudan up to April, and that was the period during which they would try to invite to their homes Sudanese officials they cared about. Their wives became sort of decoration, making tea and things like that." Most Sudanese men felt awkward with British women: "The Sudanese as a whole are not accustomed to the small talk which is polite in the presence of ladies. We were not accustomed to [the modern] emancipated women and ... did not know what to say and not to say."

One exceptional Englishwoman, whom Daud knew very well, played an active role in politics. As Daud reported, Nancy Robertson, wife of the civil secretary, Sir James Robertson, "took a very active role in politics, without the word 'politics'.... She knew the Sudanese who were friends of her husband, important Sudanese. She would invite them to tea and talk to them." According to Daud, Lady Robertson used tea-party conversation to intercede subtly and indirectly with her husband when he disagreed with Daud and other Sudanese civil servants and political figures. Daud went to her when he and Sir James had a misunderstanding. "She would do her best to prepare her husband and channel him quietly in the right direction. She understood that her husband was sometimes hot-tempered." She was, however, the exception rather than the rule.

In the eyes of Jamal Muhammad Ahmed, the great majority of British women did not fit into Sudanese society because of linguistic and cultural barriers: "Although the Sudanese were very generous with what they had, they always thought that the standard of living of the English was so high that they shied away from inviting them to their homes.... The English wives on their part always wondered if inviting the Sudanese would be a happy occasion or would be an embarrassing one, where everybody would just sit there and sip tea.... I am sure, thinking of it now, each side wanted very much to know the other side. But this cultural barrier kept the parties apart, except for the occasional family. One must never forget that there were far fewer Englishmen in the Sudan than is commonly supposed, perhaps only eight hundred in a country of one million square miles."

The contacts that did occur between Sudanese and British men and women were, according to Jamal Muhammad Ahmed, "very stuffy, formal, polite relationships. The Sudanese would be called into a British home, usually for tea. Meals were rather rare, because meals meant handling forks and knives, and for some, forks and knives were not such a great amusement. Tea was all right because you just drank tea and had a bit of cake. It was stuffy because there was this tremendous effort on the side of the hostess to keep you happy.... I can't remember at all calling anyone by his first name. It was always 'Sayyid so-and-so,' and 'Mister so-and-so'.... I even remember some sticky person telling you how to dress for coming to tea.... [He would say] 'Come in your shorts.'" Jamal only later realized that the man was trying to make the Sudanese feel comfortable: "At the time we thought it was just a way to order us about.... We resented it.... At one stage, one or two people used to go in pairs of trousers, just to establish their personalities!"

If the cultural barrier strained social contacts, it created, in Jamal Muhammad Ahmed's opinion, an unbreachable wall insofar as sexual relations between Sudanese men and British women were concerned. "They didn't excite us much, really.... There was the general view of the word *khawaja* [foreigner] which meant not the epitome of cleanliness.... The general feeling was that there are people who are different from us ... so there was nothing exciting about them at the time." Babo Nimir commented that "in their treatment of people, one did not doubt the femininity [of the British women's behavior], but one did not look at them the same way one would look at a Sudanese woman.... When you see a Sudanese woman you look at her with a certain look. I personally did not look at British women with that look. They too probably felt the same way. These things have their own eyes and their own hearts.... The right combination ... did not exist between us and the English, but of course it exists between us and the Sudanese women!"

In Daud Abd al-Latif's opinion, "we did not believe [British women] were sexually accessible. So any interest there might have been was very theoretical. The country was, in those fifty years of British rule, so 'scandal-less,' as one of [the British] said, that that itself was a scandal. No rape took place; not even a flirtation that could anger the husband or another European took place." During the brief time a British woman remained in the Sudan, Daud said, her husband "would fully insulate her. They would get together for tea or coffee in the garden and gossip. After that, they would go gardening.... Her husband was on top of her day and night, protecting her."

Amin Hassoun agreed that there was no sexual contact between the two peoples. He said he "may have heard of Sudanese very interested to see the white women and running after them, [but he did not think it ever came] to the extent of sexual relationship. I would never believe it.... Nobody would dare to do it at all ... because we had their respect. And it is in our nature that we should not do that, especially with foreigners." Amin also dismissed the idea of British men "running after ... Sudanese women." Muhammad Ahmed Abu Sinn was careful to disassociate any Sudanese-British liaisons from his home district. "We used to hear that certain British officials had relations with certain types of women in different parts of the Sudan.... But in our area, from 1935 to 1955, we heard nothing of the sort."

A few informants, however, commented on sexual liaisons. Ahmed Mahgoub knew positively of "certain instances where relations really existed between English women and Sudanese men in this country, even at the time of British rule.... Although the Sudanese looked upon them with respect, no human being is infallible." Of course, Ahmed Mahgoub was considerably younger than most other contributors, and belonged to the postwar generation. He felt that British men "always respected the position of the woman in the Sudan, as a lady in the background who didn't see men." Although very few people might be aware of affairs that were taking place, the "general consensus . . . was that it was just inconceivable for an Englishman to have relations with a Sudanese woman or vice versa."

Muhammad Abu Ranat heard about only two or three cases of such affairs during the entire period of British rule, and admitted he had no "evidence about them but gossip." Jamal Muhammad Ahmed's knowledge of Sudanese-British sexual contacts was also based on "hearsay." According to him, rumors circulated about young district commissioners in remote areas having "rubber women . . . because [the Sudanese] couldn't explain how a man could live without a woman. . . . There was that sort of story going around! Whether it was a joke or not is immaterial; it indicated that people were a little puzzled, especially in a country where you are allowed to marry four and have love affairs with about four hundred. . . . It's just this unknown life, because the DC, after doing his job . . . went back home, and the poor fellow just had to make do with what he had!"

In Daud's opinion, "most of the English were recruited from puritan families. They had a strong feeling that it was not ethically right to make any sexual contact with the natives." He referred to statistics indicating that sons of clergymen were prevalent in the colonial service. Together with sons of teachers, they were generally "people who had a strong religious inclination. Besides, they were self-sacrificing people, and the Empire was looking for people of this sort to send abroad." Muhammad Omer Beshir, who attended the interview with Daud, commented that the puritanism of Oxford and Cambridge contrasted sharply with the very relaxed attitude that military men had toward the native population. People with university and technical backgrounds, Muhammad Omer felt, were "somewhat more remote" than their military counterparts. One British soldier, Jackson Pasha,[4] was a notorious womanizer. Jackson, Daud said, would "sleep about, marry, divorce, and make a lot of noise. . . . There were others." Both Daud and Muhammad Omer, however, emphasized the exceptional nature of such incidents.

A number of contributors were asked whether they had knowledge of homosexuality among the British in the Sudan, in view of the fact that heterosexual relations were so constrained. Jamal Muhammad Ahmed, Ahmed Mahgoub, and Muhammad Ahmed Abu Sinn had heard only rumors to that effect. Jamal and Ahmed tended to believe that there was substance to some of the stories; Amin Hassoun said simply, "We lived as subordinates to them. We were not supposed to know such things."

Notes

1. Lindsay served from 1932 until 1955, when he was knighted on retirement.
2. Hartley served from 1929 to 1955, lastly as assistant Sudan Agent in London.
3. Grace Crowfoot was the author of *Flowering Plants of the Northern and Central Sudan* (Leominster: Orphan's Printing Press, n.d.), and works on spinning and weaving, including (with H. Ling Roth) *Hand Spinning and Woolcombing* (Carlton: Ruth Bean, 1974).
4. Sir H. W. Jackson served from 1899 to 1923 in a series of high posts. In retirement he lived at Merowe in Dongola.

3

Working Conditions and Attitudes

Northern Sudanese respondents generally agreed that the British were serious and devoted administrators. Even those Sudanese whose personal experiences were difficult concurred. While this is a remarkable compliment, it should be noted again that respondents were mainly from the tribal elite and of a particular generation.

Muhammad Ahmed Abu Sinn, *nazir* of the Shukriyya, painted a vivid picture of the devoted administrator. "Some of them would start working at half-past six, go to have breakfast at half-past eight, come back at half-past nine or nine, to remain in the office until two.... Then in the afternoon, they had their hobbies. Some of them worked in their gardens, some played golf, some flew kites, some rode horses and so forth. In the evening, if we had been asked to dinner, we'd find the official busy working on his research. During the meal itself, he always talked about the ideas we would have for the development of the area. 'What thing have you got in mind for the service, better service of the people?' Rarely would we talk about world politics, the United Nations Charter, and so forth.

"I remember one of the district commissioners who was touring with me. I saw him packing about thirteen books for a trip of only two nights. I said, 'One is sufficient. When are you going to read them all?' He said, 'No. If I got disinterested in one, I would change to another.' So they did their best to spend their time happily.... My other point is that the district commissioner used to spend at least three days outside the office, touring. He would go to the villages to see the people. He would sit and chat, and ask them: what are their grievances? What are their difficulties? And what could he do about them?"

A question that revealed a striking ambivalence among the Sudanese concerns the British "mission" in the Sudan: whether they were there to guide, protect, or dominate. Of course, the Sudanese assumed the self-interest that motivated the Anglo-Egyptian conquest, but they also admitted benevolent aspects of the British colonial outlook and service.

"Definitely, according to what is written in different books, they came to avenge Gordon," Muhammad Ahmed Abu Sinn declared. "That's one motivation. One must also remember that it was in the nineteenth century when they were thinking of the expansion of their empire.... Their goals were to expand the empire and to dominate the Nile Valley.... But was the expansion of the empire the only objective? Definitely not. When they came, the country was poor. People were scattered ... no security. Their first goal was to maintain security. They kept out of the Sudan the Greeks, and foreigners, generally, who wanted to obtain land. They tried to rehabilitate the people, to think of their welfare. They refused to introduce the mixed courts [of the Ottoman Empire] ... and they started to build the Sudan as a condominium, not under the jurisdiction of the minister of the colonies but to be ruled in a special way."

None of the contributors felt that the Sudan as a whole had been protected by the British. "We were not in need of protection from anybody because we had no enemies," was how Sorror Ramley put it. In Babo Nimir's words, "You think of protection against something.... There was nothing which was attacking us which they had to protect us from. If there was an enemy from outside the Sudan, then of course they would be protecting their empire, not protecting us. But there was nothing of the sort." Babo Nimir did feel that the British had been both "rulers and guides.... They gave you guidance with respect.... When they tie your hands, they tie you with silk, not with iron chains." He added that "there was a virtue in their presence, and if they were not colonialists and imperialists one would not even question their treatment." But "no man would accept" colonial rule without reservations.

Sorror Ramley described the British as "trainers to enable the Sudanese to rule themselves." Zubayr al-Malik agreed that "we were guided," but he also believed that as a chief he had "influenced *them* a lot. I felt that I was able to communicate with them well, to reason with them, and through this reasoning, I managed to do a lot of things.... They were, of course, guiding and directing us, but we too used to advise them and they used to accept our advice. There was a degree of cooperation; there was a kind of give and take."

Zubayr's son-in-law, Feisal Muhammad Abd al-Rahman, pointed out the lack of alternatives to cooperation since the Anglo-Egyptian forces were fully capable of crushing armed resistance. "Under the circumstances, you had to make the best out of a difficult situation. They opted after some time ... for a policy of indirect rule, and they had to rely on some people. There was a price for that sort of reliance, political *modus vivendi* or *modus operandi*. They probably listened to some of these people often, and often accommodated them. As the chief said, it was a process of give and take. Maybe they took more; nobody knows."

Daud Abd al-Latif described his position in the government hierarchy somewhat egocentrically: "I worked as a junior to the British and also as a senior to the British.... I had British staff in my province.... They were my juniors and I looked after them; I recommended their promotion. I wrote their reports. To me, they were ordinary human beings from a remote and different culture which I was trying to understand, and they were trying to understand my background, too." Daud observed that he "met people to whom I felt intellectually superior.... Sometimes I felt that a particular Englishman was a pygmy as far as intellect went. So there was an intellectual superiority either way, but domination was never felt by me."

Amin Hassoun, on the other hand, modestly replied that he had felt guided by the British at all times. He was impressed by British attention to detail and the respect shown to superiors: his supervisor in the Sudan Railways insisted that he retype an entire page in order to replace the word "recommend" with the milder "suggest" in a memorandum to the general manager. Amin Hassoun felt that he had benefited greatly from such an example.

Jamal Muhammad Ahmed disdained generalization. "We are talking about a hypothetical character because they were also individuals," he said. One British official might have seen each Sudanese as "a tiny little thing to be protected." Another might have recognized the individual "as a man with his own views to be respected." A third, simply "rude," might have said, "These are men from the bush who happen to be here." The Briton Jamal admired most, Robin Hodgkin, "never gave you the impression he was guiding and protecting you or ruling you."

In answer to the question of how they had viewed their rulers and whether they saw them as superior, equal, or inferior to Sudanese, the chiefs and civil servants differed. Of course, the chiefs in theory were autonomous rulers of their people with a status commanding some respect from the government. Nevertheless, they knew that ultimate power lay in the hands of the British who, ironically, justified themselves as servants of the country and its people. "They pretended to be equal," Zubayr Ahmed al-Malik said, "but one didn't really believe it. These people were people who had come to rule. Yes, they did serve the Sudan, but of course don't forget that in the first place they were serving their own country, their people, and themselves, and they knew that."

Sorror Ramley viewed the British as partners. "On that understanding, we used to work together. But, personally, I never thought of them as superior or as possessing any superior merits. And in our inner feeling, we felt we were the masters of the country. Nobody ever denied that, except perhaps some of the English who were working in the Sudan."

While Babo Nimir felt that the British were superior, presumably through authority rather than by race, he emphasized their respect for the people, especially the leaders: they were "rulers and superiors . . . but their superiority was not a tough one. . . . It was a soft, gentle superiority. They did not tell you they were your lords. But you yourself knew it. . . . There are people who tell you that they are your lords. With the English, you knew it by yourself." As Babo saw it, the British were as much guides as rulers. "They gave you guidance with respect."

Two civil servants, Amin Hassoun and Ahmed Mahgoub, stated that they viewed the British as superiors not because they were British but because they deserved the deference paid to senior officials or elders. "In our upbringing," Ahmed Mahgoub said, "your elder is your superior, irrespective of who he is," and he added that after independence he had no difficulty in dealing with the British as equals at the business table.

Jamal Muhammad Ahmed explained that the teaching profession encouraged feelings of equality between the British and the Sudanese. "The *ma'murs* and the sub-*ma'murs* used to salute so formally. With teachers, we mixed fairly frequently, and I don't think even then they gave one the feeling of being masters." The "absolutely free atmosphere" of the Gordon College student union, where students said "whatever they wanted," and the teachers, "whether English or Sudanese ... took part in discussions and everything, quite freely," explains why the students "were so vocal and articulate in the wall papers [and] in their debates. ... Things only came to a head when those very nationalistic orations were made; then students would pour out into the streets and get beaten up by the police, not by the teachers. ... There was no barrier between the teachers and the taught. But there was, of course, a barrier, a bit of hostility, between the students and the outside forces who were responsible for law and order."

Daud Abd al-Latif, once he had joined the administration and overcome the initial hostility he had felt toward the British, had the impression that "they treated me ... mostly as an equal. I also treated them as equals." Although some Britons talked (condescendingly, in Daud's judgement) "of rather small subjects" to Sudanese whom they considered ignorant of important matters, Daud stated confidently that "there was never a color bar."

Jamal Muhammad Ahmed could recall only one incident that revealed British racial prejudice. During a heated discussion at a Sudanese-British gathering, an Englishman said, "'Well, people like you we call 'wogs.' We rushed to our dictionaries to find out what 'wogs' meant." When Jamal and his friends returned and confronted the Englishman, "he jokingly told us what was meant by 'wogs.'" Jamal minimized the slur: "'Wogs' is you and me, blacks and things," he said. "But this was just a little case."

Zubayr al-Malik and his son-in-law, Feisal Muhammad Abd al-Rahman, observed that the British were extremely cautious in their relations with Sudanese. "If you take, for example, the French way of ruling a foreign country," Feisal said, "their colonial policy is almost a policy of assimilation. The chap from Senegal was taught to read about his ancestors, who had blue eyes. ... The Algerians, for instance, were considered as Frenchmen. British colonial policy was to keep a certain distance from the natives. In East Africa there was a complete color bar, in Rhodesia and those places. Apparently, when they first came to the Sudan, they tried to impose some sort of color bar. But then there were all sorts of wars and rebellions. ... The fact stands out that, although they kept aloof, they never imposed a color bar." This Feisal attributed to the

Sudan's uncertain status as an Anglo-Egyptian condominium. He also observed that "the people recruited by the colonial office [were] not a very good element. But in the Sudan, where there had been the Mahdist revolution and the Gordon disaster, and tension between them and the Egyptians on the future of the Sudan, they made a point of sending the best. British administrators in the Sudan were the top of an elite corps. . . . They considered themselves as some sort of elite. I think they were very careful not to offend the Sudanese: the way they handled the tribes, the way they gave some powers to the native administration, the way they gave tribal leaders judicial powers to dispose of litigation, and so on. Some people in the judiciary used to say that the native courts disposed of 90 percent of the cases." In Feisal's opinion, the only color bar ever established in the Sudan was at the Sudan Club which, he pointed out with some irony, later became the headquarters of the Sudan Socialist Union.

Daud Abd al-Latif was acutely aware of the British view that "most of the Sudanese, when they found money, became drunkards." Consequently, Daud and his friends in the administration "did not drink at all, to refute what was a common criticism of the Sudanese educated elite at the time," and a possible excuse for not promoting them. "Most of the English drank," Daud added, "but few of them did it excessively. . . . Nearly everybody ended the day with two or three whiskies. One of the very clear features of the evening of a DC in the Sudan was his bottle of whiskey and his book of English fiction. As soon as the sun set, the whiskey bottle and the soda and the English fiction were on the table in the garden."

Jamal Muhammad Ahmed was struck by the fact that the relationship between the British and Sudanese was always so formal. "Making a joke, for an Englishman, was not becoming," Jamal said. "After all, he was a ruler. Even if he was a teacher or a surveyor, he considered himself a ruler. . . . On our side, we were also self-conscious. We would not make a joke because we would think, 'Well, this is my superior. He may take it against me.' I was the secretary of the Sudan Cultural Center for a number of years. It amuses me now to think that in those many years, I can't remember a jocular lecture or a jocular talk in the center given by either a Sudanese or an Englishman. It was all as serious as you could make it, very instructive and educational."

Most Sudanese respondents believed that the British were acutely conscious of the country's ethnic and cultural diversity and regional loyalties, which many British officials themselves adopted. According to Ahmed Mahgoub, they "were very knowledgeable about people divided into areas, and one may . . . attribute that to the fact that a young chap would come straight from Oxford or Cambridge and be sent to a rural area, any remote place. He would study that area and know the characteristics of everybody and their attitudes toward people, which vary from one area to another. There are those Sudanese who are honest and tell the truth; there are those who mince words; there are those who are crafty—and the English knew them. They could differentiate."

Although he never heard the British make direct comparisons, Amin Hassoun believed that "the British were highly impressed with people who came from the north." Ahmed Mahjoub thought that "in nine cases out of ten they will have . . . more confidence in a southerner." Daud Abd al-Latif elaborated on this point. "There was a regional enthusiasm by district commissioners. There were people who loved the southerners very much and those who loved the northerners very much. The district commissioners and governors of the south . . . loved the southern thinking. They would analyze it and think that the southerner, because he was a man of the bush, was very careful about his first step, while the northerner, being a desert man, was only careful about the last step. This pattern became so strong that many of the district commissioners, when they went from the south to the north, would not succeed."[1] As examples, Daud mentioned King and Wyld,[2] who spent their entire twenty to twenty-five year careers in southern districts. Some British administrators felt strongly that "the south was the future of the whole Sudan." At the 1947 Juba Conference, "those who were opposed to unity were more [numerous] among the British than among the southerners."[3]

British policy toward the regions was complicated by European missionary societies which competed for influence. According to Daud Abd al-Latif, the policy of separating north and south was essentially a byproduct of religious policy: "When Kitchener came," he said, "the missionaries pushed very strongly in order to get spheres of influence" in the south, but "did not leave the door open for Islam. The conflict then emerged not with Muslims, who were denied entrance to the south," but between the Catholics and

Protestants. Islam was "associated with the north and Christianity with the south, creating a certain pattern." Ironically, many British administrators in the south opposed missionary activity, according to Daud: "I worked in Equatoria as the [first Sudanese] governor. It was the opinion of the bishop [Mason], that I was the closest governor to them, and that he was more comfortable with me, a Muslim, than he had been with a Protestant Englishman. The government files of the south are full of complaints by district commissioners against the missionaries. They would refuse to give them even a little bit of land to build a hospital. It was to this extent."

Daud concluded, "All the British wanted to do was to prevent the spheres of influence which they had given to the missionaries from being complicated by giving the Muslims the right to go to the south and establish yet another religion there. The trade control was to favor the Greeks against the northerners because the British believed that the northerners used to cheat the southerners more than the Greeks did. [The government] was not against the northerner going to the south as an official but as a trader."

Some contributors believed that British policies were divisive throughout the country. For instance, there were "those kinds of English who loved the camels and the nomads and didn't like the town people at all," Daud Abd al-Latif reported. According to Yusuf Bedri, the British often "gossiped" about one region when they had been transferred to another: "Some of them did it in an uncharitable way which aroused hostility. When they went to the western Sudan the English were told to behave in such-and-such a way because the western tribes are rather fierce and that most of them belonged to the old rebellious tribes of the Mahdiya. When they went to the east, they were told that the eastern people were wild, and they might kill a person without any cause—that life was nothing to them. When they went to the south . . . they were told that the Dinka were a very arrogant people. . . . They usually tried to give the impression that there was a great difference between the south and the north. 'You northerners,' they would say, 'are the slave traders and you treat the southerners like *abid* [slaves]. Don't call them *abid*! There are no slaves any longer.' And they would say about the southerners that they were lazy people, that they were contented with what they had and were impervious to any progress."

The two chiefs, Babo Nimir and Zubayr Ahmed, on the other hand, denied any knowledge of British discrimination among the Sudanese. "To prefer people over other people?" Babo Nimir asked rhetorically. "No, it was not their nature. No, no, never."

The British distinction between townsmen and countrymen concerned Daud Abd al-Latif. In the 1930s and 1940s "the English DC was more comfortable with the *shaykh* and sultan in traditional society than he was with the educated Sudanese. The educated Sudanese was less comfortable with the *shaykh* and the sultan than he was with the district commissioner. . . . We tried to understand why the tribal chief was appealing to the Englishman, and we discovered that the chief was appealing because he was still addressing himself to [the district commissioner's] vanity more than to his mind. But later on, the top-level administration learned that they could go nowhere with the tribal chiefs, and that their future was with the civil servants, the educated. After that, the British . . . administrator began to look down on the political movement outside the civil service. . . . There were, of course, two approaches—two political movements—in the country: the movement of those who were contained inside the civil service, who would say, 'This doesn't work and this would be better,' and the movement of those who were in the streets and who would shout, 'We want the unity of the Nile Valley' and things like that. In the eyes of the British, the outside movement was childish and despicable. . . . They took them as people completely misled, and for whom they had no use."

As to whether the British made comparisons between the Sudanese and other Africans, Ahmed Mahgoub recalled that "in the Gezira Board we had a chief mechanical officer, a very senior man, who had spent all his life in other African countries, and after great persuasion, he accepted to come and take a job here in the Sudan. He told me about the differences: to him, there was more dignity and righteousness here than he had experienced in other countries." Amin Hassoun asserted that the British indeed made comparisons, and very favorably for the Sudanese: he had "heard from many Englishmen that they were highly impressed by the Sudanese, and that the Sudanese were nearest to them, and that they were the most decent people they had met in the colonies. I don't think they were flattering me. . . . I know they are brave, they talk their heart. . . . They had many colonies, but they thought that the Sudanese were the best people they had ever met."

Comparisons disparaging to Egyptians were frequent. Jamal Muhammad Ahmed heard the British at Gordon College "poke jokes at the Egyptians, calling them 'gyppies' and so on. And, of course, we were not politically-minded, so we just took it." "They respected the Sudanese much more" than the Egyptians, Muhammad Ahmed Abu Sinn recalled. "They despised the Egyptians greatly. I have already mentioned the two reasons for which they respect the Sudanese [the bravery at Omdurman, and Sudanese hospitality]. I don't know the reasons for their despising the Egyptians." Abu Sinn stressed that particularly after 1936, the British were concerned that their legacy in the Sudan should be "to the Sudanese, not to the Egyptians."

Daud Abd al-Latif felt that the British had been "really original" in their treatment of the Sudanese, mainly because of similarities between the two peoples. "By their nature the English are shy people," Daud opined, "and they hate a man who throws his weight about. The Sudanese, too, are the same—they are very shy. Somehow, much of what makes the English laugh also makes Sudanese laugh." Furthermore, Daud said, "Sudanese don't have a color bar. Sudanese don't have a special respect for the white, or a disrespect for the black. On the contrary, the Sudanese are so confident that they are the best people in the world that it is impossible for them to think that there is somebody who can look down on them!" The Sudanese simply would not allow this, although they sometimes looked down on the British.

Several respondents asserted that attitudes and assumptions changed for the better toward the end of the condominium. Sorror Ramley believed that trust grew from cooperation in developing the country. Even Daud Abd al-Latif had eventually come to the conclusion that "there were no apparent differences between their attitude" and his. "I began to see that they were trying to improve the country, and if we could help in any way it would be better. . . . We began to achieve more by cooperating, rather than by passiveness." This was a remarkable change in attitude for one who had harbored little but "enmity" for the British throughout his school years and early career in the civil service.

"We created a clique [in the administration] which decided that 'No, sir' was as good as 'Yes, sir' if you were honest. The English too began to see that 'No, sir' was not necessarily an indication of enmity. They started to treat us as friends, and our advice began to carry weight. When we said, 'This is not acceptable to the Sudanese,' they would think twice before carrying it out."

Daud Abd al-Latif illustrated his point by recalling a British plan for the entire legislative assembly to be elected, with no appointees. Daud had feared that this system would fail to produce able ministers, and suggested that at least some ministers be appointed and automatically become members of the assembly. This frustrated Sir James Robertson and other British officials who wanted to "go the whole hog." Eventually the British realized, according to Daud, that a completely democratic process could not, at that time, produce the desired result. "It is true that the political course of Britain would not change because of our opinions," Daud said, "but in some details we did change the course."

The British civil servants and their Sudanese colleagues arrived, in Daud's account, at a "clear understanding that they were leading the country to independence and were not going to be a party to hand-over. This had a tremendous effect on the British government's change of policy in that situation. So they [the British] were that convinced and that enthusiastic about what they were doing. They had a tremendous sense of mission, most of them, a real sense of mission, and were really idealistic. These DCs came from Oxford and Cambridge just after their schooling with all the idealism of young people, and lived amongst a people who respected them and, many times, loved them—and whom they loved. Many of my friends had allegiance, really, to the Sudan. The British administrator in the Sudan was not the kind of civil servant who was transferable by the Colonial Civil Service. He was a civil servant of the Sudan. His allegiance was not to the British government; his allegiance was to the Sudan Government."

Muhammad Ahmed Abu Sinn considered World War II to have been the turning point in Sudanese-British relations. Before the war, he said, these were "artificial. After the war there was sincerity." He attributed the change to American and Soviet opposition to colonialism. "The British knew that colonialism was disappearing ... and they wanted to maintain cultural and trade relations in the mutual interest of their country and other countries." He recounted an incident in which a report was written about him because he subscribed to the *Manchester Guardian*. "The British district commissioner and I were the only readers of English newspapers. My newspaper used to be given to him, because the people of the post office thought that it was his, and he would send it back to me. But he was most unhappy.... In his report he said, 'Muhammad Ahmed Abu Sin is the hope of Shaykh Awad al-Karim, Shaykh Muhammad, and Ahmed Effendi to become the *nazir* of the Shukriya tribe. But as he is reading the English newspapers, he should not be.'" Later, "I met this man when I was a member of the Executive Council.... I said, 'I am so-and-so. Would you come and have tea with me in the Grand Hotel? I used to be a subordinate of yours." He accepted. I also invited many other people. At the tea party ... I said to him, 'My ability to speak English now is due to my keeping up the language by reading English newspapers. I'm now a member of the Executive Council; I would not have been appointed if I did not speak English!"

In many respects, Abu Sinn's anecdote illustrates the extent to which events outpaced people's vision of the future; what initially seemed strategically prudent and morally correct was soon hopelessly outdated. In retrospect the turning point was the onslaught of nationalism.

Notes

1. In fact, there were relatively few such transfers.
2. G. R. King served in Mongalla from 1929 to 1936, and in Equatoria from 1936 to 1953; J. W. G. Wyld served in the Bahr al-Ghazal from 1932 until 1951. These were unusually extended tours even for Bog Barons.
3. Cf. Peter Woodward, *Condominium and Sudanese Nationalism* (London: Rex Collings, 1979), 65–71.

4

Nationalism and Independence

The Sudanese nationalist movement differed considerably from the militant and often traumatic struggles in other African dependencies. The Anglo-Egyptian rivalry was a unique feature, not only of the constitutional status of the country but also in the development of nationalist politics. Another peculiar aspect was the pervasive influence of sectarianism, which provided mass support for political parties but kept them dependent on the patronage of religious leaders. The drive toward independence was smooth and unheroic, except at its symbolic starting point in 1924. The British claim of trusteeship, once adopted as justification for colonial rule, implied its own inevitable end, and in a sense left only timing as an issue of contention.

Jamal Muhammad Ahmed had an analytical perspective on the nationalist movement, which he saw as existing from the start: "For the educated, for our seniors," he surmised, "the British were only a passing phase; . . . even soon after the conquest of the Sudan, there were sporadic movements against the British . . . the Dinka resisting the British, Darfur resisting, and Ali Dinar resisting very much. That was soon after . . . the conquest, which goes to show that there was a feeling that this was an extraneous body in the Sudan. . . . I mean you cannot talk about a nationalist uprising, but it is an indicative sign: we resented the conquest. Then things became calmer until 1923. And then there was the army uprising in '24, in liaison with the Egyptians, of course. Only twelve years later there was the beginning of a nation, a Sudanese national movement in the [Graduates' General] Congress of 1936. . . . In 1942, when the note was presented to the British administration, and then independence in 1956. . . . So you can see that I don't think the British administrators had much peace and quiet in the

Sudan. Things happened every ten years . . . you can see the periodic upheavals, very much like somebody running a longish course, but having a breath-taking pause and then resuming the running again."

Zubayr al-Malik argued that the nationalist movement drew on the entire populace. "Some people would control their feelings, but essentially they wanted independence. There were people in whom this feeling was more obvious, and that showed their enmity against whites; those were the first people who demonstrated and spread the feeling. . . . It went through many stages, and the feeling, of course, started in small degrees. . . . It was there . . . from 1921 or 1922. It was growing very slowly in small degrees until 1924, when there occurred differences between them [the British] and the Egyptians. The feeling intensified and went on; it never stopped until independence."

At what point the independence movement actually began was a subject of controversy among Sudanese contributors. Sorror Ramley observed that "adverse ideas about the British" date from about 1919, at the time of the Egyptian revolution. He considered Egypt the source of Sudanese nationalist sentiment and spoke of Ali Abd al-Latif, who led the 1924 uprising, as the independence movement's first leader. Daud Abd al-Latif interestingly credited the British with creating Sudanese nationalism: "The British loved their country and demonstrated that immensely. That taught the Sudanese also to love his country. . . . Allegiance to the Sudan as a whole was a novel idea which the Sudanese intellectual had to grasp if he were to take over." In 1931, when he was in his third year at the Gordon Memorial College, Muhammad Ahmed Abu Sinn saw the students' strike as "the first time . . . that educated Sudanese had taken a national problem into their own hands." Sentiment was strengthened, Abu Sinn recalled, through the establishment of social clubs. "The authorities didn't allow them to speak politics, but they spoke politics. They didn't allow them to have gatherings, but, with permission, they used to give lectures, for instance during the Mulid."

Most respondents viewed the 1930s as a critical period. Daud Abd al-Latif and Muhammad Omer Beshir commented on the definite change during the governor-generalship of Sir Stewart Symes, when a policy of containment was adopted toward educated young Sudanese. According to Muhammad Omer Beshir, the British were concerned about Sudanese who read *The Nation* and *The New Statesman* and learned about groups such as the Fabian Society, fearing that these young men would turn to passive resistance. To meet the threat, the government recruited potential dissidents for the administration. This had a profound effect, in Muhammad Omer's judgement, on the Sudanese nationalist movement. "The critical minds became associated with British rule," leaving the "noncritical minds to work in the political field" and take up the banner of nationalism. Sorror Ramley discerned two strands in the movement for independence, the bureaucratic and the popular: "The difference was that those who were working within the system believed in a gradual process while those who were working outside the system were for speeding up the machine for taking over."

Avidly reading socialist literature, active in leftist discussion groups, and a visible leader in the Gordon College, Daud Abd al-Latif became a leading nationalist insider. An incident in his career illustrates the policy of containment: "After I graduated and joined the Sub-ma'murs' School . . . I gave a speech. . . . I was the first sub-ma'mur to be asked to become secretary of the Graduate Club, and as secretary I made a speech on the occasion of Sayyid Abd al-Rahman's visit to Dongola." Dongola was a stronghold of Sayyid Ali al-Mirghani, the leader of the Khatmiyya *tariqa* and Sayyid Abd al-Rahman's great rival. The British regarded Abd al-Rahman's foray into Khatmiyya territory with deep misgiving, but he argued that he was simply visiting the homeland of his father, the Mahdi. Daud continued: "I said that [the visit] was historic, because for the first time the British had allowed the sons of the country to go back to their country. This was the beginning of the nationalist movement. This was published by *The Nile* newspaper; it was translated and given to the assistant secretary of administration, [who] decided that I would be disciplined. 'First,' he said, 'you should apologize and write a letter of apology for what you said—' I said to him, 'I will not write a letter of apology—I will write a letter of resignation.' I wrote my letter of resignation and left.

"All of this went to Sir Douglas Newbold. Sir Douglas immediately said, 'Let this boy come and see me.' When I went to see him . . . he got up and met me at the door as though I were a very important man. He seated me and gave me coffee and talked to me about everything, including English literature and poetry, except the topic about which I came to him. After that, he said to me when I came to leave, 'Forget about this case. It is nothing.' I came later and found a note he had written on me. The note read as follows: 'This boy is politically-minded; he will either be with us or against us. I prefer that he be with us. Therefore, he should not be transferred except with my consent. He will be looked after by me. . . . Herewith a draft forbidding the civil servants from [engaging in] politics.'" Prior to that time, Daud said, the British has seen no danger in civil servants' being politically involved; on the contrary, they had encouraged it, fearing only that Sudanese who left the civil service would enter sectarian politics.

The uncontained nationalist movement which, in Daud's words, was "marked by various slogans . . . like '[To] hell with the British' and 'Leave the country,'" actually helped the civil servants who were "trying to convince the British of the worthiness of the Sudanese to be independent by working hard and taking over authority." In effect, "those who were in the streets helped those who were at the desks to take more responsibility. The more there was a cry, the more the British had to hand over to those who were ready to take over and do the job. . . . They [the nationalists] didn't plan it together, and there was no bridge between them. Quite a number of the Sudanese who were at the desks did not like the political movement, and they thought it was a kind of hypocritical and demogogic thing. In spite of that, these demogogues helped the one who was not a demogogue or was trained as a civil servant. . . . So there were twin movements without anybody planning it. In fact, they didn't like each other, but they were complementary to each other."

To nationalists outside the civil service, the government's gradualism was infuriating. Even Muhammad Ahmed Abu Sinn, no firebrand, spoke of Sir Douglas Newbold's dismissive reply to the Graduate Congress's memorandum of 1942 as "a big mistake,"[1] which had a unifying effect on nationalists. The Sidqi-Bevin protocol of 1946[2] brought the inside and outside nationalist movements even closer to unity. At that point, according to Daud Abd al-Latif, British administrators sided with the Sudanese. When Daud threatened to go to the streets with the political movement and demonstrate, his superior, K. D. D. Henderson, told him, "Wait, you will not be alone . . . we may go all of us into the street!" Indeed, Daud later maintained that "the government practically collapsed. This was a situation whereby, if London wanted to press the situation hard, we might have gone into a kind of U.D.I. [Unilateral Declaration of Independence] situation!"

Yusuf Bedri also remembered Henderson's "vocal and sincere" protests and gratefully acknowledged how many British officials, led by the governor-general, Sir Hubert Huddleston, and the civil secretary, Sir James Robertson, were "sympathetic with the Sudanese against any foreign intervention, whether from the British foreign office in London or from the Egyptian foreign office in Cairo. They were loyal to the Sudanese, not their condominium. All of the British civil servants, from the governor-general down, made a representation to the British government, protesting the agreement with Egypt."[3]

Several contributors played active roles in the institutions devised by the British to channel and develop nationalist sentiments along constructive lines. The first such institution was the Advisory Council for the Northern Sudan, established in 1944. Boycotted by the unionists, the council was dominated by the Umma party, followers of Sayyid Abd al-Rahman al-Mahdi, and by tribal chiefs. One such was Babo Nimir of the Messiriya, who provided a lengthy account of the council.

"The British government decided to involve Sudanese in the government. The educated here were demanding that they should have a role in the government. The English conceded the minimum. . . . We entered the advisory council through elections in two stages. We were first elected to the province councils and then the province councils elected us to the advisory council here in Khartoum. I was one of three elected from the [Kordofan] province council. . . . The agenda was prepared by the office of the civil secretary and discussions were confined to the items on the agenda. You could not deviate this way or that way. The line was clearly drawn. We came and joined this process. And we spoke for the provinces.

"The unionists, who were then known as the Ashigga,[4] and with them the liberals and others, rejected the advisory council. . . . They were cooperating with the Egyptians. We, the people of Sayyid Abd al-Rahman, were accused of cooperating with the British. And we were indeed cooperating with the British because we wanted 'the Sudan for the Sudanese.' As long as the British were in agreement with that principle, Sayyid Abd al-Rahman went along with them.... So we entered the advisory council on the grounds that independence was coming, but in stages. The unionists rejected that. Sayyid Abd al-Rahman said to them, 'Brothers, assume that a man owes you one hundred pounds. You are not able to take it from him by force. He offers you ten pounds. Do you reject the ten pounds when you cannot force him to give you the rest at once? It is better to take the ten pounds. First of all, it is a recognition of your debt. Second, it reduces the debt to ninety pounds instead of one hundred pounds. Since we cannot take the whole amount by force, it is better that we receive this amount and proceed forward from there. It will be a point of strength because it will establish our right and it will support our cause.'

"We felt that the way we were going—cooperating with the English toward the independence of our country—was much more guaranteed because, without the English, we didn't have power. They were sitting on us and on the clothes we wore. We couldn't push them away. But if we freed ourselves from them step by step, we would eventually succeed in getting free. Every time they would move, we would free that part of our garment that they would release. We would free it bit by bit until we felt we had our garment totally free. Then we could get up and move freely. That way, we would free ourselves and save our garment."

To plan further constitutional changes, the government convened the Sudan Administration Conference in April 1946. Like the advisory council, the conference was boycotted by the unionists. Eventually the conference recommended the establishment of a legislative body representing the entire country and with far wider powers than the advisory council. The resulting Legislative Assembly met first in December 1948.

Regarding the inclusion of southern Sudanese in the new body, Babo Nimir recalled his having told the government: 'I happen to know southerners better than most people assembled here. Those southerners are our neighbors; we meet quite often in intertribal assemblies. What I know about them is that we are divided only by language. But they are certainly more capable than a great many of us—far better than many of us. It is only language that is not one, but they are very capable.' Anyway, eventually the Legislative Assembly brought the whole Sudan together, north and south."

In October 1951 the Egyptian government unilaterally abrogated the condominium agreement. While this action was denounced because it had been taken without Sudanese consultation, still it appeared to strip the Sudan Government of its legitimacy. In the subsequent charged political climate, Sayyid Abd al-Rahman sent a delegation to Cairo. One of the five delegates was Babo Nimir. "We went to Egypt. We negotiated with them for fifteen days. They tried to persuade us to recognize the idea of a symbolic crown. In return they said they would give us a paper to put down all we wanted; they would sign it and send a copy to the United Nations in America. We said, 'No!'

"Our people said to them, 'As you know, we did not come with a mandate from the whole Sudan. We came representing the Umma party and the Independents. We have not been authorized to tell you this kind of thing. And unfortunately there is no democracy here. We may give you this kind of word; then, tomorrow the king may say, "I have dissolved the council of ministers." He may appoint a new cabinet. What will we have achieved? We cannot accept this. In any case, we will take your point of view to the Independents. And you now know our point of view. Maybe there will be room for further negotiations.' Then we returned to the Sudan."

Commenting generally on his experience in politics, Babo Nimir described how sophisticated politicians used naive tribal leaders for their own political ends: "As for us, we got pushed to sayyid so-and-so, and sayyid so-and-so, and we went along with them. If it were not for those sayyids, we, the people from the country out there, would not have joined political parties.... The merchant class spoke of Sayyid Ali's having formed this or joined that. We, with our people out there in the country, spoke of Sayyid Abd al-Rahman's joining this or that, and we followed. They would say, 'Sayyid Babo, Sayyid Ibrahim, Sayyid Who! Sayyid So-and-So, Sayyid Buth Diu, Sayyid Stanislaus!' We became a crowd, mainly relishing the title of sayyid. Earlier, apart from Sayyid Ali and Sayyid Abd al-Rahman, there was no sayyid. Then all of us were made to be sayyids. Does a man reject that which makes him a sayyid?"

To the question of whether his people at home were able to understand what he was doing on the national level, Babo Nimir replied: "Our people who understood all that were not many; they were few. In fact, there was a joke about my going to the coronation of the Queen. Some were reported as having said, 'Have you heard the news? Ibrahim Musa and Babo have gone to braid the Queen's hair!' I said, 'It is a great honor that I am said to have placed my hands on the Queen's head!'"

Muhammad Ahmed Abu Sinn was closely involved in the negotiations leading to independence. In 1950 he was appointed a member of the governor-general's Executive Council. He described the transaction of business at informal meetings, when the governor-general would ask advice on matters of general interest, and at formal sessions around a table that Abu Sinn recalled had the shape of a horseshoe. The council had both Sudanese and British members, but voting was not always along national lines. Abu Sinn recalled one incident in which the legal secretary planned to bring an action against a group of railway workers who had insulted the governor-general. The issue was important because the newly-unionized workers might strike and cripple the country. The council split over legal action, six for and six against. The governor-general refused to break the tie, and called new meetings until a compromise was reached: to ask the workers to apologize. Abu Sinn did not think this would work: "I said to the council: 'Apology in the common understanding of the Sudanese is not what it is among the British; it is humiliating, especially when made to a government by a worker. Tomorrow, the newspapers will attack you, saying you want to humiliate the workers. This compromise will not work.' They decided that the workers must bring their apology to the palace in person, and publish it in the press." In the end, "they didn't have to apologize. We met again after tempers had cooled. The civil secretary informed us that the governor-general had accepted the opinion of those who thought that the matter should be dropped and allowed to die."

Despite affection for and belief in the British, the Sudanese remained uncertain about the ultimate aims and loyalties of their rulers. No words, actions, or legislation could overcome these lingering doubts that the British would leave the Sudan. For many British officials, this undercurrent of uncertainty was unfathomable. Some were stoic. Others tried to comprehend, only to be frustrated by the delusion that they really understood the Sudanese. There were also those who were simply hurt, feeling that their proven integrity was unfairly questioned. This was perhaps the greatest challenge to the British in the Sudan, and one which, at the end, they met with considerable dignity. Nevertheless, the doubts were there, and many Sudanese remained unconvinced that the British would actually go until their imminent departure proved otherwise.

"It had never come to my mind that they would leave the Sudan," Amin Hassoun stated. "Although they had shown their good intentions by educating us, I didn't think that they would leave . . . so early." Amin Hassoun said he had regretted the British departure because he and his colleagues needed more British guidance. It was not until 1952 or 1953, when they were beginning to leave, that he believed they were really going. Ahmed Mahgoub agreed: "Well, when you are in a state, as we were just before they left, it never dawned on anybody that they would leave, and for that matter, so easily. They did, and I think for quite a while we really wondered whether they would not come back. It was not clear whether it was true, or a dream—but they left."

Zubayr al-Malik recalled that he had realized two years before the final British departure that "their position was weakened and that they were going." One sure sign of this, he said, was the openness of the opposition to them, replacing "caution and fear. . . . The hatred began to intensify although, up to the last minute, until the English left, no one was convinced about the end. The English were not convinced. . . . They were diehards. . . . That they should leave . . . was imposed upon them by the foreign office in Britain; the leaders in the Sudan did not want to leave."

Jamal Muhammad Ahmed recalled his first intimation that the British would someday depart: "All of us as young men . . . rallied toward the Graduates' Congress, in the famous note presented to the British by the congress in 1942. I didn't think they would leave or would not leave, but I had a feeling something was going to happen. . . . Looking at it now, I found that they started rethinking their position here as from that date, if you have to single out a date."

Muhammad Ahmed Abu Sinn related that among the Sudanese there was discussion about the possible "retardation" of the pace of Sudanization: "There were those who thought the British ought to stay as advisers, or in certain posts such as finance and defense and so on—technical positions. . . . The British knew that there was going to be a certain amount of retardation, but to my understanding they did not visualize how far it was going to extend."

Daud Abd al-Latif described the frustrations of the British in implementing their plans. "The political movement was crying that they should go while they were already planning to go." According to Daud, the British readily disclosed the extent of their plan for eventual independence to those "from whom they wanted full cooperation," but public suspicions of British intentions were exacerbated by the phrase "self-determination." In Daud's opinion, this was used by the British to "cover" their true intentions from their condominium partner, Egypt. "Many in the political movement thought we were moving toward the Commonwealth or something like that," but he believed that the British never had more in mind than "getting the whole administration of the Sudan under one system, developing it to independence, [and then allowing a] completely free and independent Sudan [to] decide for itself whether they wanted to have a certain degree of cooperation with the British" or none at all.

"It was a system where you became midwife for your own suicide," Daud observed, "and therefore it was not very popular with the short-sighted person. With those who were in on the plan it was very clear. . . . There were, of course, a number of the British who disliked this intensely because it would disturb their careers. . . . It would stop them in many cases. . . . So there were . . . people who were opposed to this kind of idea and hated the guts of all people who were working toward it."

In 1947 a conference was held at Juba to discuss the political future of the south. There, Daud said, British chauvinism engendered opposition to a united, independent Sudan. Several provincial governors, in particular Owen,[5] considered themselves "protectors of the southerners." They took a "parental attitude, and they were like a mother whose child was being taken by force to go to school or to go to another country. To them, they had their duty to the southerners, rather than to the country as a whole." On the other hand, "some of them loved the northerners and hated the guts of the southerners, and thought even making a connection was a stone around the neck of the north."

Sorror Ramley was also a participant in the "very long struggle" at the Juba conference. He later claimed that the southern chiefs, after receiving "some sort of assurance or something like that, [were] very genuine for unity." Winning over the government officials was more difficult. He told of a "complete night's work" spent trying to persuade them. "We were trying to pull together the different arguments and to give assurances to those who were a bit doubtful about the future. We made the situation clear to them. And early in the morning we agreed that we should not talk in the meeting that day and that we should just announce that we had reached agreement and that was all."

There was a general consensus among contributors—with the notable exception of Daud Abd al-Latif—that a majority of the British did not welcome their impending departure from the Sudan or approve of the Sudanese nationalist movement. Amin Hassoun felt simply that the British "were very sorry indeed; they didn't like to leave. I don't think this was because they were interested in colonizing us. I think it was because of the human relations between us, the friendships." Muhammad Ahmed Abu Sinn felt that there were other reasons for the reluctance of younger British political officers especially: "They were . . . between twenty-two and forty-five; what future were they going to have? The other thing was that they were very proud of what they had done in the Sudan, and they were very much worried that the Sudanese were not qualified for a takeover." Babo Nimir observed, "You felt that they didn't really like the nationalist movement. But they would not say ugly words to show that they felt . . . the people who worked for self-rule and then independence were really against them."

Babo Nimir witnessed instances when British animosity toward Sudanese nationalism was revealed. While he was in London for the coronation in 1953, he attended a party at Sudan House. "We were able to meet all the old administrators. . . . I met Mr. Lampen,[6] who had been governor of Darfur, and who was very good in Arabic. . . . There was another man called Davies[7]; he had been our district commissioner." Davies recalled knowing Babo as a small child: "'When I left your country, you were only ten years old,' he said. . . . Mr. Lampen asked me, 'You say you don't want the English; you tell us to go. Haven't we served you well? Haven't we done a good job for you?'" Babo felt that "his words had some blame in them. Mr. Lampen felt that we had not appreciated their work; we had not appreciated someone who had treated us well; we had not returned his favor." In reply, Babo had displayed the tribal genius for diplomacy: "I said, 'Oh, by God, you have done a good job for us in the Sudan. What you have done for us we will never forget. You have done everything well. In 1899 the Egyptians said, 'Sudan is ours.' You said, 'No! Let us bring [the Sudan] up together like our child. We will leave him alone when he has grown up enough to manage his own affairs.' Our neighbor said we belonged to him, and you said, 'No. Let us enter on equal terms to raise this child....' You preserved our own for us. Now, when we say we do not want you, we are not asking for anything other than what you have preserved for us. Now we feel we are old enough to take control of what is ours, what you have kept for us."

Babo Nimir recalled another instance in which he fought his cause with the very ideas the British had introduced to the Sudanese. "When we had learned about self-rule, I went to El Obeid. The governor was Hawkesworth.[8] He used to love me very much.... He would always welcome me very warmly. But when I voted for independence and then visited him and he was told that I was there to see him, he said, 'Let him come in.' When I went in he greeted me from a distance at his desk. A person who has committed a wrong knows it and I knew my wrong. He said to me, 'Why did you vote for this independence? What is in this self-rule?' I said to him, 'We do not know self-rule. We only know that there is the owned and the free—only the two. But you told us that there was such a thing as self-rule and that we should take our independence in stages.' He said, 'How will you explain it to the Messiriya?' I said, 'What I understand and how I voted, I will tell them in my own way....' So it is clear," Babo continued, "that they were not happy about the nationalist movement. But there were some of them who had broad, tolerant shoulders and who would allow you to go your way."

Jamal Muhammad Ahmed had been convinced "even at the time ... that [the British] acted very sensibly indeed." He remembered that an ex-governor invited three or four members of the Graduates' Congress to tea every day to discuss the issue of independence: "We sat there and argued with him logically. We were not hitting each other in the face, but we were arguing why they should go and he was arguing back why they should stay. It was as liberal as that.... We were not that wild in our demands ... and on their side they could see the general picture of the whole world.... It was under their nose: they could see that the whole world was moving toward this. Kwame Nkrumah and Jomo Kenyatta were holding their conference in Manchester and were talking about African independence—not ... about the independence of Kenya—they were talking about the independence of Africa. In

India, the British were making a hobby of jailing Nehru and unjailing him. . . . And, of course, in Egypt there was a big movement of students against the British occupation. And they could see that we were not that immune from currents coming from abroad." In Jamal's opinion, the British officials most resistant to departure were those "who thought they would protect us . . . from Egyptian hegemony over the Sudan. After all, the Egyptians were saying that the Sudan was part of Egypt, and anyway, King Farouk was called King So-and-So of Kordofan and Nubia and everything."

Sorror Ramley commented on the exceptional amicability with which the British and Sudanese parted: "The attitude . . . as the British left the Sudan was most unusual and a clear indication that there was mutual understanding on the handing over. Nobody was stabbed; nobody was killed; it was just partying. I believe it was the cheapest sort of independence ever achieved by any people in this world!"

"Even when they lost hope and were leaving," Babo Nimir recollected, "their behavior never changed. They were very faithful until the very last minute. The last day in Nahud, I met Tibbs.[9] He was about to depart. His luggage was in the car. Even then he was still working. There were files not yet completed; he took them to work on. We parted with him at Fulah, where we took a photograph with him and said, 'Good-bye! Good-bye!' He took his work and finished it in the headquarters. He deposited the files at the headquarters and then left." Zubayr al-Malik had a similar recollection: "The DC who was with us, although he was leaving the next day, was working in his office right up to the last minute."

Daud Abd al-Latif pointed out that a few departing British administrators went far beyond the call of duty when the transition actually occurred. Years before independence, the central government had directed each district, provincial, and departmental office to burn all papers which the Sudanese might find offensive upon taking over. "Some of them did that very correctly," Daud said, "but some of them thought that this letter was unfair because the records were part of the history of the Sudan," and should be given to the Sudanese. T. R. H. Owen, governor of the Bahr al-Ghazal, defied the order, turning his complete files over to Daud.

"'I was waiting to see who would be the governor,' Daud remembered Owen's telling him, 'and as you are going to be the governor, here are the keys. You will have everything, and you will, of course, never use it against us; . . . you will appreciate under what circumstances these things were written. But it will be useful to you.' And this is how the Southern Policy files were saved. The only files which we now have on the southern question, and all these books that are being written on the Southern Policy, are dependent on certain files which were at Wau . . . which I brought to Khartoum. In every other province they were burned."

Some of the British, such as Owen, took the withdrawal "very nicely," in Daud's opinion. It was those civil servants in the middle of their careers who were "a little bit irritated. . . . It was tragic because they lost a career and they were [sent] into the world without a particular skill in anything saleable in Europe. Their experience was in many cases irrelevant. . . . But they took it patiently, and we were, also, generous to that kind of person. The Sudanization Committee gave every one of them eight thousand pounds for loss of career, and eight thousand pounds was good money at that time. The young ones were not irritated at all. They thought independence was wonderful when it came. They already had the experience of five or six years in the bush, which would be useful, and could sell themselves anywhere else. For the older man, it was a completion of mission, and . . . he was proud of the mission."

In some instances, Daud believed, Sudanization was too rapid. "We got a wire saying that the army should be Sudanized in fourteen days. After a lot of words, they raised the days to forty-two. The result was that the 2,726 men, southerners all, were handed over to about seventeen northern officers who were so new that none of them knew the name of his NCO at all. That was the very first stage of a mutiny, in fact." Daud said that he wrote an Intelligence report, within three months of the Sudanization of the army, predicting a mutiny. In this he had been "tipped off" by a British colonel who had told him, " 'No army can afford this. If this happened in the British army there would be a mutiny, let alone the Sudanese army which is half disciplined, compared with the British army. This is an army which has its allegiance to the Sudan Government, not to the Sudan political movement, or to God, or to King and Queen, and you are playing havoc with it. You will have the result. . . . ' His idea was that the army was regional at the time; therefore they should be allowed at least six months for mixing the army and making it into a national army before handing it over to anybody."

Accounts of the actual departure of the British were sympathetic. Amin Hassoun received an airplane ticket from Port Sudan to Khartoum to attend the farewell party for Paul Sandison,[10] the outgoing commissioner of labor. "I went to his house to attend the farewell party and stayed until he left. During the three days I stayed, he was always feeling sorry. . . . I noticed that Mr. Sandison was about to weep when he was saying good-bye to us, and on my side it was the same thing."

Yusuf Bedri distinguished his view of the British collectively and his feelings for certain individuals. "As a whole," he said, "they were aliens." But he felt that "we were missing something" at the departure of [C. W.] Williams, the director of education and former teacher and warden at the Gordon College. "Maybe because he was the person who helped me to join the American University of Beirut. Maybe because he was the man who was on our side when we were staging our ferocious student strike. . . . Maybe for all those reasons, there was something at the back of my mind."

Ahmed Mahgoub recalled that "they all had farewell parties. . . . I think they were all very sad to go . . . they had great respect for the Sudanese. They loved them; they loved their integrity. They were attached to this country; they knew they were safe here."

"Despite our acceptance of independence," Babo Nimir concluded, "as a friend and someone with whom you have lived well . . . you feel bad when you part . . . not for love of colonial rule, but for love of them as people."

Notes

1. See 134 of this work.
2. Part of a draft Anglo-Egyptian treaty which would have recognized the unity of the Sudan and Egypt under the Egyptian Crown. Sudanese and British protests led to its abandonment.
3. See Robertson, *Transition*, 95–99.
4. Literally, "blood brothers"; the first Sudanese political party, founded in 1944.
5. T. R. H. Owen, governor of the Bahr al-Ghazal, 1948–1953.
6. G. D. Lampen served in the Sudan from 1922 to 1949, lastly as governor, Darfur (1944–1949).
7. Reginald Davies served in Kordofan, 1912–1920, and Darfur, 1920–1924, and later in a series of central government posts. He described his experiences in *The Camel's Back: Service in the Rural Sudan* (London: John Murray, 1957).
8. Governor of Kordofan, 1950–1954.
9. G. M. G. Tibbs served from 1949 to 1955, mainly in Kordofan.
10. P. J. Sandison served from 1929 to 1954, after 1942 in various central-government posts.

5
Post-Colonial Contacts and Perspectives

Virtually all northern Sudanese contributors maintained contact with former British administrators after independence, through correspondence or visits to England or both. Some of those with whom Daud Abd al-Latif had worked, such as K. D. D. Henderson, even helped him in his work through letters after they had left. Muhammad Ahmed Abu Sinn illustrated the continuing British interest in the Sudan by describing a particular district commissioner he had known in Rufaa and Hasaheisa. While in private business, this retired administrator worked to secure a sizable loan for the development of electricity in his former bailiwick.

Sorror Ramley had been to England five times when the interview was conducted; his son was in school there, and many members of his family were in the British Isles. "They go to the houses of our British friends as though they were their own homes. They go there for weekends," he said. Zubayr al-Malik "found [the British] very hospitable. They respect the Sudanese and never forget their relations. They always say that they spent what they call the best of their lives, their youth, in the Sudan. So they will never forget the Sudan.... I stayed with a number of them in their homes.... They serve you themselves.... They are very hospitable and very respectful."

On a few occasions, he said, Yusuf Bedri had found British ex-officials eager "to compare the administrative and management state of affairs during their days and during the days after they left. Some of them would be critics, and say, 'Oh, we have heard that in such-and-such a district, the people were treated badly,' or, 'You started to have this bribery.' Some of them I must admit, some of them were critics. And you would feel that the Sudanese did not live up to their expectations. You may say some of them were rather disappointed that they had wasted their time and now things were collapsing.... 'You are an African country, after all, and you are back to your African nature....' Well, some of them would say it as loudly as that; some of them would be less vocal. It is there in some of them."

Asked to give his impressions of Britain in general, Babo Nimir replied that "in manners, behavior, and courtesies," the British he had met in their native country were exactly the same as those he had known in the Sudan. "If there were differences," he said, "it was because of the nature of their duties. If one ... is the ruler of the people, there are certain things that require him to be a little tough.... But in England, of course, there wasn't that. Apart from the official position, which forced them to be a little tough, they were really very nice, kindly people."

Babo Nimir elaborated on what most impressed him about British life: "I felt that the English were a gentle ... people. When you go walking on the street ... if a person touches you by mistake, he will apologize: 'Sorry!' If he receives anything from you he says, 'Thank you,' and even when he gives to you he says, 'Thank you!' In the lifts which carried us up, even though the operator was the one carrying us, he would say, 'Thank you!'

"I said, 'What kind of people are these? When you give to them, they thank you; when you take from them, they thank you!' ... There were three things in England which are like the three virtues of Islamic prayers.... They were 'Sorry,' 'Thank you,' and 'Please.' These ... words were used all the time.... A policeman will never shout or get angry.... They are very civilized people and very gentle. One felt that the English who had been here, whose manners had been so gentle, who had never made one feel their supremacy, had truly come from this race. Such manners! Such manners!"

"The treatment I noticed among the people who were here in the Sudan," Amin Hassoun agreed, "was the same as the treatment I noticed when I went to England.... They were disciplined, organized, decent, civilized."

Zubayr al-Malik saw a change: "In their country they were very different.... We were a big delegation when we went to the coronation of the King in 1937. We saw the treatment of the English to foreigners in their country, and to their own people, and were quite astounded by it. We used to say among ourselves, 'You see, these people, when they take off their robes of power ... they change. They become very good people, very modest indeed, very, very nice people.' But there was something different when they were in the Sudan in power."

When he visited them in England, Yusuf Bedri, like other respondents, was impressed by the standard of living of former officials: "They were living in the middle class, some of them in the upper middle. But, certainly, of those I visited, none was in the range of the aristocracy." His friend, Peter Hogg,[1] a former director of local government and a senior official in British Petroleum, was living "quite a modest life." William Clark,[2] former district commissioner in Omdurman and commissioner in Geneina and Port Sudan, "had a small house in Reading, and he was telling me that he bought this house for seven thousand pounds, which he paid over the years during his stay in the Sudan. . . . It is quite a normal house. . . . He was driving quite an ordinary car." Bedri considered the unpretentious life of these officials to be "a testimony to their—not self-denial but—honesty. While they were here, they ... did not make much money to buy big estates and live in abundance."

Sorror Ramley was more impressed by the positions occupied by former colonial officials. Sir James Robertson had become governor-general of Nigeria. Another ex-official was a major; one the director of an oil company; John Seamer,[3] a Latin teacher; John Owen[4] worked in the development of animal reserves in Kenya. "They were all very happy. They gained very good experience in the Sudan and they had good employment after they left."

General experience with people in Britain elicited considerable comment from respondents. Daud Abd al-Latif related two incidents to illustrate his earliest reactions to Britain and its natives. In Bristol to study local government, he answered a notice from a woman who wanted a lodger. "I rang the bell. When she came to open it, she was stunned—she nearly fainted. This was, as I later understood, her first encounter with a colored person. I said to her, 'I am a student and I want accommodation. I read your notice and came here.'

"She said, 'My dear, it is a girl, not a man, that I want.' I said, 'I don't want to, but I could perform like a girl!' She laughed and said, 'This is very interesting.' And after a little talk I said to her, 'In our country, when you ring and anybody opens the door, he asks you to have coffee. Why don't you ask me to have a cup of coffee?' She said, 'In our country, we don't do that, but all the same, come in.' So I went in. She gave me coffee. We talked about everything, including religion, for about half an hour or an hour. Then, when I was at the door coming out, I said to her, 'Still, I will ask you to give me ten days' chance.'" Daud explained to the woman that he was leaving for London in ten days, and would not return for two weeks. If, at the end of ten days, he told her, she did not like his company, he would leave for good. The woman, telling Daud he was an "extremely persuasive young man," allowed him to move in. "On the tenth day, when I got my things packed . . . she said to me, 'No, leave your things here.'" Daud's friendship with her and her family has lasted ever since.

On another occasion, Daud and a group of foreign students were invited for coffee by Lady Wills, an heiress whose family had donated over five million pounds to Bristol University. "We had no idea of the [appropriate] manners and what to do. . . . They gave us coffee and some biscuits. When I tasted the coffee, [wartime rationing was still in effect] it was awful—it was completely undrinkable in my opinion. But to be polite I . . . closed my eyes and started to swallow the thing. While I was doing that, suddenly the lady came and asked me if it was good coffee. Unintentionally I answered, 'Was it coffee?' I spoiled the whole mission, because the mission was to entertain her and to impress her to give more money to the university. That was a kind of new experience."

Muhammad Ahmed Abu Sinn had an uncomfortable encounter or two before he began to enjoy the British on their own ground. "When I travelled from London to Hereford, they didn't speak to me for four hours. And they didn't speak to each other. I [had] thought that my color of skin or my native clothes might attract them and make them speak to me. . . . I later told Mr. Baily that I had not enjoyed my trip 'because your people don't speak to foreigners.' He said to me, 'They are not proud. They are shy. So make the first approach; you will find they're very nice.' Luckily, the next time, I sat beside a very beautiful girl. When I made the first approach, we had a very good talk, and we had lunch together."

Two incidents in particular demonstrate the depth of emotion felt by Abu Sinn toward the British. One was when "Balfour-Paul[5] brought all four of his children from different schools . . . and said [to them], 'This is the man who taught me how to deal with things in the Sudan and who helped me to know the world.'" The other was when Abu Sinn's uncle, Ali Abu Sinn, former governor of Darfur, was dying in London, and several British former colleagues visited the hospital.

Yusuf Bedri believed that tributes paid to Sudanese public figures at their deaths helped to engender cordial relations between his country and Britain. "When Babikir Bedri died in 1954, the London *Times* published a beautiful obituary. And the number of letters and telegrams of condolence we received from British people who were in the Sudan here—some of whom worked with or knew Babikir, others who [had] heard about him . . . was extraordinary."

Jamal Muhammad Ahmed felt that "sentiments of friendship between the British and the Sudanese have deepened with time: most of the Englishmen who served here are now elderly gentlemen, and they look back with a lot of sentiment to this country. You will find also that the Sudanese who had worked with them look upon them as great friends. Please don't think this is diplomatic; this is a fact." Daud Abd al-Latif agreed: "You still find them very attached to the Sudanese. It is one of the very moving things to attend the pensioners' meeting in London sometimes. You will find people who really know the country, the Sudan, and are truly devoted to it, even at the age of eighty." Contact had been maintained mainly, Daud said, by the "top few" Sudanese, those in politics, business, or cultural pursuits. The average Sudanese was no longer in contact with the British.

Yusuf Bedri had observed a very positive trend in Sudanese-British relations. When he first visited England in 1948, he described the British—in the course of an interview with the BBC—as "arrogant and reserved and not hospitable to foreigners." He later recalled walking on a street in a small town where "from a distance I heard a little girl talking to her mother: 'I see a black man.'" When he returned thirteen years later, Britain had become more of an open society. During the 1960s, while staying at Oxford, he had occasion to meet old friends and teachers as well as acquaintances of his father. "I really developed the feeling that they were Sudanese. They talk Arabic, they entertain you in their homes, they try to put you up and give you as much comfort as they can possibly afford. I never felt that I was staying in an alien home."

Several contributors felt that there had been a marked change in relations between the sexes since independence. Muhammad

Abu Ranat noted that "now there is free social intercourse between them . . . no difficulty meeting them socially and speaking to them." Jamal Muhammad Ahmed also thought that "the unnatural relations between ordinary older men and older women of that period are now over, and there is a natural contact." He observed that a number of British-Sudanese marriages had occurred. "Marriage is not the thing to go by, but from what I've seen there is no longer that remoteness on either side."

Ahmed Mahgoub married an Englishwoman. "She was my colleague in the same office, looking after students," he explained. "Our relations started with respect for one another, because there was this feeling of absolute togetherness. I mean, there was no difference whatsoever. I don't think she recognized I was a different color from her, nor did I think she was a different color from me. We just felt that with increased contact men and women of different ethnic backgrounds overcome their initial prejudices and fears and are inevitably drawn together."

The point was elaborated by Daud Abd al-Latif, who spoke of having "intimate relations with British girls" for the first time when he went to England. "One thing I noticed was that you can never understand a people well enough . . . until you are in bed with a woman. It is a time when people get over the masks they are wearing and . . . become normal human beings. No intimate sexual relations can occur without the person's becoming himself. So you learn more from a girlfriend about the actual British character and behavior than from hundreds of books on the psychology of the British nation. . . . I think the British female gave me insight into the British nation and their good nature, their lovely character, and at the same time their hypocrisy—illustrated in many ways—their shyness, and their lust. This was a new world to me, and it improved my knowledge of the British much more than I could have done by contacting the men, or reading books about the psychology of the female or their sexual nature. . . . I knew the Britisher who was a political animal rather than a human being. The picture was completed when the girl came in and started to behave as a human. You become angry, you quarrel, you become extremely intimate; the whole of life is lived with a girlfriend. . . . With a DC, the relationship is political, and both of you speak under unnatural circumstances anyhow. Where you are guarded, you are careful about what you say, and you know what to do. This is not possible in bed."

Yusuf Bedri grouped the people of the United Kingdom into three categories. "One is the old generation, of whom very few are left, and who ... have very pleasant reminiscences and are still very much concerned with the Sudan.... The second category [includes] those people who came for a short contract.... They consider their term of tenure in the Sudan just like their term of tenure in Cyprus or their term in Edinburgh or their term of tenure in Germany. They were entrepreneurs who were trying to make the best out of it before the whole thing collapsed. And the third category is the young generation, who have the feeling there was something wrong done by their forefathers, this colonial, imperial ... profession, let us call it. It was in fact a profession. They feel the British committed serious wrongs against the peoples of the colonies. 'So we must make up for that and try to build up relations with these countries, which will ... make them forget about any bitterness they [may] harbor for our forefathers, subsequently for our countries' ... you find among them the intellectuals and the social reformers."

Ahmed Mahgoub believed that the attitudes of Sudanese toward the British since independence had "always been mixed up with politics. Very, very few enlightened or elderly Sudanese would view the relationship from a human point of view, but with younger generations, it has always been a mixture of politics, with politics taking the bigger bias."

Of specific likes and dislikes about the British, Muhammad Abu Ranat singled out unnecessary reserve. He found, however, that "the ordinary man—when he tells you about something, he tells the truth; he doesn't try to cheat you." Abu Ranat also praised the British habit of going out of their way to show foreigners around their cities. "You don't find that in other countries, I mean in New York or some place."

Ahmed Mahgoub discerned a lack of imagination when he visited Britain. "Being people on an island," he theorized, "their life is patterned. You can count the whole year, day by day, and you know exactly what they are doing.... They know the weekend, what they do and so on. They can almost walk blindly to their place of work and to their vegetable markets and to their houses.... The possibility of something alien or something foreign appearing in their vicinity is a shock to them at first, but then they get adapted to it and they just carry on in the same pattern." The British had, for him, "one pattern of life they led which has no penetration from the outside . . . especially in small areas. They look upon a foreigner with a closed eye until that crust is really broken. Then, once they [establish a friendship], it becomes completely lasting."

Yusuf Bedri admired the British friendliness, once an outsider had broken the ice, and their discipline in daily life, exemplified in the orderly queues at shops and for buses. This respect for order was expressed during the colonial period in what Bedri described as "general public courtesy, to be conscious about the customs and traditions of the people and to try not to hurt or interfere with them."

Finally, contributors made general observations about British-Sudanese relations in the colonial past, the postindependence present, and even the future. Daud Abd al-Latif said this about the British: "They tried to train the Sudanese, sometimes with success, sometimes without success. Some of the Sudanese were just not ready. . . . The Sudanese who were ready were given the chance. . . . With the Sudanese who were not ready, the British put up with them with a tremendous amount of patience." This patience and dedication had, in Daud's opinion, a great impact on the Sudanese. "The have created Sudanese patriotism by example, not teaching. You would find a Britisher sitting alone in Tonj District for nine months, practically with nobody to talk to except his bottle of whiskey and his English fiction. If he could do this for his country, it would be amazing if a Sudanese young man did not love his country, too, and be ready to do the same. I think the patriotic movement and the national movement were affected tremendously by the example of the British. They created the machine which expelled them from the country." Muhammad Ahmed Abu Sinn made the same point: "When I was young, this is what I used to feel: if the Britisher, a foreigner, is working so hard for the Sudan, why don't I, a Sudanese?"

Similarly, Babo Nimir said, "I think the British were very honest. The English were serving their empire and whatever they did they did for their empire. If they were working for me, maybe I would say they were not honest people. But they were working for their empire and to that end they did their best. Everything they did was in the interest of the empire. That I call loyalty. This I consider the loyalty of a person who is working for his country."

Most contributors agreed with Faisal Muhammad Ahmed that "one has to look to the future. There is a respect between the two; there is a special relationship between the Sudan and Britain." In Yusuf Bedri's reasoning, "I'm not going to bring in the past, but I'm going to [be true to] my status as a professor bringing up a new generation, leaving some impressions—and a truthful, independent man of sixty-eight years of age should talk sense, I think." He credited the British who served in the Sudan with maintaining "a certain code of ethics, a certain standard of efficiency, and a certain loyalty and devotion to their jobs and for the people of the Sudan." The Sudanese had learned much from the British in "building up the modern state ... with their ability and ... capital, with collaboration in different spheres." He pointed out, however, that it was still a question "whether a modern state is for the advantage and privilege of the people of the Sudan, or whether it would have been much better if the people of the Sudan were living in their own traditional society, and they would not be enduring whatever problems and difficulties they are facing now." He stressed that during the entire era, the Sudanese were conscious of "self-identity and self-integrity and self-assertion."

Faisal reviewed the colonial period, giving the British credit for having "brought the Sudan from the nineteenth century into the twentieth century. They built schools, roads, railways ... in return, they got certain economic benefits, maybe political benefits, too. The Sudan fought for the British Empire in the Second World War, and some Sudanese died for His Majesty in North Africa, in Eritrea and Ethiopia. On the other hand, it's inherent in any human being, it's a sort of birthright, to pursue one's own freedom and ultimately revolt from being ruled by others in favor of being ruled by one's own kind.

"Now as far as the chief is concerned," Faisal declared, nodding in the direction of his father-in-law, Zubayr al-Malik, "I think there was a sort of ... compromise. They let him rule his people, and yet he was not the ultimate ruler. There I think lies the whole problem of indirect rule, indirect government or local administration: they give you a margin of discretion, but they have the ultimate say. I think if the British had tried to rule the Sudan directly through military rulers, the situation would have been different. After the

Reconquest, they did just that, following the Turkish pattern, and there was a revolt. . . . They therefore very wisely opted for a compromise. The British are masters of compromises. So they benefited, and after some time, when they became politically redundant, they knew it. People like . . . Zubayr al-Malik knew that they [the British] had to leave, and they left with some grace. I think the Sudanese learned a lot from the English. There were probably some bad moments—it's inevitable. But they left with grace. There was no hate."

"The English ruled the Sudan," Zubayr al-Malik added, claiming the chief's right to the last word, "at a time in which maybe, other than them, nobody would have governed the Sudan. This is a fact. They did things which history will record for them. . . . We cannot deny they have done some [good] things. But of course . . . they were colonialists. Among the things they did: they were the first people who wrote a lot about the Sudan. Some of them have written the history of the Sudan, when we ourselves have not written books about our people and our history. . . . Many of them have researched, and written about . . . the customs of the Sudan, about the languages of the Sudan, about Sudanese antiquities, about Sudanese archaeology and anthropology. And a man who reads *Sudan Notes and Records* feels that these people have really left great, memorable material for research and things of that sort. But, of course, their spirit was a spirit of colonialism. There was no question about that."

Muhammad Abu Ranat tended to agree: "I think the time will come," he said, "when the Sudanese will realize that the British here in the Sudan did many things for them. All these big Nile projects were initiated by the British, but the Sudanese knew nothing about these matters. The British left us three important concepts, which are . . . the idea of the civil service, the idea of local government, and the idea of independence . . . which were unknown in Middle East countries, and I am sure that the Sudanese will stick to these ideas."

"I think they have got a very soft heart for the Sudan," Amin Hassoun summed up with characteristic admiration for the British. "They like the Sudanese, and they hope to see the Sudan prosper and the Sudanese quite happy and nothing more. I have a very high opinion about the English people. They are very civilized, and they are so nice in their treatment of all people, in particular . . . the Sudanese."

The special position enjoyed by British commercial interests in the Sudan was the subject of Daud's concluding words: "Whatever people say in this country, they still respect the Englishman and . . . the English trader, and think that he is more direct and more honest, and is more trusted to deliver the goods than any other European they know of. . . . This is one of the reasons why their balance of trade has kept very high in their favor. The market here trusts them more. One reason—there are other reasons—but one reason is that the British behavior is appreciated in a practical way, and in Britain—as it is called a country of shopkeepers—trade is very important to them. They are getting it as a sign of the good work they have done."

Reviewing postcolonial relations between Britain and the Sudan, Daud said, "We severed our political relations twice from the British and, I'm happy to say, on issues which had no close relation with the Sudan, really: one was on Rhodesia or something, and the other was on the Canal Zone or whatever it was. We had no major difference with the British, and the British, in my opinion, kept their interest in the Sudanese more than other European countries have done [in their ex-colonies]. They are interested and they know . . . a tremendous amount of information. . . . The British ambassador has always been respected; most of them were interested in the country. We had a very large number of successive ambassadors in London—unfortunately we have had every one of them for a very short time because we change them so rapidly. We have not, in my opinion, properly used our human resources, nor have we properly exploited the goodwill created by the fifty years. If we had, we would have got more help than we have so far had from the British. And there is more goodwill, in my opinion, in London toward Sudan than in any other country. I think we have a special regard in the foreign office."

Agreeing with Daud that the British "have satisfied themselves with cultural and trade relations with this country, in the place of colonial domination," Abu Sinn felt that the challenge of the modern era was to shed the attitudes of the colonial past. "We must feel that we are an independent nation, and that we are equal to the British. We should clear from our minds that they were colonizers, and that we were under their rule. We must formulate from now on a foreign policy that establishes full friendship and cooperation between the two countries."

Jamal Muhammad Ahmed felt that that past had been "constructive" and that the present was "much more normal and healthy . . . than the previous . . . governor-governed relationship. . . . On the political and economic side . . . things have gone through a bit of difficulty . . . but now, very fortunately, are coming back" to normal. Jamal was more concerned about the future of Anglo-Sudanese relations as the human factor diminishes with the death of the generation that fostered it: "I worry about visiting, frankly speaking. The gentlemen who are mostly elderly people—pensioners, ex-Sudan governors—have done a great deal of work keeping the image of the Sudan going. What worries me is, are we going to do something to take over from these gentlemen when they retire, when they get older and die? . . . Quite a number of men and young girls are going over to England for their education, and still, for the Sudanese, England is the place to go for education. That is happening. But I don't think that is going to replace the call of these honorable men who keep the image of the Sudan going, especially in hardest times. What is going to replace that institution? These men have become institutions. What institutions are going to replace them?" Jamal offered one possible answer: "If I had the money or if I could have persuaded anybody, or had the backing of people who had money—I would have liked to see an English school on the pattern of Victoria College [as it existed] some years ago in Alexandria, in the Sudan somewhere, . . . preferably in Khartoum so that this cultural contact between the United Kingdom and this country could continue. There is no replacement for the institution I was talking about earlier, but it is to my mind one way of going about it."

In closing, Yusuf Bedri recalled the spectacular tea party in honor of the departing governor-general, Sir Robert Howe, in Khartoum. The prime minister, Ismail Al-Azhari, made a speech in which he pointed out that half a century before, at Karari, the Sudanese and the British had been committed to each other's destruction. But on this occasion "all these reminiscences did not bring the old hostility into hearts or eyes. The [farewell party] was very civilized, very intellectual, very wholesome. This has its significance, I think." The Sudanese rejected the British as rulers, but got to know them and appreciate them and in the end accepted them as good people and as friends.

Babo Nimir expressed these complex sentiments in a metaphor: "If you catch a man and hold him, if you catch a bird and hold it, when you give it a chance, will it not fly away? [The British] are wonderful people . . . but a man has an instinct for independence and freedom."

Notes

1. Peter Hogg entered the political service in 1935 and retired, as director of local government, in 1955.
2. W. T. Clark served from 1928 to 1953, ending his career as commissioner, Port Sudan.
3. J. W. Seamer joined the Sudan political service in 1936 and retired in 1955.
4. J. S. Owen served from 1936 until 1955, lastly in the department of agriculture.
5. H. G. Balfour-Paul served from 1946 to 1955.

PART 3

THROUGH THE EYES OF THE RULED:
The Southern View

1

Pre-Conceptions and Early Contacts

The southern Sudanese view of the British combined conflicting sentiments resembling those of the northern Sudanese in some respects and differing from them markedly in others. As in the north, experience with the British underwent three main phases: initial resistance to foreign rule; a period of better understanding and appreciation; and the final phase in which nationalism and eventual independence complicated what had become amicable, if ambivalent, relations. In the south there was an even greater degree of ambivalence than in the north.

The south was initially regarded by the British as wild, primitive, and unpacified and therefore as requiring of its early administration not the refined and cultured elite of the civil service but tougher military men, the "Bog Barons," with assumed discretionary powers to conquer and tame. Complicating this picture, southerners generally recognized that the British had established an effective system of law and order that restored to the south a dignity and integrity which had been violated for centuries by invaders from the north. They shared the northern view that the British were hard-working, honest, efficient, and fair, with a strong sense of honor, dignity, and integrity. While realizing that barriers between the British and southerners were never completely bridged by personal relations, mutual respect, and courtesy, they also appreciated that condescension combined with concern for protecting "primitive" and "weaker" peoples against their traditional enemies from the north. Paternalism became "conservation," relegating southerners to inferior status in the social, economic, and political life of the modern Sudan, but at least it preserved the southerners' identity.

When the time came for independence, ironically the situation in the south was not what John Phillips compared to breaking down an open door, but rather of trying to keep the door closed against the hurricane of nationalism blowing southward from Egypt and the north. The objective was to prolong the British protective role to enable southerners to hold their own against the north. But the ethnocentrism and condescension of the British toward the south, the conservative approach to southern development that kept the region on the lowest rungs of the economic ladder, and the last-minute British withdrawal without adequate guarantees for the south have remained a source of considerable bitterness among southerners.

Another factor distinguishes the southern view from the views of northerners. Because the south lagged behind the north in education, most of the people interviewed belonged to the first generation to have had formal education of any standard. The younger they were, the higher their level of education, but none had advanced beyond the secondary level. Those who were sufficiently educated to deal with the British in the cultural sphere were thus far younger than their northern Sudanese counterparts and were perhaps still very young at the time the British left the Sudan. A traditional background and limited education created greater gaps between them and the British than there were between the British and the northern Sudanese.

Southern Sudanese shared the northern preconception of the British as representatives of an awesome authority. Their numbers were, however, small; the British administrator was a rare sight to most rural Sudanese, especially in the south. He was known largely by reputation and rumors which often painted him as a strange creature, barely human in physical characteristics but deadly to anyone who dared challenge his authority. Most southern respondents had held this image until time gradually broadened their understanding of the British and their role in the Sudan.

"I used to hear that the Britisher came from the other end of the earth," Santino Deng Teeng recalled, "from across the ocean—the vast sea—from very far across the ocean, and that he flew by plane. It was also said that he had very powerful weapons, and that if any person were to make a mistake, the Britisher could kill the person from a very long distance." Andrew Wieu as a child had the impression that the British "were there as a suppressing society": he had heard stories of a great Nuer spiritual leader, Guek Ngun-Deng, who had been killed by the British.[1] According to Manoah Majok, it was said that the British would take captive those children whose lower teeth were not removed in accordance with Dinka custom: this was clearly a way for parents to encourage their children to face the painful operation or to keep them away from strangers. Chier Rian alluded to this when he said that as small children "what we used to hear was the word 'jur'—Arab. . . . The Dinka did not know the British. They knew only the Arabs due to the fact that people used to fight with Arabs." Such awesome preconceptions from childhood ensured that first encounters with the British were ruled by suspicion and fear. In some instances, this was justified, but in other cases the experience was positive.

Andrew Wieu's childhood impression of the British as oppressive was confirmed when he "came across the British district commissioner in my area, known as Mr. J. Longe.[2] The first time I saw him, he was in a canoe near my village, and he had to be carried by hand across the water and was not allowed to wade. . . . And I had the impression of a superior human. . . . The people had to carry him and his wife while others were wading in the water."

Abd al-Rahman Souley's first encounter was more serious. He was brought before the governor, Brock Bey,[3] "in connection with a gun from Ethiopia. At that time people at the border of Ethiopia and . . . Uganda used to enter Ethiopia and buy guns. They entered the Sudan through the forest near Loloro and smuggled the guns up to the banks of the river here. We bought rifles from them." Brock "wanted the gun. I told him that I did not have the gun. He gave a shove and ordered that I be tied up until I revealed where the gun was. I was tied up, but I did not produce the gun. So I was sentenced to six months imprisonment. I served the sentence and was released after six months."

Gordon Muortat recalled an experience which deeply affected his view of the government, and although the incident involved a policeman, he associated it with the British as alien rulers. *Tueny* was the name that his people, the Agar Dinka, gave to the foreigners in general. "*Tueny* could be a white man, an Egyptian, or a northern Sudanese; he could be any person who wore clothes and carried a gun or had government authority over others. I used to witness the policeman coming to our village to round up young men by force and beat them. I remember once, my uncle was beaten by policemen in my presence; I had to cry. These young men had to be taken by force to go and cut the grass for the building of government houses in Rumbek and in other towns ... It made me bitter against whoever was in charge of what you call the government, whether white men or other men. I didn't have any idea in my mind as to the racial identity of the government at that time. But later on, I learned that the government was British."

Even Chief Chier Rian, who later stressed the persuasive methods the British employed to win over the people, remembered the early days when the British "were considered to be bad people. When someone saw a Britisher, the whole village ran away. Children, women and men ran away from their homes." Santino Deng's early encounters were friendlier. He first became aware of the British as managers and law-givers. "I used to see [the new administrator] in a gathering with people in court. I saw him going to work on the road, I saw him going to count tax money, and I saw him whenever something bad had happened in an area. He would come to see who had started the trouble."

As a nephew of a chief and son of a sub-chief, Manoah Majok Deng heard a great deal about the British district commissioner in his judicial capacity. "There was a lot of talk about cases, cases concerning cattle mostly, ... how fairly the district commissioners had settled a claim or whether they had made a mistake on a certain point." But Manoah also recalled once having seen at a distance a district commissioner newly appointed to his area. "At first I was afraid. I stopped near the road. At that time I had my lower teeth, and people were saying that the *Turuk* [Turks] ... would take the children who had their lower teeth. I was with three other boys. Naturally, when they looked at us, these Britishers, we ran away. We were afraid that we were going to be put in school. And I saw them laughing."

Manoah Majok's next encounter, which occurred when he was nine or ten, was more complicated. He and his father were in court, watching a district commissioner settle cases, when that official "came around and got hold of me. He asked me whether I would like to go to school. ... I said, 'No, I will not go to school.' He looked at my mouth, so I closed my mouth. Then he said, 'Don't be afraid. I will give you milk.' I said, 'I have enough milk in my cattle-camp.' He said, 'All right, I will give you something sweet.' I said, 'I don't want it.' So he finished: 'Don't be afraid. I will not hurt you.' I sat down, and he went back to settle cases. Then the boys who were with me came back, slowly, slowly. Later on, when

I left the place, they surrounded me, asking questions. I became very important because I had talked to the district commissioner. That was the first time I talked to a white man."

As Majok's account indicates, although recruitment for school was one of the most constructive issues over which the British confronted the natives, it was met initially with strong resistance. Of course, education received low priority in the south, and it was not until the 1940s that the government established state schools there. The south was left to Christian missionaries whose primary interest was proselytizing; secular education was a secondary objective to produce a small, literate class to do routine clerical work. Considerable persuasion was nonetheless necessary to force people to send their children to school.

The earliest memories of several respondents are of help received. Chief Chier Rian himself went to school through the efforts of Titherington Bey,[4] who had arrested the Dinka rebel leader Ariath and who was known by the bull name *Makuendit* ("Great Black Bull with a White Spot on the Head"). "Titherington Bey told my father that the country would be taken over in the future by the children of non-Dinka tribes, because the Dinka were running away and hiding their children. 'Therefore,' he said, 'you chiefs should volunteer children to be taken to school. It is the educated children who will take over the administration of the country in the future. . . . ' My mother cried and violently protested, but my father . . . made sure that I went to school. Then photographs were taken and sent to my mother to assure her that I was alive!" Chief Benjamin Lang Juuk had fond memories of the same Titherington, who had personally escorted him to school: "He treated me as if I were his own child. The school was very far away at Kuajok, and when I was worn out by walking, he helped me by taking me to Wau on his horse." Although Santino Deng had seen the British from a distance, his first personal encounter was with a doctor. "I met him in 1934, when I was being taken to the hospital in Wau with an injured leg. He held my hand and kept me company."

Beyond first encounters, the picture of early interaction with the British becomes more complex, relations become more involved, and ambivalence deepens. Chief Chier Rian stressed the systematic way in which the British began to gain legitimacy. "They spent years in one area and then advanced gradually. . . . They never wandered over Dinkaland aimlessly." Whenever a British official entered an area, he "would ask members of his company who knew the Dinka language to call the people. He would tell the people that he was not there to destroy the country. He assured the people that he was one of them and said nice things. When individual Dinka came to him, he distributed beads and clothes, and tried to get acquainted with them. [Thus] they gradually won over the people until the British were liked. After that they introduced taxes. A hut was first taxed at five piasters; the following year they changed the tax. A new tax on wives was introduced. A husband was required to pay a tax of ten piasters on his first wife and five piasters on each additional wife. Again this tax was removed and another was introduced. People were required to give the government a tin of sorghum as annual tax. The grain was used to feed prisoners and the surplus was sold."

Chief Chier emphasized that an important factor in winning the rural population not only in the south but throughout the country was Indirect rule. "Local leaders took care of local administration such as settling the disputes relating to cattle. Then the British would come periodically to review the cases. When they found that a person had been penalized too severely in a particular case, they reduced the penalty to a lesser sentence. The person would have been penalized by his own people—Dinka punishing other Dinka; the British would appear not to be involved. So the Dinka began to like the British and to cooperate with them. They began to be aware of the government."

Chief Chier's tribe, the Twich, together with the Ruweng in Upper Nile, were initially administered as part of Kordofan Province. They later severed themselves from Kordofan and joined Bahr al-Ghazal Province. The Ruweng followed, leaving only the Ngok in the north. According to Chief Chier, his people had objected to occupying a position inferior to that of the Arabs. He explained his father's decision to withdraw the Twich: "When our people went to El Obeid, they were left to stand outside the office. Even clothes that were distributed to the chiefs were given to them outside. The authorities communicated with them through somebody who went into the office and brought back messages to them." According to him, the administrator in Wau, on the other hand, "would speak to the people. He would let you tell him your opinion and he would tell you his."

Although the picture that emerges from Chief Rian's account is conciliatory and humane, the image of the foreign ruler continues to clash with the pride of the Dinka and their strong sense of independence. Over the years, the British cultivated a deeper understanding of these characteristics in order to bridge the gap between ruler and ruled.

Wieu remembered the district commissioner, J. C. N. Donald,[5] who was given the Dinka bull-name *Roldit* ("Great Black Bull with White Stripes across the Shoulders"): "He was a man who would rarely laugh and who gave the impression that he was cruel." But Andrew recalled Donald's attempt to learn Dinka and his interest in the problems of students. When Andrew was in intermediate school at Atar, Donald befriended the students by going to their boarding house to give them news of their home areas which he had visited on trek. This gesture impressed Andrew. Chief Benjamin Lang recalled the methods adopted by one district commissioner, Captain Richards,[6] who "used to make the people do such work as building roads; and to advise them to wear clothes, to stop eating from calabashes, and to use plates instead. It was he who taught the people."

The evolution of cross-cultural relations in the south owed much to missionaries. Most were not British: Americans, Italians, Australians, and New Zealanders are among those remembered by contributors. One of the first white men Gordon Muortat "saw . . . at close quarters," was a missionary who visited the school at Bargel to talk to the students "about small things." Benjamin Lang spoke highly of the "fathers and the sisters. If one's son went to school, he learned to be respectful. If one's daughter went to school, she was treated with respect. They used to take care of our children as though they were their own. . . . We were very happy with their education."

There was little distinction in the early days between the teaching of religion and the teaching of secular subjects: Gordon Muortat recalled a white man who came "to class sometimes to teach religion or something like history." Manoah Majok told of two Europeans at Malek Elementary: "One was a missionary who used to teach religion. The other was a teacher responsible for a number of subjects. The one teaching religion also taught us to read books which were translated into Dinka. The one teaching the other subjects—geography and history—also spoke in terms of how good it was to be calm, to live together peacefully with other people in the area.... He lectured us on how we should be good to each other, as good Christians, and so on."

Despite his earlier praise for the missionaries, Benjamin Lang objected to the emphasis on Christianity, commenting that education in his region was "not on an equal par with that of the north.... There was a separate system for the south and another system for the north.... Religion was the main subject ... here in the south.... It was not the sort of instruction that would prepare a student for higher education."

Respondents commented on the considerable distance in student-teacher relations in the south. British teachers met their students only in the classroom or when the students worked in the school garden, according to them. Personal matters did not figure. Gordon Muortat remarked that he did not see any reason to discuss such things with his British instructors. By contrast, his knowledge of Sudanese teachers as fellow Dinkas and the connections of their respective families was an important factor in the unofficial, relaxed atmosphere outside the classroom. Manoah Majok attributed this to a language barrier. "Of course, the British believed that they could speak Dinka. Some of them could ... but they could not express it well."

Gordon Muortat strongly resented corporal punishment, which he associated with British administration of the schools: "If one was penalized for violation of some school rules or for provoking trouble with another boy, then one was paraded before this Englishman who either beat one or threatened to beat one, and who talked as a master."

Andrew Wieu had a number of confrontations with teachers. He remembered particularly Headmaster Williams, "a pleasant man, except that sometimes he was something of a dictator, trying to impose things that were not accepted." Williams insisted that boys wear the native open-style dress called *lawa*, lest they appear different from their people. Demanding shirts and shorts, the students argued that "we should not be halfway between our people and civilization. Either we are recognized as mixed or left to be like our people, but we should not be kept halfway, neither with civilization nor completely with the traditional way of life." After a week of protests, Williams agreed to appeal to the government for a change of policy.

As a student, Andrew Wieu voiced his opinions not only on school policy but also on political issues. Once he criticized the government for keeping aloof from education in the south and keeping "the southerners in an inferior position as compared to northerners." Williams replied, "You Dinka are people who have fought us, and you should have expected to be punished." Privately, Williams later compared a southern clerk who drank *merisa* and "was interested in causing trouble," with a northern Sudanese teacher who "was sober and tried to do his work well." When Andrew objected that the south should not be judged by one man, Williams conceded.

Other arguments had arisen from what Andrew considered attacks on his performance as a prefect at Atar. A South African master, J. C. Hunter, blamed him for a dish that was missing: "As this had not been reported to me when the worker had come to collect the things in the morning, I denied his claim. When he suggested that my dormitory be punished, I rejected the punishment. He took me to the headmaster, Mr. Williams. We had an encounter and I won the case.... That made him a bit bitter." Hard feelings continued for years, as Mr. Hunter reported Andrew whenever he made a mistake and even argued that Andrew should be demoted, a suggestion the headmaster overruled. Nevertheless, the two "became friends later," and when Andrew left Rumbek Secondary School and Hunter became headmaster at Atar, "we continued to correspond with each other until he resigned."

With Williams and his wife, Andrew's relations remained tense: "There was a shortage of dictionaries. As I was in charge of the store, I distributed the few dictionaries ... one copy for each class." When more copies became available, Mrs. Williams distributed them while Andrew was away and "discovered the copies I had already issued. She enquired how they had been obtained.... When I came, she yelled at me in the class: 'Andrew, you have been entrusted with the key. I am disappointed.' I went to Mr. Williams, her husband, gave him the key to the store, and said that his wife had accused me of having dishonored the key. I said I wanted the store to be audited ... stock to be taken, and if they found that anything had been lost, I should be held responsible." Mr. Williams did not respond immediately, but later called Andrew out of class and told him that he had been "disobedient and hardhearted." If he had been in the army, he would have been shot, "because you disobey your superior officers and constantly get into trouble with them." Andrew retorted, "Well, I am not in the army. I am in school, thank God!" He challenged Williams to name any teachers with whom he had argued except Mrs. Williams. The headmaster persisted: "Well, you quarreled with my wife." Andrew shot back: "'Right. Only with your wife. There are not other masters.' Then Mr. Williams broke down in tears. And I walked out."

Andrew's eventual decision to leave school in the second year resulted from yet another dispute. There had been an outbreak of chicken pox during the examination period. "I was the first to be quarantined after doing two papers. The examination consisted of eleven papers. Later several students were quarantined. But surprisingly enough, at the end of the exams, while I was still in quarantine, some of my colleagues who had finished almost three-quarters of the exam appeared on the list of absentees, whereas I was listed with those who had done the full exam and had failed. So, all of a sudden, I decided to leave the school." Andrew told Williams that he would not be "ruled for life." After all that had passed between them, Williams said, "'Andrew, I admire you.' I asked why. He said, 'Because I feel that whenever something is pressing against you, you press back; you press back.'"

Manoah Majok mentioned another aspect of life with Mr. and Mrs. Williams at Rumbek. They invited senior students to their house to teach them table manners. Mrs. Williams would explain "how one should sit . . . when one would be served, what one would take, how one should take it, and how one should eat." Students were tested at weekly dinners to which other schoolmasters were invited. Manoah Majok was not offended by any of this. Rather, the students were "very close" to Mr. Williams, and Manoah considered his own association with him one of the best he developed among the British.

The image that emerges from accounts of early interaction, whether in a tribal context or in school, is of people looked down on as primitive and backward, toward whom the British felt an obligation to teach and civilize. It was assumed that a moral and spiritual vacuum existed, to be filled with Christianity and rudimentary Western values, accompanied by a functional level of literacy and education, but not to the extent of disaffiliating the pupil from his background. To be made to wear clothes, *lawa*, or other uniform, or to be trained in table manners foreign to one's society, was in fact a step in the transition that ultimately would completely alter concepts of personal dignity and social status. Southerners increasingly came to realize that to *deny* them exposure to new ways and standards was itself to endanger their traditional pride and dignity. Overprotectiveness became a serious grievance.

Notes

1. Guek led a rising of Nuer in which a British district commissioner, V. H. Fergusson, and his retinue were killed. A government force was sent against him and he was killed fighting in 1929.
2. John Longe served from 1926 to 1953, lastly as governor, Upper Nile Province.
3. Major R. G. C. Brock served from 1913 to 1935, and as governor of the Bahr al-Ghazal from 1928.
4. Major G. W. Titherington served from 1919 to 1942.
5. J. C. N. Donald joined the Sudan service in 1930 and retired as governor of Equatoria in 1955.
6. Captain M. G. Richards served from 1919 to 1937, entirely in the south.

2
Official and Personal Relations

Official and personal relations between southern Sudanese and the British resembled the state of affairs in the north, although there was a difference in degree significant enough to approximate a difference in kind. On the whole, the evidence of the British as dutiful, disciplined, hard working, and honest outweighs southern objections to their own subordinate status. At work, as Benjamin Lang put it, "the only person the British liked was the person who did his job well." Santino Deng Teeng agreed: "The British are people who want people to work hard. Any work that was planned was implemented fully. If you did not follow the work plan, you were caught and severely punished." Chier Rian observed that "the British never left their houses and went to their offices without first going to see how work was proceeding. They used to take tea at 6 A.M. At 7 A.M. they would go to inspect the police parade and other working sites: to check up on people at the stable, building roads, and in schools. Carpenters, construction workers, soldiers, office employees—they used to go after everybody to make sure they were working. Their work was very difficult. It required a person with a lot of determination to work with them." Santino was proud that while "many people lost their jobs because of laziness," he worked in government service for fourteen years.

During the early days, as Abd al-Rahman Souley explained, "the chiefs had no salaries: they were paid according to the tasks they performed. This was an incentive to the collection of taxes, for example. The chief's pay was in the forest. If his people killed an elephant, and the government or a businessman bought the elephant tusks, the government [would divide] the proceeds between the chief and the other leading members of the tribe."

Some of those interviewed had been recruited by the British for government service. Several departments wooed Benjamin Lang, who worked first as a teacher and also worked as a council clerk. "White people used to fight over me!" he said. "The senior medical officer wanted me to train to be a medical assistant, but I declined. Captain Richards wanted to take me to Tonj to become a clerk for soldiers, but I declined." Eventually, of course, he accepted the chieftaincy of his people. Andrew Wieu, despite his history of confrontation, was recommended for public service as good executive material. During his rise from clerk to *ma'mur*, his relations with the British were often turbulent, but they improved with time.

Many of Wieu's stories involve Captain P. S. Garland,[1] for whom he worked in the Upper Nile. Garland was an ex-officer with a strong sense of his own importance, and Wieu resented being treated as a young boy. Many disputes between the two concerned minor issues of protocol. "One time while I was walking in town, he came to the guard and demanded that I should be sent for. When I came, he expected that I should salute him when I was in civilian clothes. I told him that I was not working. He said, 'You should have been dressed.' I said, 'I know that according to rules, there are special circumstances under which one should be in uniform even while off duty. But this is not one of those circumstances.' He said, 'All right.' And we parted.

"Another time, he started out on trek but returned because the road was not dry. He came back, stood out there, and sent the guard for me in my office. I was in uniform. As I approached him I saluted him. Well, he thought that I should first have stopped, like a policeman or soldier, and then saluted him. 'Andrew, don't you know how to salute?' I said, 'Yes, of course. I took the police training. I know how to salute.' He said, 'Why don't you salute me properly?' At that instant I thought it was becoming too much. I just walked out without talking to him. I went back to my office. That day went by. We didn't discuss anything."

On yet another occasion, "we met while he was on his way to a dairy, a government dairy, and I was going to the office. I was dressed in uniform; he was not dressed officially. I was wearing goggles. He stopped as I approached him. I didn't salute him. Then he said, 'You are forgetting to salute me.' I said, 'A salute is not given on demand. It's a courtesy.' Then he said, 'I am unable to see you'—meaning that I should have taken off my goggles. I said, 'I thought the glasses were clear enough for you to see me.' At that point we parted."

Garland's method of issuing orders also caused trouble. Once when Garland had sent a messenger to deliver instructions, Andrew "told the messenger to tell the district commissioner I did not hear. The district commissioner was furious about that. He thought I was rude. He sent for me. I went. He asked me, 'Did the messenger tell you what I had told him?' I said, 'What did you tell him?' He said, 'Did you tell him that you did not hear?' I said, 'Yes.' He said, 'Why?' I said, 'I am not supposed to be instructed by messengers. . . . I will never take orders from you through my employees.' Well, he accepted the point. Whenever he wanted to give orders, he would either write messages or send for me."

Another encounter involved a related matter. Captain Garland, who was going on trek, tried to circumvent Andrew Wieu by leaving administrative instructions with a police sergeant (a *bashawish*), "as if the *bashawish* were in charge." Wieu stopped the man from acting on those orders. When Garland returned and was told what had transpired, "he kept quiet. He did not ask me about it any more." On another occasion Andrew was departing by steamer for Malakal when Garland arrived to see off the assistant district commissioner, P. P. Bowcock, and his wife, who were also travelling. Second-class accommodation, to which Andrew was entitled, was fully booked. "As Captain Garland accompanied Mr. Bowcock and his wife to the first class, I was behind them. Captain Garland stopped and asked me where I was going. I said I was going to the first class. He said, 'For what?' I said, 'For accommodation.' He said, 'No, you are not supposed to be in first class. It can only be by permission of the assistant district commissioner.' 'To the contrary,' I said, 'I am entitled to travel first class when there is no second class. And it's my right.' Well, he got angry when I insisted and he walked away. The assistant district commissioner followed him.

"In the third class were prisoners, merchants, and officials, including two newly-elected members of Parliament who were going to Khartoum. . . . When the assistant district commissioner came back, I told him that we would have to divide the first class, because the other officials and above all the two MPs were entitled to travel first class, too. I said that he should have one room and the veranda in the front of the steamer and I would take the rest of the barge with the officials and the MPs. He said, 'OK.' I went and brought the rest of the officials and MPs to first class." At Fanjak, Bowcock and his wife disembarked and continued to Malakal by car. "He abandoned the steamer to me with the other people."

On yet another occasion, Wieu and Garland were to attend a meeting of officials from Kordofan and the Upper Nile provinces. "When we disembarked at Lake No, we knew that there was only one rest-house . . . and that we were going to be under one roof. He was carrying a tent with him. In his own mind he thought that I should go and stay in the tent." Andrew slept in the rest-house, where two rooms were vacant. Two days later, however, the governor and his sister arrived. Wieu chose to find another place for himself. "The governor was our superior, and since he, Mr. Garland, was the most senior—and given also the connection between him and the governor—it was absolutely incumbent upon me to allow him to accommodate the governor."

More incidents followed, and Andrew "requested to have a serious discussion with him. . . . I gave him an account of so many things which I had noted down. And then he apologized, and said, 'Well, Andrew, the first time I saw you I thought that you were a young boy, and that you would not take note of these things. But I can assure you that from now on we will work together, and these instances will not be repeated." In retrospect, Andrew felt that Captain Garland had come to appreciate his work. Much later, after his post had been Sudanized, Garland wrote to Wieu that he "did not think he would ever find [another] person who could quarrel and cooperate at the same time!"

The experience of subordination, especially with its racial overtones, embittered many of the southern Sudanese interviewed. Manoah Majok resented having to represent the ugly face of the government to his own people. According to him, the British "would let us sign search warrants and warrants of arrest and then inspect the prisons; they would go to the prisons and inspect the police. . . . They would let us do those things and then come to check. . . . They [gave] us the donkey work."

Santino Deng was more explicit: "What used to cause quarrels between us in the beginning was that [the British] sometimes treated people like children. They would call a person, and instead of letting a man walk, they would ask him to run. At times, they would insult a person. . . . Insult is not taken well by us Dinka. The person who may insult you is a person of your own age group. He can joke with you and you can joke back. When an older person insults you, when you have done nothing wrong, that causes friction between you." Santino objected to the British habit of finding "a way of aggravating you in order to test your character. [They] used to impose so much pressure on people that the weak would become overly submissive."

Ironically, Chief Chier Rian, whose family had disaffiliated their people from Kordofan because they had expected better treatment from southern administrators, observed that "relations with the British were not good. They used to treat chiefs and senior officials as though they were their servants. When a person made a slight mistake, they slapped him. . . . We cannot even talk about insults. They insulted even chiefs." By his own admission an outspoken man, Chief Chier recalled difficulties with Captain Richards,[2] who "was like a madman; he smoked opium." Captain Poole, who later married a Dinka girl, would "hit a person" if annoyed. "The only Britisher who treated me kindly," Chier Rian reported, "was a certain Mr. Hunter,[3] who was district commissioner in Gogrial in the 1940s." Chier taught him how to travel during floods in a Dinka canoe and how to tend cattle, and although Chier said "there was no single Britisher who would like you to the point of telling you his secrets," Hunter was a valued associate.

While educated southerners were resentful of alien rule, they were frequently reminded of their backwardness, poverty, and dependence. Benjamin Lang recalled that whenever southern officials explained that salaries were too low, "the British replied that we were working to build our country and that our country had no money. They used to tell us that we were poor. . . . The money that was available came [through taxes] from our brothers in the north." For a people who regarded themselves as the richest (in cattle, the most noble symbol of wealth, for which they felt themselves envied by others), this was insulting.

Benjamin Lang spoke too of racially-motivated disrespect toward southerners. According to him, prior to independence and especially before the Juba conference in 1947, "the British did not show southerners much consideration. . . . When the British ruled the country, they ruled us as a different people. Their color was different from ours. There was no close relationship between them and us as there is today." Benjamin noted, however, individual officials, Desmond Hawkesworth and G. R. I. Dees,[4] as sensitive and helpful: "I used to give them my advice and they took it," he said. "Those two people—our hearts and theirs were in harmony."

Andrew Wieu's propensity for confrontation extended to his relations with instructors during a professional course in the School of Administration at the University of Khartoum, following years of practical experience in the field. He once confronted Mr. Whitlock, who taught criminal procedure, over the issue of special treatment for a convicted individual. When Andrew asked under what circumstances a judge might recommend such treatment, Whitlock replied, "My friend, the special treatment is not applicable to your part of the country." Andrew did not react, but when they were discussion the "taking of evidence on commission," Andrew proposed a case "where the accused was a Britisher" and let Whitlock know "that I was taking revenge for what he had said last time by making the Britisher an accused—a criminal!"

Southerners' replies to the question of whether close personal relations existed between them and the British indicated a much greater social distance between ruler and ruled in the south than there was in the north. Gordon Muortat replied, "I used to know them; they used to know me; but our relations were more or less confined to work. They were not personal relations. I never had any personal relations with the British at all, no particular friendship." Chief Benjamin Lang pointed out that "their way of life . . . is not the same as ours. It is not the same as our black people's way of life." Andrew Wieu objected to the word "close," maintaining that the nature of the system precluded close friendship even when harmonious working associations were established.

The accounts of most respondents reveal that British-southern Sudanese social relations were generally tense and artificial. "There was not that relaxed atmosphere of equals," Andrew Wieu explained. "People discussed matters of their responsibility. They talked about what England was. People discussed what would happen to the Sudan. But there was a limit." "When mixing," Manoah Majok observed, "one would be on guard. Especially during the first encounter with them, one would make sure he was behaving well, according to the manners he had been taught. . . . It was not a social event at which one would talk freely." In Abd al-Rahman

Souley's view, a Briton, if given a choice, would "not sit down with black people in the same place." Chief Chier Rian more discreetly pointed out that if the British "had had tea with the people, the relationship would have been closer."

The meeting of cultures in the southern Sudan involved women only occasionally. Mrs. Williams, wife of the headmaster at Atar Intermediate School and later Rumbek Secondary School, herself a teacher, was a striking exception. But the majority of contributors noted the barriers to interracial relations between men and women. Referring to the role of British women, Santino Deng and Chief Benjamin Lang differed, and their views indicate the mystery surrounding British women who were visible but distant and isolated.

"We used to meet their wives occasionally when there was work to be done," Deng Teeng said, "but they kept to themselves a great deal. They were always busy; as you know, that is their way of life. The work a wife had to do in her house never gave her a chance to take a walk, meet people, and hold a conversation on other matters. She had no free time. Whenever one went to her house, she was found working. There was nothing the British wives could not do. They farmed, grew vegetables, cleaned their houses, and washed clothes by themselves. They even performed difficult tasks that men usually do. The wives were very highly educated and they did everything." Benjamin Lang disagreed: "At home, the British wife supervised the preparation of food for her husband. That is all the women did. They did not work as hard as our women do. Our women are enslaved to a great extent. . . . They fetch water, pound sorghum, cook, cut grass, and thatch houses."

In any case, the number of British women in the south was very small, partly because young administrators were discouraged from marrying, partly because of the hardships of the south. Married officials brought their wives for only part of each year, when the climate was tolerable. Delayed marriage prompted Benjamin Lang to observe that British administrators would "start to go grey" before they chose to marry. If one took a wife, he would seldom complicate his work by encouraging her involvement. Chief Chier Rian spoke of Mrs. Wilson, who was practically anonymous. "When Mr. Wilson went to court, his wife did not go. When he had finished working, they both stayed home." In the words of Gordon Muortat, "many of these officials used to work for several years, and when they left, they'd go without people knowing the names of their wives." "In the southern Sudan," Andrew Wieu concluded, "their wives were in a category by themselves."

Given the social barriers between the British and southern Sudanese, the scarcity of British women, and racial sensitivities, relations between southern men and British women were virtually out of the question. Between British men and southern women, relations were extremely rare. When they occurred out of wedlock, they caused scandal. If marriage occurred, celebrated according to local custom, it was regarded as anomalous but acceptable and respectable; any children that might result were fully recognized by the girl's relatives as legitimate.

The best-known marriage was of Captain Poole to a Rek Dinka girl. The wedding was celebrated according to Dinka law and custom. Poole paid a large number of cattle as bridewealth. A son was born, Arthur Agany Poole, a light-skinned boy raised as a Dinka and later called by his peers *Madhrub-Bohya* or simply *Madhrub* ("The Painted"). When Poole left the Sudan he left behind his family, itself a comment on such marriages. But he arranged a job for his wife as head of the Tonj Primary School's local employees and ensured the education of his son. Arthur Poole became a successful businessman and maintained contact with his father in Britain.

While Poole's marriage was the most prominent, there were others, less well-known and less accepted. Among the Bor Dinka, Manoah Majok said, there was a district commissioner who married a Dinka girl. Although she was not ostracized, there was feeling among the people that she was "loose, because she had been married to somebody not of her skin." Her isolation was aggravated by her husband's denial that the relationship was a proper marriage. "She was given a small room outside, in the servants' compound. . . . She would not appear in the house if there were other Britishers around. It appears that this man did not want the other Britishers to know that he had a Sudanese wife. . . . It was kept a secret in the servants' quarters." Despite all this, Manoah said, the marriage was accepted because the husband "after all . . . was a human being."

Most other instances were remembered in little enough detail to have the status of rumor. Gordon Muortat spoke of an administrator named Payne who invited Dinka girls to his house to "chat" with them. Andrew Wieu remembered a teacher in Rumbek who went on picnics to a place called Pacol for reasons suspected to be sexual. Captain Alban,[5] who had a child with a Nuer woman and then left his family to return to England, is also the subject of stories. Gordon Muortat recalled having heard a great deal about "somebody called Mr. Beer [who] used to dance with the people; he used to attend Dinka dances and put ivory bangles on his arm. He was very much interested in Dinka social life. People went to the extent of saying that he had relations with some Dinka girls. But there was no proof as far as I am concerned." According to Santino Deng, anomalous liaisons were not uncommon. "Although they married our women, they never took them home to their country," he said. Nevertheless, Santino concluded, "they left their children with a lot of cows. They sent them money and they educated them well."

Despite these half-remembered examples, all agreed that male-female relations among the British and southern Sudanese were limited. Most British, in Benjamin Lang's opinion, "did not court the girls, nor did they covet other people's wives." And Abd al-Rahman Souley maintained that only servants and guards employed by the British "could see such things" even if they did in fact take place. Chier Rian was impressed by the discipline and self-restraint of British administrators: they "were never found walking the streets at night. They were not many: there used to be only one Britisher in a district, so that they had nobody to talk to. They used to sit alone at night near a burning lamp and when they got up, they went to bed. . . . I do not know how they handled their lust for women."

Regarding known or reputed homosexuality, Gordon Muortat responded with an emphatic no. Manoah Majok said that homosexuality is unknown among his people, the Dinka. Santino Deng conceded that "there may have been people like that [but] it never happened in our part of the country among the British who were with us." Andrew Wieu gave an exceptional account of an assistant district commissioner with two homosexual servants on his staff and who "went naked with the local people." The same man associated with a local policeman whom "he escorted to the extent that they were suspected of living together" and whom, when he left the area, "he recommended to a colleague who was of the same character." Nevertheless, Wieu confirmed that the incidence of homosexuality was negligible.

Notes

1. P. S. Garland served in the Upper Nile from 1950 to 1955.
2. See 173n.6 of this work.
3. J. M. Hunter served from 1938 to 1955.
4. Dees served from 1949 to 1955.
5. A. H. Alban served in the Sudan from 1921 to 1942, entirely in the south.

3

Working Conditions and Attitudes

One aspect of colonial rule that greatly impressed southerners was the energy the British devoted to work and the satisfaction they seemed to derive from it. "It was a matter of pride in the Empire," Andrew Wieu said. "They served as such, carrying the flag, with a show of force, as a mandate." He described British efforts to understand the area and the people and to study their law and languages: "They undertook their duties with pride and interest."

Manoah Majok and Gordon Muortat both pointed out that British administrators were "masters of the situation; they were ruling the people." Enjoyment of their work, in Muortat's opinion, was enhanced by a three-month annual leave. "I never observed any situation in which a Britisher . . . appeared miserable or homesick." In the southern view, the British were well paid and lived in reasonable comfort. According to Manoah, "a Britisher had four or five people working from his own pocket. They cleaned around the house, washed clothes, took care of horses, and made up his bed . . . that was a long time ago when money was more scarce than it is now."

Contributors were asked if the British were there to guide, to protect, or simply to dominate the Sudanese. Here, the tide of critical sentiment was at its highest. Santino Deng Teeng gave an emotional response. "There were British who cheated. There were malicious ones who bullied as if they were waging a blood vendetta, as if some of their family had died here. They seemed to be harboring grudges. Some were bad to the extent that if they saw you, they would frown and make some comment. We were forced to ask that kind of person why they seemed to hate us, what we had done wrong."

Other southerners did not display Deng's anger but said essentially the same thing. "They were considered as rulers," Manoah Majok said. "The people respected them not because they liked them, but because they were afraid of them." According to Muortat, the British administration was never regarded as "a sort of holy mission or blessing to the people. [We] accepted colonial rule because [they] had guns, and they had planes—it was unreasonable for anybody to think that he could defy them.... They were there as a matter of right of conquest, rather than to help the people. I didn't see any help that they were giving to the people; instead I saw and heard of people suffering from diseases which could have been treated. Women died giving birth without any facilities being made available.... There was forced labor.... It wasn't until 1946 that the British for the first time started to pay people for road work. And the pay was really very little."

Chief Chier Rian found a discrepancy between the British image of mission and the reality. In words almost identical to Manoah Majok's complaint, he said, "In towns, if there was unpopular work to be done, implementation of a government order, such as demolishing of houses, they pushed junior administrators who were Sudanese from the north to do the job and remained behind the scene masquerading as protectors of the people's interests. The British did not leave their own country because they heard there were some helpless people somewhere who were in need of education. No, they came to rule. They ruled the country by force in such a way that they slapped or insulted any person they found. What chief did they respect? What chief will say that the British respected him?

"We saw the British as masters. We did not see them as our friends. They were not related to people. They were foreigners.... Nowadays, I know that the commissioner in Wau and I are of the same people. If he were to visit, I would address him as commissioner, but I know him and I know his father. He will not condescend to me. He respects me because he knows me—that I am Chief Chier Rian. But the British did not know who I was. They did not respect my father or my brother Monywiir, who became chief after my father. Therefore, I cannot say that they respected me."

The very nature of conquest, according to Chier Rian, explains the oppressive nature of British rule: "They conquered the country with soldiers.... The character of a soldier is not the same as that of a civilian. Our soldiers now, military people, respect people here because they know we are brothers. But if they were taken to rule another country, they would treat the citizens of that country in a military fashion. In a drill, when they tell soldiers to turn, they turn; march, they march; stop, they stop. This is the way the British used to give orders."

The collection of tribute was particularly offensive, according to Gordon Muortat. "Some of the people who were called upon to pay taxes were very poor, and if they didn't pay, their cows would be taken and sold, or they would be put into prison." Most Dinka, though poor in cash, possessed sufficient cattle to exchange for the required cash. But "it was not explained that the taxes they paid were to be spent on services or were necessary for their welfare. It was perfectly known by the Dinka that whatever they paid as a tribute or tax was a sort of ransom to relieve themselves of more oppression."

Some contributors saw British rule as an inevitable part of a larger picture: the Scramble for Africa combined with the particular circumstances of the Sudan. As Andrew Wieu put it, "There was the pain of Gordon's death at the hands of the Sudanese. They could not let the land in which the British blood had been spilled be seen to go to another power."

Ambivalence is reflected in Benjamin Lang Juuk's view of British motives in the Sudan. "When the British ruled our country, they ruled as one would attend to his personal affairs, or maintain family property.... They used to warn people against going wrong as one would lecture his own child.... Such was the case when the British used to discourage those who went to the cattle camps to drink milk and neglect their farming.... [They] would drive people out of the camps, and if anybody caused so much trouble that he deserved to be shot, he was shot." On balance, however, Chief Benjamin praised the British for their good work rather than condemning them as aliens: "Theirs was a mission to educate, to advise against fights, to ensure that nobody stole anybody else's property, that nobody killed another person. They also taught people not to get angry [and retaliate] if something was taken from them.... Whether the results were good or bad, I personally think they came to teach us. They did not come to plunder our wealth. It was not for the purpose of cheating the country of its wealth that they stayed here. They don't cheat.... There is nothing the British did that was bad. If they did, it was in good faith."

Indeed, the majority of southern contributors viewed the British mission in much the same light as the British viewed it themselves. "The British . . . gave the impression that they were there to help the people," Gordon Muortat said; had they not come at all, "the people would have suffered very much, or their condition would have been very bad, or perhaps, as a result of tribal wars, people would have destroyed one another."

The fact that the British were generally in senior positions of authority meant that many contributors had considered them as superiors, at least in rank. "When the British worked with us, they were above us," Benjamin Lang asserted. "They worked as people above us and as our masters. We were never equal to them." Gordon Muortat confirmed that "right from the beginning . . . I regarded the British as superiors. The way the missionaries used to appear before the school. . . . And as time went on, through all the rest of my life, and working in the government. . . . I don't mean superior in nature, but their position was that of a superior, not a junior."

Andrew Wieu distinguished between superiority in rank and superiority in character, culture, and race. As human beings, he said, the British were regarded as equals. In terms of the quality of their work, Wieu argued that they were not always superior. He recalled that "Mr. Bowcock[1] in Bentiu did not understand things as I understood them," and delegated a great deal to Wieu, even asking him to check the contents of all letters to the governor. Wieu concluded that "he was the boss as a matter of policy respecting the two societies; one was governed, and the other was governing."

Abd al-Rahman Souley chose to compare the two nationalities on the basis of cultural development. "Of course, the British are superior to the Sudanese," he said. "Why are they superior? Because they have been advanced for a long time. When did the Sudan develop to reach the level of the British?"

Such issues were insignificant to some. As Deng Teeng put it, "We had lived in our country before [the British] came and we still lived in it. We saw ourselves as better than they were. We looked down upon them because they were from another country." Deng almost repeated the words of Sorror Ramley[2] in saying that "the British . . . were working for us, and they lived on our resources.

They helped us only with medicine, but the medicine was bought with our money. Some people who were weak—those who were cowards, who did not know better—allowed themselves to feel inferior to the British. But those who knew better told them that this land was not their country and asked them what they wanted and whether they did not have a country of their own. Among the Dinka, there were bad elements and there were people who understood things—men who held up their heads and spoke with pride."

The question of how the British regarded themselves evoked a wide variety of responses. From their behavior Gordon Muortat had believed that an assumption of superiority was based solely on British dominance: only when he heard of racial discrimination as an issue did he become sensitive to arrogance based on color or culture. Andrew Wieu commented that many British considered themselves better than Africans because of their view of Sudanese civilization. They based general judgements on first impressions of individuals and peoples. Wieu believed that the British saw the Nuer as savage because of their revolt. "With the Dinka, they thought the people were proud for no reason. Their initial view of the Sudanese was that they were an inferior people who didn't really mean much to them."

According to Wieu, Sudanese were viewed as people with potential. The British respected and made use of the governing ability of traditional rulers and institutions. A recognition of the Sudanese as men of value was reinforced by the African fighting record in the Second World War. "I think they began to realize that a time was coming when they would look on Sudanese as human beings, and even as equals." Andrew considered even Captain Garland's attitude the result mainly of his military background. "As a military man, he always thought in military terms. And before I really came to confront him, in the course of my work as an official, Captain Garland was known to act as a dictator. Even with merchants in the market, whenever he came around walking, he expected everybody to stand up. Later on, he calmed down when he realized that he was not alone to do as he wished and to go unchecked. But even with his officials he acted as a dictator, insisting that everything be done the way he wanted it to be done. That was, of course, an element of oppression or dictatorship. He didn't want things to go the way other people thought they should, but only the way he saw them. And that was the point of conflict between me and him. I believed that things should be done in the normal way of the people, who should be viewed as equals."

Relevant to consideration of attitudes is the question of whether the British discriminated in the administration of justice. We have seen evidence that although fair, the British were concerned to avoid undermining their image as an imperial race. Andrew Wieu said, "A Sudanese official would never have been given a right over a Britisher openly; it would be done very, very secretly, confidentially. No one would know that such a thing had happened which might run contrary to the British image as rulers or to the assumptions about their superiority and seniority over the subordinate Sudanese. They made sure that there were not conspicuous concessions." According to Wieu, a Sudanese would lose sympathy if he quarreled with the British in public, no matter what the reason. "Any confrontation with a Britisher among others was looked upon as insubordination. They would not forgive you for that."

Chief Benjamin was, on the other hand, quite emphatic in praising the British sense of justice. "The Britisher did not discriminate between people, saying that this was his brother—white—or that was a black person." He cited the case of a British doctor who forced a Dinka woman to testify in court. When the woman's newborn baby, who had been left behind, died for want of its mother's milk, the British district commissioner told the doctor to pay compensation.

All contributors acknowledged that the British ranked themselves first on the ladder of racial stratification. Among the Sudanese, in Chier Rian's view, "the British used to see the Dinka and the Arabs alike as their slaves. They did not distinguish between people." But other respondents argued that some Sudanese were considered inferior to others. Chief Lang Juuk contended that "the British thought more of our brothers in the north than they did of us." Gordon Muortat and Andrew Wieu agreed that northerners occupied a position just below the Egyptians. In the civil service, northerners were given posts as officials, and southerners "used to do the horse and donkey work." Wieu conceded that this attitude began to change after the Sudan Administration Conference in 1946. Abd al-Rahman Souley, generally an ardent defender of the British, said that even foreigners received better treatment than southern Sudanese: "For instance, if a black person had a case against a Greek, during the trial the Greek would be seated and the southerner would remain standing, whether he was right or wrong."

It was Souley's contention that British distrust of southerners began in 1924. When Egyptian troops were ordered to leave the Sudan following the assassination of the British governor-general in Cairo, some southern Sudanese troops refused British orders. Following that episode, Souley said, the British began to believe Arab claims that "if they had not given the 'slaves' preference, and had taught their [Arab] children instead, their children would not have revolted against the British."

That the British tried to prevent the cohesion of different ethnic groups was a theme of more than one respondent. In Manoah's view, "there was between the northerners and southerners . . . a way of playing one against the other." According to Wieu, northeners enjoyed the superior position and "in that sense, the British really had a policy of divide and rule." Gordon Muortat added that as well as making it "quite clear that Africans, Arabs, and so on each had a special position, [the British] also created differences between the Dinka, for example, and other tribes. They tried to give the impression that some tribes were dominant over others." He was sure the British did this "as a policy of divide and rule—to weaken, to keep people always in conflict."

Several contributors elaborated on ways in which the British seemed to fan hostilities. Andrew Wieu said, "To northerners they talked of southerners as being lazy, or people who would come to the office drunk. They gave northerners the impression that southerners did not have any significant value. And to southerners— well, they kept reminding them of the Mahdi, the slavery, and all that. They . . . said they came to help the southerners out of slavery; of course this fanned something in the minds of southerners. Therefore, there remained some hatred." Gordon Muortat noted that "no statement [was] made openly by any of the British officials, saying that northerners were better than southerners. But they used to hint all the time that the northerners would replace southerners if the southerners did not receive political safeguards. . . . Some of them used to give hints that the domination of the southerner by the northerner [could] not be avoided [in a unitary system] because northerners are superior to southerners." Gordon recalled that T. R. H. Owen "was very open about it." He said, "Northerners were not good people.... He argued that a leopard would never change its spots, nor would men in a pack. And if the Arabs of the north used to enslave southerners and oppress them, was it possible, after half a century, that they would change and accept southerners as equals?"[3]

To what extent did attitudes change in the course of time? Northern Sudanese responses indicated an obvious improvement. To a lesser extent this was also true of the southerners. In Chier Rian's opinion, change was impossible. "If a snake comes along, and somebody said it had no teeth, one would still run away from it. The British never changed a bit." Abd al-Rahman Souley agreed that it was only after independence that the British would greet a person with respect. Others described a more dynamic process. In some cases, close working relations resulted in better understanding. In others, individuals grew apart as their differences sharpened, especially on political issues: time played both a cohesive and a divisive role. Andrew Wieu's case exemplifies the mellowing effect of experience. But Gordon Muortat and Manoah Majok argued that Sudanese political awareness aggravated tension in terms that had been based on fear. Gordon dates his own change in attitude to 1944 when his class at Loka struck to protest differences in treatment between northerners and southerners. "When this consciousness came to us, it affected our relations with our masters, and made us look on the way we were being treated in school as the effect of the policy which the British were maintaining in the administration generally. My understanding of the British changed and became actively that of resentment."

"People became aware," Manoah Majok said, "that if you were behaving yourself, you were left alone. If you were trying to say that you wanted something better than what you had, then they were very cruel." Manoah thought that increased contact between northern and southern Sudanese and among southerners eroded the British image as rulers. In the workplace, individual Sudanese asked more questions and ceased to "obey blindly the orders given him by his superiors." In his view, "people began to be critical of the British for not giving them their rights as individuals."

Notes

1. P. P. Bowcock served from 1951 to 1955. See Part One, *passim*.
2. See 120 of this work.
3. Cf. 65–66 of this work. It will be recalled that despite Owen's desire to protect the south, he stated a preference for the Arab peoples when asked, in the course of these interviews, to make a comparison. His explanation was that Islam was closer to Christianity, whereas southerners, as pagans, were culturally more remote from him.

4

Nationalism and Independence

The period of the nationalist movement was particularly confusing in relations between southern Sudanese and the British. Southerners resented British colonialism but felt they needed its protection against the north. The British had similarly mixed emotions, wanting to protect the south and resenting the echoes there of nationalist voices from the north. Tensions persisted to the very end and still featured in the accounts of southern Sudanese, the first southern generation to be politically conscious in the modern context, long after the event.

Andrew Wieu saw the nationalist movement as "resistance to interference; a resistance to separation; and a resistance to deprivation of our right to be free.... The government could be there, but as long as it did not interfere with people's lives, nobody could interfere with it either. But the government wanted to impose taxes and to take such measures as would ensure people's loyalty to foreign rule. And, therefore, it was a conflict of the authority seeking to subdue and the resistance of people fighting to remain free." Wieu also saw the movement as a struggle for fundamental rights that united Sudanese of various tribes and cultures, northerners and southerners alike. As the spirit of nationalism developed, Wieu said, "people realized that they had a common enemy and that collectivity was necessary to defend their right [to free themselves] to pursue the course of life which they had pursued as independent people."

Benjamin Lang Juuk also emphasized the unity of the movement: "When we took over our country—when our big, educated brothers rose and contacted us in the south, and it was agreed that we should rule our country by ourselves—we liked it. Our brothers in the north and our brothers in the south were agreed on one thing: the British should leave and we should govern our country."

Other respondents differed, emphasizing that southerners were left out of the nationalist movement at the beginning and were far from unanimous in supporting it when their "big, educated brothers" did contact them. "The north advanced and we here did not know," Chief Chier Rian said. "They were first given the authority to try cases. Then they were given local government councils. . . . Later, they had provincial councils, and we in the south were not informed. Finally, they reached the level of a governor-general's council. . . . That is when they became powerful, at least until the British left." In the south there were no councils, and it was not until after the Juba Conference that a secondary school was built. "Those in Khartoum . . . got educated and we were left behind. They did not want us to unite. That was the British policy. That is why they left us behind and pushed the north ahead."

Most southerners agreed on the goal of independence, but the issue of when and how was complex and divisive. Gordon Muortat asserted that the nationalist movement split along north-south lines: "There was no 'Sudanese Nationalism' as an entirety or as an integral whole," he said. "As soon as the south came into the picture, it started to develop its own nationalism in opposition to that of the north." The northern movement, manifested in the Graduates' Congress and the Advisory Council, was institutionalized by the time contact was made with southerners in 1947. Northern nationalists "simply demanded a meeting between the north and the south without consulting the south," Gordon Muortat said. "They always spoke as if the south did not exist, as if the Sudan as a whole was their own, and the other people were not important. . . . This actually alienated most of the southerners." Abd al-Rahman Souley agreed that it was northerners, instigated by Egyptians, who were "in a hurry" to achieve independence, and that the Juba Conference was convened only when the British insisted the southerners should be consulted.

At Juba, southern representatives were initially opposed to participation in a Legislative Assembly that did not recognize regional interests. According to Souley, they were won over by the issue of salaries: "Southerners hated the British [because] the British did not pay good salaries. . . . The highest paid civil servant was making three Sudanese pounds a month. . . . That is what caused the southerners to say that the British should leave." Manoah Majok said that for "the first two days of the conference, the consensus was that the southerners wanted to stay alone." They were persuaded to send representatives to Khartoum primarily by Judge Muhammad Salih Shingeiti, the future speaker of the house.

Chief Chier Rian was one of those at the Juba Conference who believed the south should develop separately until it achieved a standard comparable to that of the north, at which time the issue of full unity would be considered: "How we spoke at the conference will be found by literate people in the records.... The reason I was not happy about [the British] departure was not that I liked them. It was because they had raised the standard of the north and left us behind. I knew that when they left, the north would replace the British and dominate us. That was why I said they should teach us first; so, I did want them to stay. I wanted them to teach us so that when they left and we remained with our brothers, we would be equal."

The bitterness of British administrators in the south at the rapid move toward independence is clear in the account of Andrew Wieu's experience. "When the Cairo Agreement [of 12 November 1952] was signed, we were directed to celebrate the occasion. Captain Garland was on trek. So, I sent him the telegram that had come, and I proceeded to make arrangements for the celebrations: I distributed bulls to the prisons and other institutions. And when he came he found everybody dancing and celebrations going on. He thought there was nothing of interest to the people of Bentiu that should have caused them to celebrate. So he called me in and asked me what was going on. I said, 'Well, you got the telegram and my note that there were to be celebrations.' He asked me, 'Do you think the Nuer understand all these celebrations? What benefit are they going to get out of it?' I told him that we might not get anything out of it, but one thing was clear. I said, 'In the past, you have been speaking on our behalf. But now, you have taken the responsibility from your neck and placed it on our neck, and we'll be speaking on our own behalf. That in itself is a gain that should be celebrated. Whether you see it that way or not is another matter. And that is why we should celebrate. You have ceased to be responsible as spokesmen for us. We will be our own spokesmen.'

"Well, he didn't appreciate that. So he went to Malakal and brought the governor, Mr. Longe. And Mr. Longe came and asked me the same question. And I replied to him the same way. Then, to my surprise, Mr. Longe said that in fact I had no future because an administrative assistant had no future. I said, 'If you don't give me a cause, and I have no future, I'll never change.' Then they went to Abiemnom, where there was an interprovincial conference attended by the acting permanent undersecretary, Mr. Beaton,[1] the last of the Britishers. They brought Mr. Beaton. After taking the salute, Mr. Beaton asked me what I would like to do. I told him that I understood that I had no future as administrative assistant. What I would do was opt for another career, where I might find a future. So he said, 'Well, you people can go on courses and improve yourselves.' In the end, he went back and wrote a letter to the effect that all should go on courses and that courses had been arranged."

While the educated class and the urban population were becoming politically minded, the bulk of the tribal populace remained in the dark. Andrew Wieu told of a meeting with an old Dinka in Bentiu in 1953. "I asked [him] whether the district commissioner had not been telling them of what was going on. He asked me what was going on." When Wieu explained political developments, the old man said, 'Well, the district commissioner has not been telling us. But, you know when the Dinka go to the cattle camps ... it is not the blind man who leads the way. So you people who are educated and therefore know something, it is for you to tell us what is going on and what we should do. When the district commissioner comes, we will use your views as our own views.'"

Even the educated were not necessarily politically minded. The first time Gordon Muortat, then a police cadet, witnessed "Sudanese nationalism in action" was in 1951, when he went to Khartoum. Manoah Majok realized that change was imminent only when newspapers and radio became accessible, and the British began to discuss politics—unheard of in earlier days.

Most respondents dated full southern participation in the nationalist movement to 1952. The option of the south's autonomy within a united Sudan began to receive serious consideration. Many southerners, including Manoah Majok, were convinced this was necessary to guarantee that southerners would not become a "Second People." The Constitutional Amendment Commission, which tabled its report on 23 January 1952, recommended creation of a Minister for the Southern Provinces and a Board for Southern Affairs. The proposal was rejected, but a federal structure became increasingly popular as political organization developed among southerners.

The Southern Liberal party was formed, Abd al-Rahman Souley said, when missionary-educated southerners complained about the lack of consultation prior to the 1952 agreement. The governor "gave a simple and short answer. He said that the south had not been included in the agreement because we had no political party." Souley was made leader of the party by default: "Younger members of the party said that they did not want party positions because no money could be earned from it. There was none among them who would leave his job to become leader of the party." During the 1953 southern elections, Souley, on the advice of British officials, tried to persuade his colleagues "that the then three southern provinces should unite and go to Parliament in the north as one unit to present southern demands to the Parliament."

Many southerners' view of the British was profoundly affected by the lack of official support for federalism. According to Andrew Wieu, "the British were wary of accusations from Egypt and the northern Sudan that they were working to separate the south, had they been receptive to the southern claim to special status within." But the long-standing Southern Policy had left southern Sudanese at an extreme disadvantage in the new union. Not a few saw sudden British withdrawal and "neutrality" as a reversal and a betrayal.

"I felt that the British had sold us," Gordon Muortat said. "When they were given the option of keeping the south as a colony and perhaps benefiting from it through colonial exploitation, they thought that it was better to forget the south and pursue other advantages they valued very much. These included their military bases in Egypt and their general oil interests in the Arab world. Of course, they also liked the northern Sudanese. They thought that if they allowed the northern Sudanese to dominate the African population, the northern Sudanese would be devoted to them for a long time, and this is true. The southerners, of course . . . concluded that the British had sold them out in order to stay in the Suez Canal area. This was the first thing. So the southerners knew that the British were going—going away from the Sudan, without caring very much about southerners and their position—in order to retain control over the Suez Canal."

Gordon Muortat explained that southern Sudanese were unhappy about the British departure "not because we wanted to be ruled by the British forever, but because we feared the consequences for us in the south. We knew that if the British left before the southerners were brought to the level of the north in education, social development, and so on, there was a possibility of the northerners taking over the south. . . . Most of us used to view the going away of the British as a recolonization of the south by the north." Chief Chief Rian expressed a similar view: "We were familiar with British administration, but our northern brother was unknown to us. We were afraid that the Arabs would mistreat us after the British were gone. We knew that we were not going to find jobs. We, the chiefs, were very apprehensive that our children would not get a fair deal." Chief Benjamin Lang spoke of the lonely position he took up in Parliament: "'Now that the British are leaving, and the level of education in the north is not the same as that in the south, why don't we let the British stay a little longer to teach the south?' My proposal was defeated by our brothers who were in Parliament with me."

Santino Deng Teeng differentiated between the reaction of educated men and that of the Dinka in the villages when word of the nationalist movement reached his area. "The best reason we saw for their departure was the way they had arrived," he said, summarizing the argument of the educated. "They came and took over the country by force and conquered the people. We gave in and accepted their conquest, and they became our masters and ruled us according to their law. If something was prompting them to leave, many people argued that we should seize the opportunity, that we should be free, that we should remain alone. By remaining alone we would open our eyes and prove ourselves equal to the Arabs. That was what we had to do." The average Dinka, however, "understood that the Egyptians and the Arabs from the north had decided to expel the British so that they could take over the country. Many of our people feared that the Arabs and the Egyptians would enslave us. They would cheat us because they were educated and most of our people were not."

"Before the British left," Gordon Muortat said, "the southerners tried to present their case. They tried. They didn't have the means at that time to send a delegation to Egypt where negotiations were taking place; they had to confine themselves to writing memoranda and petitions. They petitioned the governor-general and they petitioned the British government, making an appeal that the southerners should not be handed over to the north because the result would be disastrous. If the British wanted the north and the south to be together, they should remain for another ten years and speed up development in the south, at least to bring it onto a par with the north.... It would then be for the southerners to decide whether the political boundaries should include southerners and northerners in one Sudan.... Northern domination ... was the plan and that was what happened. The British made it purposely by keeping the south backward and developed the north as a part of the Arab world. We knew this, but we also thought that the same British who had made that wicked policy should undo it before leaving."

There were attempts to reassure southern Sudanese "in order to appease us," Chier Rian said. "The Arabs promised to promote those who were clerks, who had been educated, to become administrators." But independence brought little advancement. "When Sudanization was completed," Gordon Muortat pointed out, "90 or 99 percent of the civil service was taken over by the northern Sudanese. The army too was taken over by the northern Sudanese. It shocked people, and there was not any doubt in the mind of all the southerners that this was nothing but a change of masters."

Among the southerners who supported immediate independence, despite awareness of problems to come, was Andrew Wieu. "The issue for us was to first get rid of the superior power that was suppressing us and then turn to the next. The British were the largest power. We should tackle them first in solidarity with the north and Egypt. The north was a lesser power which we could tackle alone, as we eventually did."

Developments after independence added to the disillusionment of southerners. Federation was ruled out. The military took over and tried to silence southerners. In 1964 all Christian missionaries were expelled. "The missionaries were the ones helping us," Chier Rian said. "The missionaries were doing an excellent job of teaching us.... They were expelled because of politics. It was said that the south rebelled on the instigation of the missionaries. That is when we had disturbances. This is what caused the expulsion of the missionaries." Manoah Majok noted "the behavior of the northern administrators ... who were transferred to the south.... They behaved as people who were better than southerners. As soon as one would begin to ask questions, he was subjected to being followed under the suspicion that he wanted the south to separate from the north.

Abd al-Rahman Souley was of the minority view that the civil war was no fault of the British: "Certainly there has been death," he conceded. But "we brought death on ourselves, we the southerners, through our confusion. We do not analyze things. Now, if you court a girl, she will not accept you on the first date. She will try to learn more about you. . . . But we in the south, whenever anything appears to be good, we rush into accepting it. That is the characteristic which has caused us a lot of deaths. Up to now it still prevails."

British Southern Policy had an impact on relations between individuals. Some respondents were bitter. Gordon Muortat looked upon the British as rulers whose day had ended. Manoah Majok, whose British colleagues left before the majority, went to the railway station to watch the last armed contingent leave. "I just saw the people go away," he said. "I did not have much attachment to them." Chief Chier said simply, "Nobody cried when the British left."

Andrew Wieu, while welcoming the departure of the British, would miss "individuals who had been intimate. If they had remained behind as part of the new system, rather than as rulers, one would have been happy." Andrew concluded, "They felt at home and we felt at home with them, as individuals. . . . Some of them really left weeping. . . . They had developed a love for the Sudan." Those Wieu remembered most vividly agreed with the southern majority view that they were leaving too soon. One district commissioner in particular forecasted impending strife. But even the more optimistic had a sense of leaving loose ends untied. "They had outlined a program for Sudanization which would have lasted until 1961," Wieu said. "It was now abruptly interrupted. They didn't think they had completed their mission to develop the Sudan and to hand it over in the way they would have liked."

Southern bitterness against the British for neglect of development paradoxically combined with the sadness a dependent feels when abandoned by his source of security. Gordon Muortat articulated this when he said, "I was not sorry because our good masters were leaving. I was sorry because I foresaw that their departure was going to lead to a conflict between north and south."

Note

1. A. C. Beaton joined the service in 1927 and retired, as permanent undersecretary in the ministry of the interior, in 1954.

5

Post-Colonial Contacts and Perspectives

Given the distant relations between the British and southern Sudanese, it was to be expected that personal contacts were for the most part severed at independence. Some individuals corresponded or exchanged visits, but with few exceptions contributors held the British responsible for their plight since independence. And yet the British were still praised for achievements in law and order, peace and security, and for providing cohesion and stability.

Both Manoah Majok and Andrew Wieu corresponded with a number of British following independence. Manoah and Williams exchanged letters until Williams's death in the late 1960s. Wieu corresponded briefly with P. P. Bowcock, the last district commissioner in the Upper Nile, while the latter worked in Northern Rhodesia. This correspondence ended, however, when Wieu reminded Bowcock "of the things we used to discuss and our differences, including my own view about their power in the Sudan and the way they had treated the southern Sudanese and the south as an area. The last letter I wrote to him was after the mutiny and all the confusion that had taken place. I told him, 'Your country will be cursed because of all you did for the south, leaving the south in chaos!' He never replied to the letter."

Since most southern Sudanese contributors were young men with rising prospects at the time of independence, their careers later took them to the United Kingdom where they met their former British rulers. In Britain, Andrew Wieu found that many ex-officials "maintain vividly in their minds a love for the people of the Sudan." He had been honored at a number of dinners hosted by Dr. Slade, whom he had met in the Upper Nile hospital, and Philip

Ingleson, the former governor of Darfur, among others. Manoah Majok, who first went to England in 1964, found the British very friendly, far different toward Sudanese from the way they had been in the Sudan. "They wanted very much for us to stay in their places.... And they were, of course, trying to show off." The British asked many questions about people in the Sudan, and "it appeared they were following what was going on ... very closely."

Chief Lang Juuk told a surprising story about the attitude of British former administrators toward a delegation of Sudanese parliamentarians. Accompanied by four Arab chiefs, they toured Britain as well as Belgium, France, and Italy in 1956. They were impressed by the "advanced level of development" but, in Britain at least, by the lack of warmth on the part of the people. D. H. St. Clair Biggs[1] was the only former administrator to contact them and invite them to his home. The others "who had known us hid from us. When we recognized some of them and reached out to them as people who had once worked with us, they denied knowledge of us and pretended to be different people!"

Another southerner profoundly disappointed by England was Gordon Muortat, although the circumstances of his visit were different, as he had left the Sudan for political reasons and chosen to oppose the Addis Ababa Agreement from Britain. He recalled experiencing particular problems in renewing contacts with the British he had known in the Sudan. A former district commissioner, G. R. I. Dees, contacted Gordon after his arrival in 1972, following publication of an article about him in the *Daily Telegraph*. Apart from that, no one had been in touch with him. He believed that former British associates avoided him for political reasons on the advice of the British-Sudanese Association.

It is ironic in the light of his personal history that Andrew Wieu was most positive about relations with the British in England. Despite problems, he felt there was a basic understanding between the two peoples: "I think the British loved the Sudan and continue to love the Sudan.... They feel proud of the Sudan. And they think that the Sudanese people, with their generosity, with their frankness and openness, will remain good friends.... They have never changed their attitudes about the Sudan or the Sudanese.... And the Sudanese feel the same way toward them. Whatever anti-imperialism slogans are popular at home here, we still remain quietly good friends of the British."

Regarding the standard of living of British administrators when they were in Africa and their status in England, Andrew Wieu said that a large number "had been better off in the Sudan because of the many amenities or facilities accorded to them." A number had taken jobs there "just to earn a living."

In summarizing the British achievement, Chief Benjamin Lang paid special tribute to them as peace-keepers. Comparing the current situation to what prevailed during the British era, he was very positive about the colonial experience: "The way the British taught the people, there was no confusion; there was not the degree of confusion that there is now ... that our children have become educated.... People are now being killed—50, 100, 200. It is our children who have brought on this kind of thing. It did not exist during the days of the British." Chief Chier Rian agreed: "During the British era, it used to be ten years before one would hear that somebody had killed another person in the whole of Gogrial District.... Now, the Arabs are taking care of themselves well.... No Arabs are dying in Arab-land. It is the Dinka, Nuer, and Shilluk who are dying."

This confusion and bloodshed in Nilotic societies was partly attributed by Chier Rian to a breakdown in authority after the abandonment of indirect rule. "The Dinka have a lot of freedom. Even a commoner can now insult a chief. During the British era, the Dinka respected their chiefs. When a chief asked them to go and work on the road, they went. If the chief told a person to return a cow that he had taken from somebody, he returned it. But now, the Dinka respect only the soldier, because of the gun." Even Deng Teeng, a critic of British rule, lamented the change: "When we Dinka analyze it, the British way of life resulted in making people take good care of themselves and respect each other. The mutual deference was one thing they emphasized."

Several southerners praised British law enforcement. Abd al-Rahman Souley said, "They would sentence you if you contravened the law, but if a Britisher knew that you were familiar with the law and you committed a crime, he would punish you more severely because you intentionally broke the law.... The British did not just try people at random. [Moreover], the police ... were well-disciplined.... If a policeman were sent to fetch a labor crew from a particular chief within a distance of twenty miles, he would simply go and bring the labor crew. He would not mess around there. He would not beat the people, nor would he engage in any destruction." Manoah Majok also praised the legal and administrative framework the British established. The Sudan Penal Code, Sudan Code of Criminal Procedure, Law of Tort, Law of Contract and models of local government have all been modified, but, according to Manoah, "we are still basing our real work on what they laid out."

On the role of the British in economic development, Benjamin Lang stressed a positive contribution, citing in particular construction of roads in swampland. He mentioned doctors and teachers among the people he remembered most vividly for their human qualities. "The senior medical officer . . . loved his patients. He never left their bedsides night or day. [Nor did] the British teacher . . . leave the children who were being taught."

Abd al-Rahman Souley went into most detail about the work done by the British: when the district commissioner found villagers "suffering from some serious disease, he would give instructions not to drink bad water, or not to do this or that so as to make sure the disease did not spread in the village. Also, at the end of the year, the British would summon the chiefs to come to Juba and get an agenda of work for the government. The chiefs also gave annual reports about the state of affairs in the villages so that the government could determine the needs of the people and provide supplies such as medicine for areas far from town. There were also January meetings in Juba of people from remote areas during which the district commissioners would give details about such matters as agricultural programs and forest protection."

Souley credited the British with establishing agricultural and irrigation schemes and with developing transportation. "Before trucks were introduced, the Bari used to carry rocks and gravel on their heads," he said. Souley conceded that "the south is still backward. We cannot match the northerners now. The north is far ahead of the south. What do we have here in the south? Who, here in the south, knows the tricks of northerners?" But he did not blame the British: "If you were a teacher, and you had two classes to teach, you could not run back and forth trying to teach both classes at the same time. What you could do is teach one class first and then go to the second one after you had taught the first class. The British did not stay here for a long time. They were here only for some forty-plus years, and the Sudanese kicked them out, saying that they had learned enough. They should have taught the northerners and then moved to the south to teach the southerners."

Others did not share Souley's enthusiasm. Chier Rian had harsh words for what he saw as British failure to develop the south: "There is no good thing that the British did in the Sudan. They kept people in the dark so that they might have a longer time to exploit the country. They did not build a well-equipped hospital. They did not build a bridge across any river, as we did later in Wau. They did not give any responsible position to a citizen.... They were foreigners, but if they had taught us well, they would have done nothing wrong. They did not teach us well.... Learning how to settle disputes over cows is not an education which can help a country.... This is an area where the British have been. Those who are found here with me, what in their livelihood has changed? Are they not still as they were in the days of your grandfather?"

Andrew Wieu, in many ways positive about British rule, also contended that the British had left the Sudan "more primitive than they left Uganda, for example, or Kenya. In Kenya they had their own settlements: Kenya was almost part of their home. In Uganda it was slightly different, because Uganda was a protectorate. Ours was a condominium which had no place in the British Empire.... It was something anomalous or strange to the British system."

In summarizing their views, Gordon Muortat and Manoah Majok stressed the belief that British administration was a source of conflict in the Sudan. "We are still suffering from the policies of the British in the southern region," Manoah said. Muortat emphasized the British impact in encouraging the language, culture, and system of government of each separate tribe: "This made each tribe resent the interference of other tribes. It resulted in a lot of conflict under the British administration. It prevented political harmony and political maturity and even delayed nationalist development in the south." Andrew Wieu, on the other hand, did not lay primary blame on the British for the upheaval that followed independence. If the Sudanese themselves had not "allowed our own mistakes and our selfishness to let our religious and our cultural differences ... result in devastating conflict, I believe the Sudan would have been a happier place in which to live."

Chief Chier Rian was impressed by the close attention the British paid to financial matters. "The Sudanese are careless with their money. Ten people are assigned to do a simple job.... Nobody keeps a record of the money that comes in and the money that is spent.... That is what will bankrupt the Sudan." Chier Rian went on to say, "The British did not want to take anything from the Dinka. When they had no milk, it was their servants who went and asked the chief for some, which they took with their tea."

The positive influence of British training also impressed the chief: "If there were two people, one who had worked with the British, you would find that he knew how to administer the country while the other person did not. The way the British ruled us, the Dinka favor even to the present day. If you went out and asked an older person who were the better administrators—our Sudanese who now rule the region in Juba (our people, not the Arabs) or the British—he would tell you that the British were better."

The most serious charge leveled against the British was of racism, and it was made by Gordon Muortat, who believed that the tendency to discriminate on the basis of race is stronger in the British than among any other Europeans. "The British think that they are the best, that they are superior, and that other races are inferior. They will never believe that Africans, for example, could develop to the present level of the British." In political terms, he said, this resulted in a "double standard ... affecting Africa," for while the British supported independence for former colonies, they also supported white minority control in Rhodesia, Namibia, and South Africa.

Gordon described ties between Britain and the independent Sudan as "friendship between the British and the northern Sudanese, not us." He indeed believed there was a "lot of evidence" that the Addis Ababa Agreement, which ended seventeen years of civil war between north and south and established the Southern Regional Government, "was designed by the British in a way that would not benefit the southerners.... Negotiations were designed in such a way that they should take place between those who were favored by the British, other imperialist countries, and the northern Sudanese. So when negotiations took place, it was under favorable conditions, involving selected southerners whom the British knew would not insist on terms that were unacceptable to the north."

Abd al-Rahman Souley was perhaps the least ambivalent about the British: "I hear Muslims say that Christians do not know God," he remarked. "But this is just word of mouth. The British knew God.... The British policy was always to do right so they could remain masters of everybody and leave their position to their children, grandchildren, and so forth. . . . Even now, I, who have been around long enough and have worked with the British, when I see what is going on now I would say that change has been very destructive. Yes, by God! . . . Just say that Sudan is ungrateful! If the Sudanese were grateful, they would have thanked the British."

Gratitude is what Chief Lang Juuk felt toward the British. "We should thank them because they did a lot of work," he said. "Even if they made some mistakes, their good work was sufficient compensation. How could it be said that they were not building the country? In everything they did, there is nothing for which we cannot thank them. I praise them in everything. No matter in what department a Britisher worked, he did his work very well."

Andrew Wieu suggested that in order to appraise British rule in the Sudan more equitably, it would be useful to view it in a wider colonial context. In the field of education, for example, he contended that "the French system . . . was based on the principle that there was no difference between French and Africans. So they imposed their own language on the Africans. . . . There was nothing done to develop an African identity in the people they ruled. [British colonialism was] a good system. . . . I feel we were lucky that we were ruled by them because of their systematic dealing with the people, through institutions. They did not use force as the means to achieve their ends, but as a last resort, to pacify the situation. That is the difference between the British and the other powers that we have known in the Third World or in Africa. . . . As a people they have a message to give to others in a way that should be appreciated. Their different institutions, the way they process their institutions, the phasing out of their colonial power in Africa and elsewhere in the world, has been systematic and with respect for the people they were leaving. They always intended to leave as friends rather than as enemies."

How does one reconcile such a wide array of views and sentiments? Perhaps Andrew Wieu's formulation is a useful guide. He argued that given a choice between freedom and rule by a foreign power, the Sudanese would obviously not have been ruled by the British. But "we have been in a more advantageous position than any African state that was not under the British." The Sudanese resisted colonial rule from the start; when it became established, they saw positive aspects of British rule even as they criticized it and continued to resent government by a foreign power. In the end, a yearning for freedom brought independence. The strongest argument against the British was merely that they were a colonial power. Chier Rian concluded, "They were foreigners . . . I, Chier, . . . know that what they did was not bad. But they ruled people as though they were their slaves. They were teaching the people, but the way they were teaching the people was that of a foreigner. . . . The British will never come back. The country has now been taken over by its citizens." But even the chief could remark, with a bitter irony, that the south's way of protecting itself, after the end of colonial rule, "was guerrilla war."

Note

1. Biggs served in the Bahr al-Ghazal from 1950 to 1954.

APPENDIX A

THE QUESTIONNAIRE

A. Questions for the British

1. Introduction of the subject matter: an examination of cross-cultural interaction through relations in the colonial context.
2. Name, age, area of origin in the U.K., family background, and present occupation.
3. Please enumerate without elaboration the positions you held during the British rule in the Sudan.
4. Would you give an account of any views you might have held or heard expressed about the Sudanese before meeting them?
5. What circumstances led to your selecting or being selected to serve in the Sudan?
6. Who was the first Sudanese you met and under what circumstances did you meet?
7. Please describe your journey to the Sudan, what you envisaged to be the nature of your mission, the circumstances under which you arrived, and your initial impressions about the country and the people.
8. What was your first assignment in the Sudan, and under what circumstances did you get it?
9. Did the nature of your job put you in close touch with Sudanese?
10. Were all the Sudanese in your occupation your subordinates or did you have professional equals?

11. Did you get to know any Sudanese closely? And what did it mean to be close to Sudanese?
12. What other positions did you hold and how did they compare?
13. Were there any British near you? If so, how close were you to them and how did your socializing with them compare with your socializing with your Sudanese friends and acquaintances?
14. If you or any of your British friends were married, could you give some account of how their wives fitted into the situation?
15. Whenever any social mixing was involved, what significant differences did you observe in the cultural expression in socially mixed situations as compared to exclusive British or Sudanese social occasions?
16. Could you say whether there were any man-woman relationships between the British and the Sudanese and how they were viewed?
17. Were there any known or reputed affairs between the British and the Sudanese?
18. In view of the isolation of many British administrators in the Sudan, especially in terms of man-woman relationships, did any homosexual tendencies develop as a result?
19. To what extent did interest in, and liking for, your work make up for lack of amenities and opportunities to mix socially?
20. How did you view the nature of your mission vis-a-vis the Sudanese: to guide, dominate, or protect the Sudanese?
21. How did you think the Sudanese viewed your mission?
22. Did you regard yourself as a superior or an equal to the Sudanese? Please be absolutely frank.
23. How do you think the Sudanese viewed you?
24. Did your attitude toward the Sudanese or the Sudanese attitude toward you change as you got to know them better?
25. Did you used to see the Sudanese in comparative terms, for instance, Sudanese as compared to Egyptians or other Africans, or even internally, such as northerners compared to southerners?
26. Could you give an account of the Sudan nationalist movement for independence and what views you held on it at its various stages?
27. What was the position of the Sudanese closest to you on this issue of nationalism?

28. When did you first feel that the British might leave the Sudan and when did you estimate they would in fact leave?
29. When it became apparent that the British were leaving, how did you feel about the whole issue?
30. Could you give an account of the circumstances under which the British in general and you in particular left the Sudan?
31. Have you kept contact with the Sudanese? If so, in what form—letters or visits?
32. If you have been back or been in contact with Sudanese, what comparative changes have you observed in the occupational positions of the Sudanese you had known? Had you expected they might ever attain such positions or fail to achieve as they have done?
33. Did you observe any changes in the attitudes of the people toward the British?
34. What things do you particularly like or dislike about the Sudan and the Sudanese?
35. What is your general evaluation of the British rule in the Sudan?

B. Questions for the Sudanese

1. Introduction of the subject matter: an examination of cross-cultural interaction through relations in the colonial context.
2. Name, age, area of origin in the Sudan, family background, and present occupation.
3. Please enumerate without elaboration the positions you held under the British.
4. Would you give an account of any views you might have held or heard expressed about the British before meeting them?
5. Who was the first Britisher you met and under what circumstances did you meet?
6. If you had any British teachers in school or college, please give an account of your relationship with them, especially in comparison with non-British teachers.
7. What was your first employment under the British and under what circumstances did you obtain it?
8. Would you give an account of your working relationship with the British under, or with, whom you worked?

9. What other employments did you have under the British and how did they compare in terms of the job and the working relationships?
10. Did you have any British subordinates or equals in the employment or were they always your seniors? What comparisons can you make between your various positions and working relationships?
11. Who were the British closest to you and what did it mean to be close to them?
12. Were any of the British you knew married? If so, how did their wives fit into Sudanese society?
13. Whenever there was any social mixing between the Sudanese and the British, did you observe any significant differences as compared to exclusive social occasions?
14. Were there any man-woman relationships including reputed affairs between the British and the Sudanese? If so, how were they viewed?
15. In view of the isolation of many British administrators in the Sudan, especially in terms of man-woman relationships, were there any known or reputed homosexual practices or tendencies among them?
16. To what extent did interest in, and liking for, their work make up for lack of amenities and opportunities to mix socially?
17. How did you view the nature of the British presence in the Sudan? In particular, did you think the British were there to guide, protect, or dominate the Sudanese?
18. What did you think was the British view about the nature of their presence in the Sudan?
19. Did you regard the British as superiors, equals, or inferiors?
20. How do you think the British regarded the Sudanese: as inferiors or equals?
21. Did your attitude toward the British or the British attitude toward the Sudanese change as you got to know them?
22. Did the British used to evaluate the Sudanese in comparative terms, e.g., northerners compared with southerners, or Sudanese compared with Egyptians or other Africans?
23. Could you give an account of the Sudanese nationalist movement as you witnessed it and what you thought about it at its various stages?

24. When did you first feel that the British might leave the Sudan and when did you estimate they would actually leave?
25. What views or feelings did you hold about the prospects of their leaving?
26. When it became apparent that they were actually leaving, how did you react to the situation?
27. Did you entertain any special feelings about the British you knew or did you feel about them as a collectivity?
28. Could you give an account of the instances under which the British in general and those closest to you in particular left the Sudan?
29. What were your feelings and those of the British you knew as they left the country?
30. Have you kept in contact with the British you had known in the Sudan?
31. If you have been to England, what were your impressions about the country and the people? Were they as you had expected?
32. If you visited after independence, did you meet any of the British you had known in the Sudan? If so, under what comparative circumstances and were they as you had expected?
33. Have you observed any changes in the attitude of the British toward the Sudan and the Sudanese since independence?
34. What do you particularly like or dislike about the British?
35. What is your general evaluation of the British role in the Sudan?

APPENDIX B

BIOGRAPHICAL NOTES ON CONTRIBUTORS

To help the reader place the responses in their appropriate individual context, we have prepared these biographical notes primarily from the information furnished by the contributors themselves, supplemented in the case of the British members of the Political Service by the information in the book *Sudan Political Service, 1899–1956.*

BRITISH CONTRIBUTORS

Gawain Westray Bell, C.B.E. Born 21 January 1909. "My family is originally from the north of England where they were sheep farmers, owning their own land. They immigrated to the coast where they became masters of sailing vessels and prospered from selling sails and ropes and so forth. In due course, they became quite a well-to-do middle-class people.

"My father was educated in a secondary school in the northern part of England. He did not go to a well-known public school, but he began his life in the city and ended up a stockbroker. He worked for a number of years in South Africa as the representative of a shipping company. My mother's family came originally from Austria, but my father met my mother in South Africa, where he married her."

Bell himself was educated at Winchester and Hertford College, Class II, Modern History. Member of the Oxford University Rifle Club VIII and IV 1929–31 (Captain, 1931). Joined the Service in 1931 and served two-year probationary period in Kassala. Having passed Arabic and Law examinations, was posted to Kordofan for four years as Assistant District Commissioner, Easter Jebel's District in the Nuba Mountains, living principally at Talodi, part of the time in Rashad, and for a short term in El Obeid. In 1938, was seconded to the Government of Palestine. Commissioned General List in 1941, served in the Blue Nile, 1941–42; then to the Government of Transjordan on secondment to the Arab Legion, 1942–45. Returned to the Sudan in 1945 and was posted as District Commissioner at El Obeid, then as District Commissioner, Western Kordofan, headquarters En-Nahud up to 1949. Went to Egypt as Deputy Sudan Agent in Cairo, 1949–51. Returned to the Sudan and served as Assistant Civil Secretary (Political) 1951–53, then Deputy Civil Secretary, 1953–54 and finally after self-government as Permanent Undersecretary, Ministry of the Interior. Retired 1955.

Philip Parnell Bowcock. Born 1927. Eldest of three sons of a farmer on the Staffordshire/Shropshire border in the West Midlands. One grandfather secretary of a building society and the other headmaster of a school. Went to local direct grant grammar schools, Newcastle-under-Lyme, and then by scholarship to St. John's College, Oxford, Class II, Modern History. Began service on secondment to Middle East Centre of Arabic Studies in 1950. In 1951 served as Assistant District Commissioner, Khartoum at the Headquarters (Muderia); then spent two years as Assistant District Commissioner, Western Nuer, Upper Nile Province, and one year as District Commissioner, Zeraf District, 1954–55; retired 1955. Joined H.M. Overseas Civil Service in the Provincial Administration and, subsequently, the judiciary in Northern Rhodesia (now Zambia). After ten years there, joined the administrative class of the Home Civil Service with the Ministry of Technology. After three years, qualified as a solicitor and joined a family practice in Leek, Staffordshire; was a senior partner at the time of response to the questionnaire.

George Richard Frederick Bredin, C.B.E. Born 8 June 1899 in Valparaiso, Chile, of British parents. Father a doctor. Educated at Clifton and Oriel College, Oxford. Distinction class. Litterae Humaniores (shortened war course). Oxford University Rifle Club VIII, 1920. War Service: Royal Engineers, 1917–18 (France and

Flanders). Appointed to the Political Service in 1921: White Nile 1921–22; Kordofan, 1922–26; Assistant Civil Secretary (Administration) 1927–29; Darfur, 1930–31; Deputy Governor, Blue Nile, 1935–39; Deputy Civil Secretary to Sir Douglas Newbold, 1939–41; Governor Gezira (later Blue Nile), 1941–48; member of the Governor-General's Council 1945–48, and also Chairman of the Council of the University College of Khartoum. Retired 1948. After retirement became Assistant Registrar, University of Liverpool, 1948–49; Fellow and Bursar of Pembroke College, Oxford, 1950.

Lawrence Medlicott Buchanan. Born 3 February 1906. Educated at St. Edward's, Oxford and Christ Church, Oxford (Exhibitioner); Class IV, Classical Honour Moderations; Class II, Jurisprudence. Service: Nomad (Beja) Administration, 1929; Kordofan, 1930–31; Darfur, 1931–32; seconded to Legal Department, 1932–36; Northern Province, 1936–38; Civil Secretary's Office, 1938–42; Northern Province, 1942–45; Blue Nile Province, 1945–48; Deputy Governor, Northern Province, 1948–52; Civil Secretary's Office (Director of Local Government), 1952–54; retired 1954. Subsequently served as Commissioner for Local Government, Uganda Protectorate, 1955.

Derrick Charles Carden. Born 1921. Area of origin: Hampshire in south England. Father was Anglican clergyman. Spent 25 years in India. Mother's forebears had worked in various occupations in India in the nineteenth century. Family middle class. Educated at Marlborough and Christ Church, Oxford. War degree. Distinction in Greek Philosophy. Oxford University Hockey Club, 1941. Service: Governor-General, temporary commission as Bimbashi in Sudan Defence Force, 1942–43; Assistant District Commissioner, Northern Kordofan, 1943–47; Finance Department, 1947–50; District Commissioner, Central Nuer District (Fanjak), Upper Nile Province, 1950–54. Resigned 1954. Joined H.M. Foreign Service, 1954. Position when interviewed: Ambassador to the Sudan.

Anthony Wemyss Moore Disney. Born 28 November 1903 in London. "Father a barrister who became one of London's Stipendiary Magistrates." Educated at Marlborough and Hertford College, Oxford (scholar); Class II, Classical Honour Moderation; Class III,

Litterae Humaniores. Service: Assistant District Commissioner, Fung Province, 1926-31; Personnel Section, Civil Secretary's Office, 1931-35; Assistant District Commissioner and then District Commissioner, Wad Medani, Blue Nile Province, 1935-37; District Commissioner, El Fasher, Darfur Province, 1937-42; District Commissioner, Fung District, Blue Nile Province, 1942-46; Assistant Director, Department of Economics and Trade, 1946-49; Director, 1949-53. Retired 1953. After retirement, Managing Director, Blue Nile Brewery Ltd., Khartoum North, 1953-57.

Arthur Douglas Dodds-Parker. Born 5 July 1909 in Oxford "where my father was surgeon and taught anatomy for 40 years." Educated at Winchester and Magdalen College, Oxford; Class II, Modern History. Service: Assistant District Commissioner, Eastern Kordofan, 1931-33; Western Kordofan, 1934; Assistant Private Secretary to Governor-General, 1934-35; Assistant District Commissioner, Southern Fung, 1935-38; Assistant Director, Public Security, Khartoum, 1939; "I resigned to help fight Fascism in 1939 [and] returned to help restore the Emperor to Ethiopia in 1940-41." After retirement: Member of Parliament for Banbury Division, 1945; Chairman, British Empire Producers' Organization, 1947-50; Joint East and Central African Board, 1947-50; Joint Parliamentary Undersecretary of State for Foreign Affairs, 1953-54; Parliamentary Undersecretary of State for Commonwealth Relations, 1954-55.

James Donaghy. Born 1907. Senior Lecturer in English, Gordon Memorial College and University College, Khartoum, 1945-55.

William Marshall Farquharson-Lang (formerly William Farquharson Marshall Lang). Born 2 July 1908, area of origin, Aberdeenshire, Scotland. "My father and many of my forebears were ministers of the Church of Scotland and three of them (including my father) rose to the highest position of the Church. On my mother's side, we were landowners." Service in the Sudan: seconded to Education Department, 1931; transferred to Education Department, 1938; Gordon Memorial College, 1939-43; Governor-General's Temporary Commissioner in Sudan Defence Force, 1940-41; Inspector, Education Department, 1943-44; Headmaster, Wadi

Seidna 1945–50; Assistant Director of Education, 1951–55. Retired 1955.

Jean-Pierre Greenlaw. Born in Paris in 1910 of French mother and English father (manufacturer of ties); public school education, Imperial Service College, Windsor. Travelled widely in Europe, speaking fluent French and Italian and understanding of German and Spanish. Artist. Service in the Sudan: Inspector, Handwork and Art, Bakht-e-Ruda, El Duem from 1936–44. Responsible for introducing art and craft education in 40 school curricula. Founded the School of Design in 1946 as part of Khartoum University. Left the country in 1951 before pensionable age for reasons of conscience in colonial ideology and religious matters.

V. L. Griffiths. Born 1902. "Oxfordshire. Father Welsh, a clergyman with a farming background, and a small family with no tradition of going abroad. Mother, English, fifteenth in the family of clergymen, with a tradition of going overseas, mainly to British territories." Service in the Sudan: Assistant Master of Method, Gordon College, 1929–30; Inspector, Education Department, 1931–34; Principal, Bakht-e-Ruda, 1934–50.

Edward Christopher Haselden, C.M.G. Born 14 August 1903. "Family originally from Liverpool. My father's father went from Liverpool to Alexandria in about 1860 to work with a British company buying cotton. He married an English woman there and they lived in Alexandria for many years and had several children. My father was born there, and after education in England and Germany returned to work with a British company trading in Egyptian cotton." Educated at Cheltenham and Pembroke College, Cambridge (Exhibitioner); Class II, Mathematical Tripos; Class I, Mathematical Sciences Tripos. Service in the Sudan: Kassala, 1926–28; Khartoum, 1929–32; Public Security Intelligence, 1932–35; Kassala, 1935–42; Governor-General's Temporary Commission as Bimbashi in Sudan Defence Force, 1940; Darfur, 1942–45; Sudan Agent in Cairo, 1945–53. "I retired from the Sudan in 1953 and worked for some years in occupations which interested me, including a charity helping former British residents in Egypt."

Kenneth David Druitt Henderson, C.M.G. "But ever since my first day at Oxford, for some reason, everybody has always called me Bill. I was born in London, 4 September 1903, to Scottish parentage. My father was a doctor. A large number of the Sudan Government officials were the sons, for some obscure reason, of doctors and clergymen. I imagine there were more clergymen's sons in the Sudan than any other profession. I was educated in Scotland at Glenalmond and then at the University College, Oxford (Exhibitioner); Class II, Classical Honour Moderations; Class III, Litterae Humaniores; and then in the Sudan." Service: Blue Nile, 1927–30; Kordofan, 1930–36; White Nile, 1936–38; Civil Secretary's Office, 1938–44; Principal of School of Administration and Police, 1944; Secretary to Council, 1939–44; Kassala, 1944–46; Member of the Sudan Government Delegation at hearing of Egyptian Case, Security Council, 1947; Governor, Darfur, 1949–53. Retired 1953. After retirement, Secretary, Spalding Trust.

R. A. Hodgkin. "I am now [1981] 65, and was born to a Quaker family during the First World War. My father was a Christian pacifist: and, indeed, both parents came from Quaker origins with a strong tradition of social service and of Christian pacifism. My father died during the First World War while on a mercy mission to Armenian refugees. This took him through Iraq, and it was there that he died when I was only two years old. . . . This was one of the reasons why there was in our family a fascination for both Eastern countries and the Arab world. Father was just one aspect of this. My stepfather, when my mother married in 1932, had been Director of Education in Iraq. He did not know my father personally, but he brought into our family an interest in matters Arabian and also Oriental.

"I was educated at a Quaker public school and at Oxford, and my wife at Cambridge. Both my wife and I studied geography at the university. In my case, this interest was combined with a passionate wish to explore and climb mountains; and though one cannot exactly claim that the Sudan is a mountainous area, I think, in various ways, we both came to the country with a tremendous interest in travelling in wild country and in getting to know people of different backgrounds.

"I started in 1939 at the Old Gordon College in Khartoum as a so-called tutor, teaching mainly geography and English. This was almost my first teaching job, and it lasted until about 1943. Then for a year or two, I was concerned with the very early beginnings of the new Khartoum University, and I was the first lecturer in geography there. This lasted for two years. I then joined V. L. Griffiths at Bakht-e-Ruda Institute of Education, and was appointed along with my Sudanese colleague, Awad Satty, to open jointly the Publications Bureau, which was designed partly to handle the production of books from Bakht-e-Ruda, but much more importantly, to develop reading material of a wide range for youngsters who had left primary schools, but were not likely to go on to intermediate or secondary education. In 1949, when Griffiths retired, I was appointed to succeed him as Principal of the Bakht-e-Ruda Institute of Education and of its satellite colleges. I stayed there until 1955, when my post was Sudanized and my place was taken by Sayed Osman Mahgoub, who had up to that time been vice-principal."

Paul Philip Howell, O.B.E. Born in London, 13 February 1917. Father's family of Welsh origin who moved to the city of London in the early 19th century—but many members of the family went into the Indian Civil Service or Indian Army. One distant cousin, A. B. B. Howell, served in the Sudan. Father a regular soldier, first in Guides Cavalry (Indian Army), then commanded IVth Hussars, then Brigadier General, Chief of Staff to General Allenby (Cavalry Corps), General Jacobs, etc., killed in action, age 37 in 1917. Was also *Times* Correspondent in Balkan Wars, 1912. Mother (née Buxton) of well-to-do Norfolk family with Quaker origins; bankers, brewers, politicians.

Educated at Westminster School, Trinity College, Cambridge. (Senior Scholar, M.A., Ph.D); and Christ Church, Oxford (research student, M.A., D.Phil). Sudan Political Service, 1938–55: Assistant District Commissioner, Khartoum North, 1938–39; Aide-de-Camp and Assistant Private Secretary to Governor-General, 1939–41; Governor-General's Temporary Commission as Bimbashi in Sudan Defence Force, 1940–41; seconded to O.E.T.A. (Eritrea), 1941; Assistant District Commissioner, Zeraf District, 1942–44; District Commissioner Western Kordofan, 1946–68; Upper Nile (Chairman, Jonglei Investigative Team), 1948–53; Chairman, Southern Development Investigation Team (rank and status of Deputy Governor), 1953–55. Retired 1955.

After retirement: "Assistant Chief Secretary, Uganda, 1955; Permanent Secretary, Commerce and Industry, 1957–61. Head of British Middle East Development Division, Foreign Office and later Ministry of Overseas Development (Beirut), 1961–69. Director of Development Studies, University of Cambridge. Fellow of Wolfson College, Chairman Faculty Board of Archeology and Anthropology, Member of Governing Body, Institute of Development Studies, Sussex; Member, Council Overseas Development Institute, etc."

A. W. Ireland. South Midlands. Born April 1916. Government Meteorologist, 1927–55.

John Wynn Kenrick, O.B.E. Born 22 January 1913 "of mixed Welsh, Scottish, and English origins. Father qualified as a doctor at the London Hospital and then served in the Indian Medical Service." Educated at Wellington and Trinity College, Cambridge; Class II, Modern Languages Tripos; Class II, History Tripos. Service: Probation period in Torit, 1937; Assistant District Commissioner, Juba, Headquarters Equatoria Province, 1939–41; Aide-de-Camp and Assistant Private Secretary to the Governor-General, 1941–43; Governor-General's Temporary Commission as Bimbashi in Sudan Defence Force, 1941–44; Assistant District Commissioner, Talodi, 1944–46; District Commissioner, Rashad, 1946–49; District Commissioner, Omdurman, 1949–53; Assistant Adviser to the Governor-General on Constitutional and External Affairs, 1953–55. Retired 1955. "After leaving the Sudan, I went into the personnel function in industry and finished as Personnel Director of Philips Industries (U.K.).

Maurice Stanley Lush, C.B., C.B.E., M.C. and Bar. Born 23 November 1896 "in southern England, middle class parents, father a solicitor, grandfather a doctor; won scholarship at British Public School; read classics; intended to go to Oxford, but First World War intervened; entered Royal Military Academy, Woolwich; served in France with British Army, 1916–19; promoted Captain." Service: seconded from the Egyptian Army to the Political Service, 1919–20; appointed to the Political Service, 1920. Secretary to H.B.M.'s Minister in Ethiopia, 1919–22; Deputy Assistant Director, Intelligence (Sudan), 1923; Assistant District Commissioner, Gadaref, Kassala Province, 1923–26; District Commissioner, Khartoum, 1926–27; Assistant Civil Secretary (Personnel), 1927–29; Private Secretary to the Governor-General, 1929–30; Deputy Governor, White Nile Province, El Dueim, 1930–32; Deputy Governor, Upper Nile Province, 1932–35; Sudan Agent in Cairo, 1935–38; Governor, Northern Province, 1938–41; seconded to British Army as Brigadier to become in succession Chief Political Officer, Ethiopia, 1944; Military Administrator, Madagascar, 1942; Tripolitania, 1942–43; and Executive Commissioner and Vice-President, Allied Commission in Italy, 1943–46. Retired 1946.

John Franklin Madden. Born 19 September 1901 "in Cairo. Father surgeon in Egyptian Government Medical Service for 30 years. Educated at Rugby and Magdalen College, Oxford (Demyship); Class I, Classical Honour Moderations; Class II, Litterae Humaniores. Service: Red Sea Province, 1925–26; Deputy Assistant Civil Secretary (Personnel), 1929–32; Darfur Province, 1932–37; Equatoria, 1937–42; Civil Secretary's Office (Police), 1942–44; Deputy Governor, Darfur, 1944–46; Deputy Governor, Northern Province, 1946–68; Governor, Northern Province 1948–51. Retired 1951. After retirement, appointed as Justice of the Peace for West Suffolk in 1955. Later Secretary of the Magistrates Association. Finally retired in 1955.

John George Mavrogordato, C.M.G. Born in London, 9 May 1905, of Greek parentage. Service: Deputy Assistant, Legal Secretary and Lecturer in Law at Gordon Memorial College, 1944; Advocate-General (Attorney-General), 1946; Legal Adviser to Governor-General, 1954. After independence, Legal Counsel, Ministry of Justice, 1958–61.

William Crockett McDowall. Born 16 October 1917. Father a senior member of the Indian Civil Service. Educated at Glasgow Academy and the Queen's College, Oxford; Class II, Philosophy, Politics and Economics. Service: Kassala, 1939–43; Equatoria, 1943–46; joined Legal Department, 1946; Police Magistrate, Khartoum, 1946–47; Deputy Legal Secretary in Advocate-General's Office, 1947–50; Barrister-at-Law, Gray's Inn (called 1950); Judge of the High Court, 1951–55. Retired 1955. After retirement joined ICI and eventually became Chief Executive of one of its subsidiary companies. Retired 1979.

Frederick Douglas McJannet. Born 9 January 1914 in Edinburgh. Father a lawyer, mother of an eminent medical family. Educated at Glenalmond and Oriel College, Oxford; Class II, Modern History. Service: White Nile, 1936–38; Blue Nile, 1938–40; Governor-General's Temporary Commission as Bimbashi in Sudan Defence Force, 1940–48; Equatoria, 1943–45; Upper Nile, 1945–49; Northern, 1949–54; Deputy Governor, Upper Nile, 1954–55. Retired 1955. After retirement, worked in the Education Department of Suffolk County Council until retirement in 1979.

Thomas Holliday Baskerville Mynors. Born 1 August 1907. Family originally from Herefordshire "where ancestors were small landowners, parsons, etc." Educated at Marlborough and Oriel College, Oxford, (Scholar); Class II, Classical Honours Moderations; Class II, Litterae Humaniores. Service: Mongalla, 1930–35; Kassala, 1935; Khartoum, 1935–36; seconded to Legal Department, 1936–38; Blue Nile, 1938–44; Civil Secretary's Office, 1944–50; seconded to Gordon Memorial College as Dean, School of Administration and Reader in Public Administration; Assistant Director of Local Government, 1950–54; Deputy Governor, Blue Nile, 1954; Governor, Blue Nile, 1954–55. Retired 1955. After leaving the Sudan, 13 years with Shell International (partly in the Far East and West Indies, partly in London); then last 13 years (writing in 1981), County Councillor and member of many public health and education and labour relations bodies.

Henry Alleyne Nicholson. Born 11 October 1900. "My father was a well-known Edinburgh doctor and we lived in comfortable circumstances." Educated at Edinburgh Academy and Trinity College, Oxford (Scholar); Class III, Classical Honour Moderations; Class II, Litterae Humaniores. Service: Fung, 1924–26; Mongalla, 1926–27; Berber, 1927–29; Dongolla, 1930–32; Upper Nile, 1933–35; Department of Economics and Trade, 1939–41; Khartoum, 1941–45 (Deputy Governor, 1943); Deputy Governor, Upper Nile, 1945–48; Governor, Equatoria, 1945–49. Retired 1949.

Thomas Richard Hornby Owen, C.B.E. Born 23 May 1903. Father was a colonel of artillery—British, "not Scots or Welsh!" Educated at Repton and Corpus Christi College, Oxford (Scholar); Class I, Classical Honour Moderations; Class II, Litterae Humaniores. Service: Bahr-el-Ghazal, 1927; White Nile, 1928–32; Kassala, 1932–36; Civil Secretary's Office, 1936–39; Kordofan, 1939–45; Equatoria, 1945–48 (Deputy Governor for Bahr-el-Ghazal Sub-Province, 1946); Governor, Bahr-el-Ghazal Province, 1948–53. Retired 1953. After retirement, Assistant Warden, Game and Fisheries Department, Uganda.

John Fleetwood Steward Phillips. Born 16 December 1917. Father and paternal grandfather army officers; paternal grandmother a Stewart of Galloway. Maternal grandfather, Sir Alexander Pinhey, born of long-established Devonshire farming family, was in Indian Political Service; he married Violet, daughter of Sir Henry Gordon, brother of General Charles Gordon, killed in Khartoum, 1885. Educated at Brighton and Worcester College, Oxford; Class II, Honour Moderations. War Service: Army, 1939–40. Sudan Service: Assistant District Commissioner, Kordofan Province Headquarters, El Obeid, 1945–46; Assistant District Commissioner, East Jebels (Nuba) Talodi, 1946–47; Assistant District Commissioner, Jebels (Nuba) District, Kadugli, 1947–49; Assistant District Commissioner, Southern Gezira Wad Medani, 1949–51; District Commissioner, Southern Gezira, Wad Medani, 1951–52; District Commissioner, Dueim, 1952–54. Retired 1955. Subsequently joined H.M. Foreign Service. Served as Ambassador in Aden, Amman, and Khartoum.

Anthony William Polden. Born 1924. "[Born] Dublin, the Republic of Ireland. Father wholesale leather merchant. Mother country doctor's daughter. Secondary education in Dublin school with classical headmaster. Matriculated in Trinity College, Dublin, and qualified as Member of the Royal College of Veterinary Surgeons from the R.C.V.S., Dublin, in 1948. Service: Veterinary Inspector, Wad Medani; Veterinary Inspector, Fangak; Acting Senior Veterinary Inspector, Upper Nile."

George Edward Russell Sandars. Born 19 October 1901 in Cheshire. "Brought up in a country rectory, my father being a canon of

Chester Cathedral and Rector of Davenham parish." Educated at Winchester and New College, Oxford (Scholar); Class II, Classical Honour Moderations; Class III, Litterae Humaniores. Service: Kordofan, 1925–26; Kassala, 1926; Deputy Assistant Civil Secretary (Administration), 1927–28; Nomad (Beja) Administration, 1929; Kassala, 1930–33; Private Secretary to the Governor General, 1933–37; Blue Nile, 1937–41; Sudan Agent, Cairo, 1941–45; Deputy Governor, Khartoum 1945–45; Deputy Civil Secretary, 1946–48; Governor, Blue Nile, 1948–51. Retired 1951.

Alan Buchan Theobald. Born 19 July 1906. "Brought up in Sussex. Father and mother were both missionaries in India. On retirement from there, my father was a parson in England." Educated at Varndean School, Brighton and University College, London (Scholar); Class II, History. Service: Education Department 1929–36; "Tutor at Gordon Memorial College, then a secondary school. I was in charge of Wingate House which contained about 40 boys. I taught history and English." Province Education Officer, Northern Province, 1936–39, and for one year (1940) at Kassala. Bimbashi in the Sudan Defence Force, attached to the 5th Indian Division as an Arabic-speaking Intelligence Officer, 1940–41. "In 1942 I returned to Gordon College and remained there throughout its development, first in the School of Arts when it became the High School, then in the Faculty of Arts in the University College of Khartoum (linked to the University of London), and finally in the independent University of Khartoum. For five years I was Vice-Principal (Administration) while Sayed Ibrahim Ahmed was Vice-Principal (Student Affairs). I then returned to teaching. I was Head of the History Department; Dean, Faculty of Arts, and for three years I was also the sole Vice-Principal of the University College. During my last three years, 1956–59, I voluntarily resigned as Dean and Vice-Principal in favour of Sudanese colleagues, and concentrated on teaching and research only."

R. C. Wakefield. "Born 1906 in Lancashire. Father a country doctor. Family background one of enterprise. My great-great-grandfather founded a bank and his collateral, Edward Gibbon, was the founder of modern New Zealand. An uncle was on an early Everest expedition in 1922 and a brother served in the Indian Political Service until 1947. Another brother settled in Rhodesia after the

1914–18 war and opened up new territory to farming." Service: Inspector of Surveys, 1929–46; Director, Survey Department, 1946–54; Survey Consultant to Sudan Government, 1954–55; Chairman of Unclassified Wages Commission, 1951; Director, Equatoria Projects Board, 1949–54; Councillor without Portfolio in the Legislative Assembly and Member of the Governor-General's Council, 1952–54.

John Winder. Born 22 August 1905. Lancashire and Yorkshire. Father an engineer. Grandfather on father's side a solicitor. Mother came from cotton spinning and weaving industry. Educated at Oundie and King's College, Cambridge; Class II, Historical Tripos. Cambridge University Fencing Team (Foils), 1927. Service: Halfa, 1927; Red Sea, 1928; Port Sudan-Suakin Administration, 1929–30; Mongalla, 1930–33; Khartoum, 1933–36; Upper Nile, 1936–42; Northern, 1942–46; Upper Nile, 1946–51 (Deputy Governor, 1948); Assistant Civil Secretary (Departmental), 1951–53; Governor, Upper Nile, 1953–55. Retired 1955. After retirement worked as a land agent and for a short time in commerce.

NORTHERN SUDANESE CONTRIBUTORS

Ahmed Mahgoub. "My age is 48 [recording 1973]. My ancestors came from the Egyptian side of the northern Sudan, but I was brought up in Khartoum North. . . . I started as a junior clerk with the British. Then I became a clerk librarian for the Sudan Cultural Centre. I went to London in 1948 to join the Sudan Agency, as it was then known, in the capacity of a student welfare officer. I then returned to become a public relations officer for the Gezira Board in the Sudan. Then I went back to London to represent this board as agent in the cotton market. I am now the director of one of the government corporations."

Amin Hassoun. My age is now 60 [1973]. I come from the Northern Province, Dongola District. We came from Shallal originally. My grandfather left Shallal and settled in Dongola. My father was a shore master in the Sudan Railways at Karima. His father was a leader of ships and steamers. After graduating from the old Gordon Memorial College, I joined the Sudan Railways as a typist. Later on, I was transferred to the Labour Department, where I worked under two or three Britishers. From the time I was in the Sudan Railways, I used to give private lessons in Arabic to Britishers and I got to know many of them. I am now on pension and I run a small business, managing a clearing and forwarding house in Port Sudan."

Babo Nimir. "My real name is Osman; Babo is something of a nickname. I was named after my uncle, Osman Ali Julla. When I was small my grandfather took a special interest in raising me and I was more or less living with him. He would call me 'Osman.' My Uncle Osman would respond, 'Yes!' Then my grandfather would say, 'Not you, I mean, Osman, the Babo.' In our Sudanese customs a small child is referred to as 'Babo.' So, he would call me 'Osman, the Babo.' The name 'Babo' began to spread and spread until it overshadowed the name Osman.

"As for my age, I was born in 1910. My area in the Sudan is Kordofan Province, Fulah District. I was the Paramount Chief of the Missiriya; now [after the May Revolution] I am an ordinary farming citizen.

"Before the Mahdiya, we had a chief called Ali Massar. He was the uncle of Ali Julla, my grandfather. When the Mahdiya became established, tribal leadership was absorbed into the Mahdiya. People all joined the Mahdiya. After the Mahdiya, people went back to their respective areas and looked for a man who would be a good leader. Our people looked around for a man who would benefit the tribe; they chose Ali Julla who was from the Ajaiyra, the section that had originally held the leadership. After a while, the Falaiyta chose their own chief separately from the Ajaiyra, even though both were sections of the Homr. Ali Julla continued as chief of the Ajaiyra until he became an old man. He then handed over the chieftainship to his son, Nimir, my father.

"My father became chief in 1918 and died in 1924 on the 13th of January. Out of the whole of 1924, he lived only 13 days. I was 13 years old. The tribe, the Ajaiyra, heard about it and met at Abyei to select his successor. Chief Kwol of the Ngok Dinka and Chief El Haj Ajbar of the Falaiyta were there. The district commissioner, Mr. Crawford, also attended. They went as far as Abyei and met with the whole tribe. The Ajaiyra all assembled and said, "We want this son of Nimir." So it is not as people say these days, that chieftainship is a matter of heredity. It is not so. True, the sons of the late chief are looked to as contenders, but they are not imposed on the tribe."

Daud Abd al-Latif. "I was born in 1914. I have no birth certificate, of course. There were no certificates at that time in our small village of Wadi Halfa. My village is 22 miles from the boundary with Egypt. I was a civil servant for 28 and 1/2 years, part of it under the British rule and part of it under the self-government and part under independence. I left the service after being governor of two southern provinces, Equatoria and Bahr-el-Ghazal, and in the end, under secretary in the Ministry of the Interior. I am now retired from the government, but I am at present the managing director of the Sudanese Tractor Company, which controls the caterpillar equipment. I am also the chairman of Air Lekeed, which works in oxygen and acetylene and welding machinery. I also have interest in other companies."

Jamal Muhammad Ahmed. Age 58 [in 1973]. "My area of origin is Wadi Halfa. My family background, like that of all people from Wadi Halfa, is a farming background: my father was a farmer, my grandfather was a farmer, and as far as I know, the whole lot of them were farmers. The same is true of my mother's side, although my mother comes from a different village. I went to Sudan Government schools: the elementary school in my village; the intermediate school in Wadi Halfa; and the Old Gordon College in Khartoum, and then Exetor in the southwest of England, then affiliated to London University, and finally to Balliol College, Oxford. My contact with the British was chiefly through education and later in the administration of education. I am currently Ambassador in the Ministry of Foreign Affairs [Later Minister of State for Foreign Affairs and finally the Minister of Foreign Affairs]."

Muhammad Abu Ranat. Age 67 [in 1973]. "I come from western Kordofan. I was born in a village near Nahud called Abu Homeida. My father originally came from an island called Abu Ranat in Merawi District. He went to Nahud as an ordinary citizen. There was then nobody in Nahud. So he collected around him people of different tribes from the Northern Province and they founded Nahud town. He was then appointed Omda [Mayor] of Nahud.

He continued as such until his death in 1937. Then my elder brother, Ahmed, took over. He was both the Omda of Nahud and the President of the Native Court.

"I received my intermediate education in Khartoum. My first contact with the British was in January 1925 when I was appointed translator.... I joined the School of Law in October 1935 and graduated as District Judge in November 1938. The first station I worked in was Hassaheisa in the Blue Nile Province. In November 1944 I was appointed District Judge of the First Degree. I was also appointed at the same time Deputy Assistant Legal Secretary and Inspector of Local Courts. I was therefore holding three posts at the same time, two administrative and one juridical. In 1950, after I had a short course of training in England, I was appointed Judge of the High Court. In February 1955, the time of self-government, I was appointed Chief Justice Designate and actually took over as Chief Justice from Sir Robert Lindsay in June 1955."

Muhammad Abu Sinn. "I was born January 1915 in Rufaa. I had my elementary and intermediate education at Rufaa. In 1929 I went to Gordon Memorial College. That was the first time I saw the British—as tutors. I am of the Abu Sinn family who have been leaders of the Shukriya tribe for centuries. I am now the head of the tribe and have been for the last twenty-two years. I was a member of the Legislative Assembly, later the representative of the tribe to the first Sudanese Parliament and Minister of Social Affairs. I left politics in 1958, but I have kept working for the tribe through the local government."

Sorror Ramley. "I am 63 [in 1973]. My village is Wad Ramley, north of Khartoum.... We have been working for the welfare of our people since we established this village, which was named after my grandfather, Sorror Ramley, now also my name. I took my father's position after he died in 1930. At that time I was in my final class at Gordon Memorial College. The people and the government were both interested that I should go back home. I went and took my father's position and continued until 1969 when I resigned. A few months after my resignation the new regime came into power. So my resignation was in line with the government policy that the tribal system should cease."

Yusuf Bedri. Age 62 [in 1973]. "We are originally from the Northern Province. But my family moved to Rufaa in the Blue Nile. I was born and brought up in Rufaa. My first encounter with the British as in Rufaa and later at the Gordon Memorial College, where most of the teaching staff were British. I then met the British again in my work as a pharmacist, and later, in the then Department and Ministry of Education, as a teacher and administrator in education."

Zubayr Ahmed al-Malik. "My family is a very old one. My ancestors were kings on the island called Argo for 300 years. Argo is part of Old Dongola. The last king reigned until 1881. When Mohammed Ali came to open the Sudan through his son, Ismail, all the kings stepped down. That was how we lost our kingdom.

"I finished my education in the Old Gordon Memorial College in 1924 and graduated at the beginning of 1925. My original idea, when I joined the college, was to become an engineer. I was in the Engineering Department when the government decided to take people from the college to be part of an improved administration. Four of us were selected: I, Abu Ranat, Ahmed Kheir, and Ahmed Bukhari. I did not welcome the idea, but I was pressured into accepting. When we graduated we were each sent to our province with a letter that said that we were to be close to our fathers, that we needed a special training, and that we had been chosen for that particular purpose. I went to Merowi.

"After eight months I heard that a clerical post in the office of the governor-general was available. It was required that the man to be nominated for the post should be of a particular age, educated to a certain level, and from a known family background. I found these considerations applicable to me. So I accepted the post. I spent four years in the office of the governor-general, doing mostly translation work.

"Then the British decided to Sudanize those positions in Finance that had been held by the Syrians. Many Sudanese with the required level of education applied. I was chosen and given a post in the Personnel Section in the Ministry of Finance.

"Then my father died at the beginning of 1934. My people asked me to leave the government job and become chief. This was the wish of all the people in the area. In those days, people with our level of education preferred government service because it offered a better future. And truly, government service offered a better life. But I sacrificed everything to become chief of my people."

SOUTHERN SUDANESE CONTRIBUTORS

Abd al-Rahman Souley. "My tribe is Baria. My home is Jebel Lado. I don't know my date of birth, but I can approximate when I was born. I was born when the Belgians were still here in this part of the country. When the Belgians left and the condominium of the British and the Egyptians began, I had matured and was able to see and listen to things around me. I think I was about 12 or 13 years old at that time. I saw the Belgians with my own eyes and could, at that time, speak the Belgian language. When the British entered the country, I used to ask those who could read and write what year the Belgians left, and was told that they left in 1910.

"During the Belgian era my father was a chief in his own right. When the British came I was still small. In about 1927 or 1928 I became an assistant to my father. In my village I was like a chief. When I came to town I became a sub-chief to Chief Gadum Ibrahim. By 1937, when Mongalla and Rejaf were transferred to Juba, I left the position of sub-chief, came to Juba and then went to Uganda. When I returned from Uganda in 1940 I became a businessman here in Juba.

"I obtained a trading license and I used to slaughter cows (beef) here in Juba as a butcher. In 1940 political activities began here in the south. By 1953 there was a lot of political activity in this part of the country. Our people heard news from northerners that the British were leaving. They said that an agreement had been reached in Khartoum and in Cairo, and that the British were leaving. So, missionary-educated southerners went to ascertain this news from the British governor. They told the governor that they had heard that an agreement had been reached between the Arabs, the British, and the Egyptians. They wanted to know why the south had not been consulted. The British (governor) gave a straight answer. He said the south had not been included in the agreement because we had no political party. The northerners had participated because they had political parties such as the Umma party, the National Unionist party, and the Peoples' Democratic party. That was why they had taken part in the negotiations. So southerners, at that point, came down from the governor's office and formed a political party. That party was called the Liberal party.

"Then the problem was who would lead the Liberal party. Younger members of the party said that they did not want the job because no money could be earned from it. They said that they could not leave their present jobs to become leaders of the party. That was when one of the Dinka fellows called Gordon Apach Ayom nominated me to be leader of the party. He said, 'Sayed Abderahman, come and be the leader of the party.' That was when I was made leader of the party."

Andrew Wieu. Age 54 [in 1981]. "I come from southern Sudan, Upper Nile Province, of a Dinka family. I am a descendant of Ayuel Longar, the legendary ruler of the Dinka—the so-called Dinka Holy Son. I am now the Regional Minister of Education in the Southern Region of the Democratic Republic of the Sudan. I started first as an administrative assistant trainee, taking police training, clerical training, accounting training as a prerequisite to my administrative training. Having gone through this program of training, I was appointed administrative assistant in February 1952 and I started my work in western Nuer, District of Upper Nile. I then began further training in 1954 in Khartoum University College where I assumed the position of sub-ma'mur after the course and was promoted to ma'mur in 1955. Sudanization came while I was ma'mur in Bor District of Upper Nile Province, and I was promoted assistant district commissioner on independence."

Benjamin Lang Juuk. "I am the chief of the Akuar branch of the Twich Dinka on the border of Bahr-el-Ghazal, Upper Nile and Kordofan Provinces. I became chief in 1941. First I was a school teacher in 1933. In 1936 I became a clerk in the Council at Gogrial. In 1941 I was chosen by my people, while in Gogrial. They said, 'We want the government to send our son to us to administer our affairs.' And, indeed, I have administered our area without any problem. During my tenure I often met with Ngok and Nuer chiefs. I worked very closely with my brother-in-law, Chief Deng Majok Kuol. When he died in 1969 we had worked together for many years. I also worked together with other chiefs in the border areas.

The person who worked with them first was my elder brother, Ring Juuk. He was the first to be chief. Then when he retired, I was placed in his position by our people."

Chier Rian. "I was educated by an Italian because the missionaries who used to teach in our area here were Italians. Our teacher was called Father Nebel. At Wau Intermediate School our teacher was Father Mason. Mason later became the Bishop of Bahr-el-Ghazal, and then Bishop of Kordofan; he was transferred from Wau to El Obeid. The Britisher who took me to school was called 'Makuendit' in Dinka. He was the one who caught the great Dinka leader, Ariath. Titherington Bey was his name. Bey was an Egyptian title. It was he who came to my father. My father at that time had retired from the chieftancy. My brother, Monywiir Rian, was the chief. Titherington Bey told my father that the country would be taken over in the future by the educated children of the non-Dinka tribes because the Dinka were running away and hiding their children from education. 'Therefore,' he said, 'you chiefs should volunteer children to be taken to school. It is the educated children who will take over the administration of this country in the future.' That is when I was caught and taken to school. My mother cried in protest, but my father did not agree. He made sure that I went to school. Then photographs were taken and sent to my mother to assure her that I was alive. Kuajok, where the school was, is far from us. When the school year ended, I was placed by the government in the care of a policeman to take me to my father. When I returned to school, my brother Monywiir, who took my father's position, provided his police to escort me back to school. That was the way children were looked after.

"After I left school, the first job I held was that of a teacher. I taught for three years at Kuajok. The language of instruction was Dinka. On 1 January 1931 I became a clerk. I was the first among the Dinka of Aweil, Gogrial, and Tonj districts, including Abyei, to occupy such a position. I was the first son of a chief to go to school and I was the first to become a clerk. I worked as a clerk responsible for Gogrial for fifteen years. I began on 1 January 1931 and worked until 15 April 1946. If you check it, it adds up to fifteen years. After the big assembly in Abyei, people turned to Wunrok. The district commissioner of the Arabs and Chief Deng Kwol of the Ngok Dinka remained in Abyei. The Twich came and met and told the district commissioner in Gogrial that their cases were not being settled well in our area. I was in Gogrial at that time. They said that they wanted me to come and be the president of the court. The senior district commissioner in Tonj said that I should not leave Gogrial. He said that if I left, Gogrial would suffer. But the junior district commissioner in Gogrial, on the other hand, said that if I did not become the president of the Twich court, the cases would never be straightened out. Lang Juuk, Bol Chol, and Monywiir, my brother, were chiefs then. All Twich people said they wanted me. Then the district commissioner went to Gogrial and told me what my people wanted. He said that Gogrial District Headquarters needed me, but my people also needed me. He said they would let me go to become court president."

Gordon Muortat Mayen. "My age at present [1981] is approximately 58. I come from Rumbek District of Agar Dinka. My father was a leader of a section called Patiop or Domgel. He was the sub-chief under Chut Dhuol. And he was outstanding in local affairs involving tribal customs and politics until he died in 1955. I graduated from the Sudan Police College at the end of 1951 and became a police inspector; I remained in that position until the British left the Sudan."

Manoah Majok Deng. "I was born in Wan-Wan in 1928, according to medical assessment. I come from Bor area, Kongor District. I come from a family called Nyang in Kongor section of the Bor Dinka. I left school late in 1951 and joined the service in 1952, first as an accountant; I was in Khartoum for some time. Later on, after a year, I joined a course of chartered accounting in Khartoum, in the auditor-general's office. At that time they were all British, of course. This course was to be run in England, and I was to go to England in June. Then they decided to bring the lecturers to Khartoum to the Technical Institute where the lectures were being held. Later on, toward the end of 1952, I applied to join Administration. I then came into contact with the British. All the lecturers, of course, were British. The person with whom we were in contact at that time, with whom I was working, was the Financial Secretary. later, I joined the office of the Civil Secretary. All my work and all my studies were directed by the Civil Secretary. My career continued in the field of local government. My present [1981] occupation is that of a deputy minister, an advisor to the president of the High Executive Council on local government affairs."

Santino Deng Teeng. "I am 52 years old [1973]. I come from Abiem section of the Malual Dinka in Aweil District. I am from a clan called 'Panoon.' We came from Apuk a long time ago. The village called Panhomweth was founded by us. Then we came to Aguok, then to Paliet, with our land extending up to Ajuong. My father's people were farmers and cattle herders. They were also people who defended the territory. Whenever there was a threat, such as an attack by outsiders, they would lead a force to fight the aggressors. That is why my father was named Teeng. Because he fought very well, my father was named Teeng by my grandfather. 'Teeng' means those who lead an attack and fight with others. So we are people from the village. We farm and keep cattle and live our Dinka way of life."

Santino Deng initially worked in the government as an agricultural technician and later joined politics, holding various ministerial posts in a succession of governments. At the time of the interview he had this to say about his occupation then: "My work now is to travel throughout the countryside to show and encourage the people, our Dinka people to the villages, how to farm well. That is what I am now doing."

Index

Abd al-Khaliq Mahjub, 74, 84n
Abd al-Rahim Abu Daqal, 44, 60n
Abd al-Rahman al-Mahdi, 39–40, 42, 60n, 73, 133, 135–36, 137
Abd al-Rahman Souley, 165, 175, 180–81, 183, 188, 190–91, 192, 196, 199, 202, 207, 208–9, 210–11, 236–37
Abdullah Khalil, 30
Abdullahi, Khalifa, 3, 15, 69, 91
Addis Ababa Agreement (1972), 4, 206, 210
Advisory Council for the Northern Sudan, 135–36, 196
Al-Ahfad College, 111, 112
Ahmed Abdullah, 89
Ahmed Mahgoub (Mahjub), 110, 115–16, 122, 125, 127, 139, 145, 152, 153–54, 231
Ahmed Umar, 24
Ahmed Uthman al-Qadi, 90
Akout Atem, 87
Alban, A. H., 183, 184n
Ali Abd al-Latif, 72
Ali al-Mirghani, 73, 133, 137
Ali Abu Sinn, 23, 42, 64, 151
American University of Beirut, 105
Amin Hassoun, 107, 110, 112, 115, 117, 121, 122, 125, 127, 139, 141, 145, 148, 156–57, 231–32
Andrew Wieu, 164, 165, 169, 170–72, 176–78, 182–83, 185, 187, 188, 189–90, 191, 192, 195, 197–98, 199, 201, 202, 205–6, 207, 209, 211–12, 237
Anglo-Egyptian Condominium Agreement, 3, 5–6, 136–37
Anglo-Egyptian conquest, 3
Anglo-Egyptian Treaty (1936), 72, 128

Anglo-Sudanese Association, 85, 206
Arabic, 16, 20, 21, 22, 23, 24, 30, 42, 45, 47, 48, 62, 107, 110, 151
Arabs, 1–2, 165, 168, 190, 191, 192, 193n, 200, 201, 210
Ariath (Makuendit), 167
Ashigga (Ashiqqa), 40, 60n, 74, 135, 145n
Atar, 169, 171, 181
Atbara, 41
Awad al-Karim Abu Sinn, 130

Babikr Bedri, 98n, 111, 151
Babo Nimir, xii, 101, 102, 109, 112, 114–15, 120, 122, 127, 135–36, 137–38, 141–42, 145, 148, 154–55, 159, 232–33
Baggara, 45, 50, 51–52
Bahr al-Ghazal, 143, 168
Baily, R. E. H., 45, 47, 55, 60n, 150
Bakht al-Ruda (Institute of Education), 59, 63
Balfour-Paul, H. G., 150–51, 159n
Bara, 20
Bari, 208
Beaton, A. C., 198, 203n
Bell, G. W. (Sir Gawain), 8, 13, 14, 16, 18–19, 20, 24, 27, 30, 33–34, 42–43, 47, 51, 57, 61, 64, 65, 66, 69, 71, 73, 77, 78–79, 85–86, 87, 91–92 96–98, 219–20
Beni Amer, 21
Benjamin Lang Juuk, 167, 169, 170, 175, 176, 179–80, 181, 183, 187, 188, 190, 195–96, 200, 206, 207, 208, 211, 237–38
Bentiu, 197, 198
Bentley, Oswald, 54, 60n
Berber, 21
Biggs, D. H. St. Clair, 206, 212
Bog Barons, 163

Bowcock, P. P., 17–18, 22, 28, 56, 61, 68, 80, 83, 177–78, 188, 193n, 205, 220
Bredin, George, 17–18, 19, 21, 43, 50, 53, 73, 75, 76–77, 78, 79, 81, 85, 90, 109, 220–21
Brock, R. G. C., 165, 173n
Buchanan, L. M., 14, 17, 21, 24, 28, 35, 51, 74, 75, 80, 92, 221
Buth Diu, 76, 87, 137

Cairo Agreement (1952), 197, 199
Cambridge University, x, 3, 42, 129
Carden, D. C., 8, 13, 14–15, 20, 25–26, 29, 31n, 36–39, 44, 48, 54, 57, 62–63, 68, 76, 78, 80, 87, 93, 94, 95–96, 221
Carless, T. G. G., 105, 110–11
Chier Rian, 165, 166, 167–69, 175, 179, 181, 183, 186–87, 190, 192, 196, 197, 200, 201, 202, 207, 209–10, 212, 238–39
Christianity, 1, 97, 126, 172, 193n
Civil war, 4
Clark, William, 149, 159n
Colonial Office, 3, 92
Constitutional Amendment Commission, 198–99
Crawford, 102
Cromer, Lord, 3, 14
Crowfoot, Grace, 112, 117n
Cox, Christopher, 15, 31n
Cultural Centre, Khartoum, 41, 124

Darfur, 2, 47, 51, 54
Daud Abd al-Latif, 40, 87, 102, 104–5, 110–11, 113, 115, 116, 121, 123, 124, 125–26, 127, 128–29, 132–35, 139–40, 141, 143–4, 147, 149–50, 151, 152–53, 154, 157, 233
Davidson, Elmer, 56
Davies, Reginald, 141, 145n
Deane, L. A., 54, 60n
Dees, G. R. I., 180, 184n, 206
Deng Majok, xii
Deng Teeng, 207
Dinka, 3, 54, 126, 165–69, 170, 171, 179, 182, 183, 187, 189, 190, 191, 198, 200, 210
Disney, A. W. M., 13, 16, 20, 26–27, 30, 67–68, 71–72, 81–82, 86, 89, 96, 221–22
Dodds-Parker, A. D., 14, 19–20, 24, 35, 50, 62, 81, 82, 86, 87, 222
Donaghy, James, 74, 86–87, 222

Donald, J. C. N., 169, 173n
Dongola, 110, 133
al-Dueim, 23
Dupuis, C. G., 45, 47

Eastern Arab Corps, 20
Education, 15, 19, 21–22, 23, 24, 26, 36, 38, 64–64, 102–4, 180, 196; women's, 64, 87–88, 98n, 111–12; Southern, xi, 3, 4, 96–97, 164, 166–67, 169–73, 196, 201
Egypt, Egyptians, xiii, 4, 18, 72, 73, 75, 77, 81, 128, 132, 135, 136, 137, 140, 141–43, 191, 196, 199, 200, 201
Equatoria, 126
Erkowit Study Camp, 63–64
Ethiopia, 165
Evans-Pritchard, E. E., xii
Executive Council, 109, 130, 138

Fadlallah Khayrallah, 36
Farquharson-Lang, W. H., 13–14, 17, 19, 23–24, 26, 28–29, 31, 36, 49–50, 52, 57, 62, 63, 65, 69, 74, 77–78, 87, 89, 90, 112, 222–23
Feisal Muhammad Abd al-Rahman, 121, 123–24, 155–56
Female circumcision, 35
Foreign Office, 3, 92
"Fuzzy-Wuzzy," 13

Gaitskell, Arthur, 63
Garland, P. S., 176–78, 184, 189–90, 197
Gawamaa, 24
Gedaref, 20
Gellaba. See Jallaba
Gezira Scheme, 22–23, 63, 88–89
Gillespie, Ian, 54
Gogrial, 54, 207
Gordon, General, 24, 120, 187
Gordon Memorial College, 23, 24, 103–4, 106, 123, 128, 132, 133. See also Khartoum University College
Gordon Muortat Mayen, 165–66, 169, 170, 180, 182, 183, 185, 186, 187, 188, 189, 190, 192–2, 196, 198, 199–201, 202, 206, 209, 210, 239
Goss, F. H. 105–6, 108n
Graduates' General Congress, 72–74, 84n, 131, 134, 139, 142, 196
Greenlaw, Jean-Pierre, 15, 17, 23, 43–44, 49, 53, 56, 64, 69, 75, 86, 223

Index

Griffiths, V. L., 30–31, 40, 43, 55, 59, 60n, 61, 63, 90, 223
Guek Ngun-Deng, 164, 173n

Hadendowa, 17
Hamar, 24
Hancock, G. M., 42, 60n
Hantoub, 87
Hartley, J. A., 110, 117n
Haselden, E. C., 35, 78, 223
Hawkesworth, Desmond, 106, 108n, 142, 180
Henderson, K. D. D., 8, 13, 15, 22–23, 28, 29, 36, 39–40, 41–42, 44, 45–47, 51, 53, 54–55, 57–58, 60n, 64, 65–66, 70, 72–73, 75, 79–80, 81, 82, 87, 88–89, 90–1, 134, 147, 224
Henderson, Mrs. K. D. D., 47, 82
Hibbert, D. H., 103, 108n, 111
Hodgkin, Robin, 8, 15, 31, 49, 58–59, 62, 63–64, 67, 94, 107–8, 122, 224–25
Hogg, Peter, 149, 159n
Homosexuality, 56–59, 116–17, 183
Howe, Sir Robert, 158
Howell, P. P., 13, 22, 34–35, 57, 66–67, 76, 83, 88, 89, 92–93, 96, 225–26
Huddleston, Sir Hubert, 135
Hunter, J. C., 171
Hunter, J. M., 179, 184n

Ibrahim Musa, 138
Independence, 4, 18–19, 23, 65–67, 71–83, 129, 131–45, 156, 157–58, 163–64, 195–202
Indian Civil Service, x, 14–15
Indirect Rule, x-xi, 4, 9, 25, 70, 127, 168
Ireland, A. W., 35, 50, 92, 226
Islam, xiii, 1, 2, 3, 35, 54, 56, 68, 97, 126
Isma'il al-Azhari, 74, 77, 82, 83, 97, 158

Jaafar Muhammad Nimeiri, 87
Jackson, H. W., 116, 117n
Jallaba, 66, 70n, 83
Jamal Muhammad Ahmed, 103, 107–8, 113–14, 116–17, 121–23, 124, 128, 131–32, 139, 142–43, 151, 152, 158, 233
Jamieson, W. B. M., 111–12
Jonglei Canal, 4
Juba Conference (1947), 125, 140–41, 179–80, 196–87

Kababish, 25–26
Kamlin, 21
Kenrick, J. W., 19, 34, 44, 48, 56, 64–65, 71, 76, 82, 95, 226
Keun, Odette, 97
Khartoum, 21–22, 34, 37–38, 41, 47, 49, 52, 62, 74, 79, 90, 104, 158, 196, 198
Khartoum North, 22
Khartoum University College, 64
Khatmiyya, 73, 74, 133
King, G. R., 125, 130n
Kipling, 13
Kitchener, 125
Kordofan, 2, 20, 52, 54, 142, 168, 178, 179
Kosti, 21

Lampen, G. D., 141, 145n
Lawrence, James, 81
Legislative Assembly, 129, 136, 196
Lindsay, William, 82, 110, 117n
Longe, John, 165, 173n, 197–98
Lugard, xi
Lush, Maurice, 17, 24–25, 28, 30, 34, 43, 49, 50–51, 53, 226–27

Madden, J. F., 31, 227
Mahdia, 2–3, 15, 44, 69, 91, 101, 124, 126
Mahdists, 73, 74
Malakal, 49
Malek, 169–70
Managil, 88–89
Manchester Guardian, 129–30
Manoah Majok Deng, 164–65, 166–67, 169–70, 172, 178, 180, 182, 183, 185, 186, 191, 192, 197, 198, 201–2, 205, 206, 208, 209, 239–40
Mason, Bishop, 126
Mavrogordato, J. G., 16, 23, 28, 69, 91, 96, 227
McDowall William, 15, 18, 23, 43, 56, 57, 61, 66, 69–70, 76, 78, 80, 82, 88, 94–95, 227–28
McJannet, F. D., 18, 50, 61–62, 78, 228
Mekki Abbas, 56, 69
Missionaries, 3, 4, 97, 125–26, 167, 169–70, 201; Catholic, xii, 125–26, 169; Church Missionary Society, 112, 125–26; Verona Fathers, xii
Missiriya, 45–47, 142
Mongalla, 21

Monywiir Rian, 186
Muhammad Abd al-Rahim Abu Daql, 44
Muhammad Ahmed (ma'mur at Talodi), 36
Muhammad Ahmed Abu Ranat, 101, 104, 110, 116, 151–52, 153, 156, 233–34
Muhammad Ahmed Abu Sinn, 8, 101–2, 104, 106–7, 109, 112–13, 115, 119, 120, 128, 129–30, 132, 134, 138, 139, 141, 147, 150–51, 154, 157–58, 234
Muhammad Ahmed b. Abdullah (the Mahdi), 2–3, 191
Muhammad Khalifa Sharif, 39
Muhammad Omer Beshir, 116, 132–33
Muhammad Salih Shingeiti, 197
Muneim Mansur, 24
Muslim Brotherhood, 74
Mynors, T. H. B., 21, 24, 55, 66, 67, 76, 81, 228

Nadel, S. F., xii
al-Nahud, 39, 41, 44
Nationalism, xiii, 4, 18, 65–70, 71–83, 90–91, 123, 131–45, 154, 191–92, 195–202
Newbold, Sir Douglas, 38, 54, 58–59, 60n, 63, 72–73, 75, 79–80, 84n, 95, 96, 110–11, 113, 133–34
Nicholson, H. A., 18, 28, 31, 34, 40–41, 44, 50, 66, 69, 79, 81, 89, 228
Nilotics, 68, 87
Nimeiri regime, 4
Nomad-Beja Administration, 21
Northern Nigeria, 30
Nuba, 2, 66
Nuba Mountains, 51, 54, 76
Nuer, 29, 39, 68, 76, 164, 183, 189, 197
Nyerere, Julius, 90

Omdurman, 44, 77
Omdurman Secondary School, 74
Ottoman Empire, 2, 120
Owen, J. S., 149, 159n
Owen, T. R. H., 14, 15, 17, 18, 22, 29, 35–36, 53–54, 66, 69, 79, 80, 93, 94, 140, 143–44, 145n, 191–92, 193n, 229
Oxford University, x, 3, 15, 16, 28, 42, 58, 85, 129, 151

Parliament, 199, 200
Phillips, J. F. S., 14, 15, 18, 19, 26–27, 30, 31, 36, 48, 53, 54, 56, 62, 66, 67, 68, 75, 80, 81, 82, 86, 88, 89–90, 93–94, 163–64, 229

Polden, A. W., 23, 76, 78, 85, 229
Poole, Arthur Agany, 182
Poole, J., 54, 179, 182
Port Sudan, 16, 41, 49, 77
Power, G. W., 107
Pridie, Sir Eric, 106, 108n

Raby, 56
Rhodesia, 63, 157
Richards, M. G., 169, 173n, 176, 179
Richardson, J. N., 102, 108n
Robertson, Sir James, 72, 75, 95, 113, 129, 135, 149
Robertson, Nancy, 113
Rufaa, 102, 147
Rumbek, 166, 171–72, 181

Sandars, G. E. R., 31, 61, 66, 68–69, 79, 80, 229–30
Sandison, Paul, 145
Santino Deng Teeng, 8, 164, 166, 167, 175, 178–79, 181, 183, 185, 188–89, 200, 240
Savile, R.V., 13, 31n
Seamer, John, 149, 159n
School of Administration, 70, 180
Scott, G. C., 38, 59, 60n
Shukriyya, 119, 130
Al-Sibyan, 107
Sidqi-Bevin Protocol (1946), 134–35, 145n
Slatin Pasha, 44, 60n
Slavery, 2, 69, 97, 98n, 126, 191, 192, 200
Sorror Ramley, 103, 120, 122, 128, 132, 133, 140–41, 143, 147, 149, 188, 234
Southern Liberal Party, 199
Southern Policy. See Sudan Government
Southern Provinces Regional Government Act, 4, 210
Stack, Sir Lee, 72, 191
Stewart, Sir Herbert, 14
Sub-Mamurs' School, 133
Sudan Administration Conference, 136, 190
Sudan Civil Service, x, 3, 156, 190, 196–97, 201
Sudan Club, 124
Sudan Courtesy Customs, 40
Sudan Cultural Centre. See Cultural Centre, Khartoum
Sudan Defence Force, 6–7, 47, 88, 106, 144–45, 201
Sudan Gezira Board, 56, 127
Sudan Government, 3, 6; Language policy,

xi-xii, xiii; Legal department, 23, 28, 82; Religious policy, 3; Southern policy, xi-xii, 3–4, 76, 96, 125–26, 140, 143–44, 163, 170, 172–73, 199, 202; Survey Department, 67, 70n
Sudan Medical Services, 105, 106
Sudan Notes and Records, 156
Sudan Political Service, x, xi, 3, 4, 6–7, 9, 14–15, 16, 29, 30, 50, 51, 52–53, 65, 80, 93, 95, 129, 141, 144
Sudan Railways, 18, 107, 110, 121
Sudan Socialist Union, 124
Sudanese Communist Party, 74
Sudanization, 23, 80, 139, 144, 178, 202
Symes, Sir Stewart, 18

Talodi, 36, 61, 62
Theobald, A. B., 18, 21, 26–27, 35, 56, 57, 62, 103, 230
Thorp, Mrs., 112
Three Towns, the, 52, 73
Tibbs, G.M. G., 143, 145n
Titherington, G. W., 167, 173n
Tokar, 21
Turco-Egyptian regime, 2–3, 60n, 69, 91, 101

Ubayd Abd al-Nur, 34–35
Udal, N. R., 103
Uganda, 165, 209
Umma Party, 73–74, 135, 137
Unionists, 73–74, 75, 127, 135, 136
University of Khartoum, 180. *See also* Khartoum
University College
Upper Nile Province, 68, 87, 168, 176, 178

Victoria College (Cairo), 158

Wad Medani, 22–23, 56, 88–89, 105
Wad Ramley, 103
Wadi Seidna, 36, 77, 87
Wakefield, R. C., 16, 34, 67, 74–75, 78, 230–31
White Flag League, 72
Whitlock, 180
Williams, C. R., 110
Williams, C. W., 103, 108n, 145
Williams, Mrs. C. W., 112
Williams, Headmaster, 170–72
Wills, Lady, 150
Winder, John, 16, 34, 41, 49, 57, 75, 76, 83, 87, 231
Wingate, Sir Reginald, 13–14, 31n
Wise Bey, 14
Women, British in Sudan, 45, 47–49, 54–55, 112–14; British relations with Sudanese, 35, 44, 45–47, 50–56, 182–83; Sudanese relations with British, 43–44, 45, 48, 49–50, 54–56, 112–16, 151–53, 181–83
World War I, 51
World War II, 16–17, 18, 73, 80, 105, 129, 155, 189
Wyld, J. W. G., 125, 130n

Yahia al-Fadli, 40
Yusuf Abu Saad, 23, 39, 42
Yusuf Bedri, 102, 103–4, 105–6, 111–12, 126, 135, 145, 147–48, 149, 151, 153, 154, 158–59, 235
Yusuf Ian Gillespie, 54

Zalingei, 64
Zubayr Ahmed al-Malik, 102, 103, 106, 109–10, 113, 120–21, 122, 123, 127, 132, 139, 143, 147, 148–49, 155–56, 235–36

"BONDS OF SILK"

Production Editor: Julie L. Loehr
Design: Lynne A. Brown
Copy Editor: Jo Grandstaff
Proofreader: Loretta Crum

Text composed by Delmas Typesetting, Inc. in 11 pt. Goudy Oldstyle and Goudy Oldstyle Italic.

Printed by McNaughton & Gunn, Inc. on 55# Glatfelter Natural and smyth sewn in Roxite B Vellum